Everybody Marries the Wrong Person

Everybody Marries the Wrong Person

Everybody Marries the Wrong Person

Turning Flawed into Fulfilling Relationships

by Christine Meinecke, Ph.D.

New Horizon Press
Far Hills, NJ

New Horizon Press
P.O. Box 669
Far Hills, NJ 07931

Meinecke, Christine
Everybody Marries the Wrong Person: Turning Flawed into Fulfilling Relationships
Cover design: Wendy Bass
Interior design: Susan Sanderson

Library of Congress Control Number: 2009944175

ISBN 13: 978-0-88282-319-5
New Horizon Press

Manufactured in the U.S.A.

2014 2013 2012 2011 2010 / 5 4 3 2 1

Author's Note

This book is based on the author's research, personal experiences and clients' real life experiences. In order to protect privacy, names have been changed and identifying characteristics have been altered except for contributing experts. For purposes of simplifying usage, the pronouns his/her and s/he are sometimes used interchangeably. The information contained herein is not meant to be a substitute for professional evaluation and therapy with mental health professionals.

Contents

Part 1

What It Means

Chapter 1

Out with the Old

Everybody marries the wrong person. Yes, *everybody.* Not just reckless, unsuspecting people. Not just clueless teenage people. *You* married the wrong person and your spouse did, too.

What a Crazy Notion!

Some readers are thinking, *What a crazy notion*! Unlike everybody else, you believe you married the *real* Mr. Wonderful or Ms. Perfect. If, for any reason, your first reaction is to reject the premise that everybody marries the wrong person, please, keep reading. Your marital future depends on it.

An Open Mind

Some readers are thinking, *I've never heard that before*. Since new ideas interest you, you're keeping an open mind. And since keeping an open mind is the bedrock of psychological development, you could be well on your way to an "ah-ha" moment.

Ah-ha!

Some are thinking, *Ah-ha! There could be something to this*. You're not as happily married as you expected to be. You're tired of drama and dysfunction. Yet, nothing you've tried seems to show your spouse the error of his or her ways.

Longtime Companions, Too?

Some are wondering whether this crazy notion applies to longtime companions, too. Yes, it does. *Everybody Marries the Wrong Person* is for all, regardless if you are married in a traditional or nontraditional sense, living with a partner, seriously involved though not living together, straight, gay, lesbian, bisexual or transgendered.

Going Wrong with Old Thinking

Nobody *wants* to marry the wrong person. In fact, most of us are determined to marry the *right* person. We go wrong, because we are blinded by love and misled by myths and misconceptions. We go wrong, because we follow conventional guideposts (just as everyone before us has) and fail to ask ourselves, *Where exactly is this leading?* We go wrong because we base our expectations about marriage on old thinking—the myths and misconceptions of conventional wisdom.

According to conventional wisdom, marrying the *right* person is the key to marital success. Although we hear that 40 to 50 percent of first marriages and 60 percent or more of second marriages end in divorce, we also hear that true love conquers all. So, we squeeze shut our eyes, cross our fingers and hope that of all the people choosing partners, we will choose most wisely.

We also hear that marital bliss turns to marital distress, because partners do not try hard enough. So, we vow not to be matrimonial slackers. We tell ourselves that of all the couples trying hard to avoid disaster, we will try hardest.

Paradoxically, couples expect to gain an *un*conventional result (marital success) by following conventional wisdom. *Everybody Marries the Wrong Person* reveals what is old and self-defeating about conventional wisdom and how we damage romantic relationships by basing our expectations on old thinking. After reading this book, you will know how to gain the *un*conventional result.

What Not to Do

Here's a preview of what lies ahead. Let's consider the pros and cons of advice offered by a columnist:

> **Stop holding emotions inside**
> Stop censoring yourself, start speaking up and see what happens. When in doubt, frame it in terms of your feelings. "Your constant lateness makes me feel like I don't matter."… all these things help you feel out the limits of productive communication.[1]

I think this advice is flawed. I believe there are better ways of improving your relationship. Let's break it down bit by bit.

Stop holding emotions inside. Neither myself nor some of my fellow psychologists hold onto the old belief that we somehow damage our mental or physical health by "holding emotions inside." We do not believe that we undermine our power in relationships by failing to make our feelings known.

- *Stop censoring yourself.* I believe that unless you're in a life-threatening situation, ALWAYS censor yourself. Our brains are hardwired for survival, which, in turn, predisposes us to the concept of shoot first and ask questions later. Mentally healthy partners hold their fire and utilize the rational mind.
- *Start speaking up and see what happens.* Speaking up in some situations can be a problem. Just tune into any reality show on television. Instead, start behaving rationally and see what happens.
- *When in doubt, frame it in terms of your feelings.* When in doubt, I think it's best to frame it in terms of rational thoughts.

Your constant lateness makes me feel like I don't matter. One statement. Three kinds of wrong, however, in my opinion.

"Your constant lateness" guarantees a defensive reaction.

"Makes me feel" fails to take responsibility for your feelings.

"Like I don't matter" begs for trouble.

Helps you test the limits of productive communication. In my experience, blaming your partner for your feelings *is* the limit of this. A save can be made only if your partner practices more emotional restraint than you do.

The problem with staking marital futures on conventional wisdom is that conventional wisdom is often wrong. As it has been repeatedly demonstrated, humans are prone to the world-is-flat assumptions. In the sixth century B.C.E., Pythagoras believed the earth to be round, yet at the end of the C.E. fifteenth century, public consensus was that Columbus would go sailing off the edge of the earth. Or maybe this belief about Columbus' contemporaries is simply today's conventional wisdom. Regardless, from Pythagoras to the contemporary bestseller *Freakonomics,* challengers warn that conventional wisdom is "a web of fabrication, self-interest and convenience" and "not necessarily true."[2]

So, why do people go on believing things that are not factual? How, in the information age, do we remain uninformed and misinformed? Are we so preoccupied with the mundane that we fail to register profound new facts? Are we intellectually lazy? Ideological rather than logical?

Twenty-first century answers to such questions can be found in the burgeoning body of knowledge about how the brain works. Daniel Gilbert contributes by pointing out in *Stumbling on Happiness* that our conclusions can be fundamentally wrong due to shortcomings of brain functions such as imagination, memory and perception.[3] Today, if Joe Average holds fundamentally wrong beliefs about the shape of the earth (spherical versus infinite plane), it is relatively inconsequential to his daily life. If, however, Joe Average happens to be married and holds fundamentally wrong beliefs about romantic relationships, the consequences to his daily life are many, varied and harsh.

Going Wrong with Failed Marriage Models

Divorce statistics and clinical anecdotes document the relevance of the countless volumes written to address failed marriage models. If interested in a comprehensive summary of what-not-to-do paradigms, read *Marriage, a History: How Love Conquered Marriage* by Stephanie Coontz. This highly informative work describes a few thousand years of humanity's trial-and-error approach to "the highest expression of commitment in our culture."[4]

Throughout *Everybody Marries the Wrong Person,* real-life experiences of modern couples make the case against failed models. You will recognize troubling aspects of your own experience, because you are caught, like everyone else, in endlessly repeating, disappointment-laden patterns. In order to extricate ourselves, we must expand beyond familiarity.

Although couples live out unique and ingenious specifics of going wrong, archetypes provide basic structures. The Good Wife, The Good Provider, The Trophy Wife, The Sugar Daddy, The Social Climber and The Breeders are models familiar to generations of couples. Whether we look to the famous and infamous or to our own family members, we see couples tracing combinations of the same templates, playing out similar dramas and grappling with unhappy outcomes.

The Good Wife

Let's review two failed paradigms: The Good Wife and The Good Provider. Although most wives aspire to be good wives, The Good Wife model defines goodness as obedience and subservience. Generations of women have followed this model—some because it was imposed upon them, others because they held themselves to this standard. Children raised by Good Wives copied the model. Girls expected to grow up, get married and be The Good Wife. Boys expected to grow up and marry The Good Wife.

Traditional wedding vows taken from *The Book of Common Prayer* (composed in 1553 by Archbishop of Canterbury, Thomas Cranmer) clearly reference this model. The question: "Who giveth this woman to be married to this man?" assumes that a father or other male guardian offers the dependent woman to the husband she will serve and obey.

Later in the ceremony, the man takes the woman's hand and "plights his troth" then releases her hand, symbolizing the woman's final opportunity to refuse to go through with the marriage. If the woman chooses to "plight her troth," she takes the man's hand. After the pronouncement of marriage, words taken from St. Matthew are spoken: "Those whom God hath joined together let no man put asunder." Although some hear poetry in these words, others hear purveyance.

During the 1960s, oral contraception and Second Wave feminism[5] inspired many to take a critical look at The Good Wife model. Women imagined alternatives to obedience and subservience. Couples aspiring to gender equality altered traditional wedding vows or composed their own. Brides refused to march down the aisle to Wagner's *Wedding Chorus* and balked at being "given away" by their fathers. Wives kept their maiden names or couples hyphenated. Today, despite five decades of societal change (some superficial, some profound), The Good Wife archetype continues to shape marital expectations.

The Bride/Dead Girl

Several years ago, I saw a 150-year-old painting by Gustave Courbet called *The Preparation of the Bride/Dead Girl.* This work impressed me not only because of its striking imagery but also because of its metaphorical backstory. There is definitely something odd about the scene depicted on this large canvas. Is the central figure a bride or a dead girl or both? Does she look so lifeless because she is being forced into an arranged marriage? Has she swallowed poison on her wedding day? Are the twelve servant women around her attending a bride and preparing a wedding feast or preparing a corpse and a wake?

When Smith College acquired Courbet's painting *The Preparation of the Bride*, authenticators discovered no evidence that Courbet ever produced such a painting. Instead they found information about an unfinished and presumed-lost canvas titled *The Preparation of the Dead Girl*, which depicted customs of Courbet's native region, the Franche-Comte. Then, X-radiographs of *The Preparation of the Bride* revealed deliberate repainting in critical areas. The central figure, originally nude, had been given a dress. Her head, originally slumped, had been lifted. Her left hand had been raised and a mirror placed in it. Smith College had, in fact, acquired Courbet's *The Preparation of the Dead Girl* altered by an unknown artist, probably to conceal the somewhat morbid content, and renamed prior to auction in 1919.[6]

The bride/dead girl analogy offers insight into why The Good Wife model failed. On balance, the cost to women is too great. Married women with dead girls beneath the surface are all too common. Groom/dead guy can be experienced, too.

The Good Provider

Although most husbands aspire to provide for their families, The Good Provider model defines goodness as excellence in breadwinning and procuring as many material luxuries as possible. Generations of men have followed this model—some because it was imposed upon them, others because they held themselves to this standard. Children raised by Good Providers copied the model. Boys expected to grow up, get married and be The Good Provider. Girls expected to grow up and marry The Good Provider.

Traditional wedding vows place the husband in charge of the wife. As has been discussed, there is a major downside to this for women. There is also a major downside for men. Think groom/dead guy.

Today, being a good provider is pretty much synonymous with being in charge. If a man is, in fact, a good provider, he feels that he has earned the right to be in charge. If he is not a good provider, he may act overly in charge to compensate.

Even though most couples now aspire to equality, the legacy lives on. In the modern parade of life, men are still the likeliest candidates for the partners in charge floats. Society grants feminists and female politicians their own in charge floats, but true equality, though it exists in certain microcosms, has yet to parade down Main Street.

The effect of The Good Provider model on marriages is two-fold. Husbands are judging themselves against this standard, as are wives.

Pete's Story

In his early thirties and married for six years, Pete has a two-year-old son and a daughter on the way. Both my client Pete and his wife, Toni, are employed full-time. Notably, he is the cook in the household and a very hands-on dad.

Pete: My wife has been talking again about quitting work and staying home after the baby is born.

Dr. M.: Say more.

Pete: Well, the truth is I wish I could stay home with the kids. You know how much I love my little boy.

Dr. M.: (Smiles and nods.) I do know that. So, what does your wife say about it?

Pete: She says, "No way. I'm the mom. If anyone gets to stay home, it's me."

Dr. M.: And?

Pete: There's not much I can say to that. The whole world basically agrees with her and somebody has to bring in the money, so I guess it's me.

Dr. M.: You're unhappy about this.

Pete: I sure am.

On June 20, 2009, in honor of the one hundredth anniversary of Father's Day, President Barack Obama conducted a White House town hall meeting about the ethics of responsible fatherhood. Among his comments:

- "[W]e need fathers to step up…to understand that their work doesn't end with conception."
- "[I]f I could be one thing in life, it would be to be a good father."[7]

You don't get much more in charge than president of the United States and yet, President Obama's attitude about being a husband and father reflects his understanding that a man's responsibilities go far beyond bringing home the bacon.

Just as The Good Wife model limits women's lives, The Good Provider model limits men's lives. Up to this point, couples who sought new marriage models simply tried on each other's equally limiting, gender-stereotyped roles. *Everybody Marries the Wrong Person* offers a new, gender-neutral option: Self-Responsible Spouse.

A New Marriage Paradigm

Many people imagine that their marriages will be better than their parents' and grandparents' marriages. Since observation teaches us a lot about what we do *not* want, we can be emphatically specific about spouse-choosing criteria (e.g., blue-eyed Kansans, born on odd-numbered days need not apply). At the same time, most of us are surprisingly nonspecific about what opens us to constructive, long-term relationships. We then rely on conventional models to guide us through everyday married life. Fortunately, any couple can enjoy marital success by refuting conventional wisdom and adopting this new, universally applicable and constructive marriage paradigm.

Sounds Too Hard

As daunting as becoming a self-responsible spouse may sound, the concept is simple. Being self-responsible in romantic relationships means taking responsibility, minute-by-minute, for our own happiness and unhappiness. In other words, self-responsible spouses meet their own needs and wants and manage their own fears and dark moods. In order to do so, three mental adjustments are essential.

Adjustment 1: Change Expectations

Expectations based on fairy tales and wishful thinking must be replaced by expectations based on reality. We stop pretending that finding the right person will overcome the near impossibility of happily sustaining romantic love. We stop deluding ourselves that failed models will, in our particular case, produce success. We abandon conventional wisdom's impractical goal of finding or fashioning the ideal mate.

Adjustment 2: Change Reactions

According to *Stress in America*, a survey published in 2007 by the American Psychological Association, 73 to 83 percent of participants across age groups ranging from eighteen to over fifty-five report that a relationship with a spouse/partner is a moderate to high stressor.[8] Reacting to a partner as a significant source of stress fosters drama and dysfunction. Partner-blame must be replaced by self-responsible reactions that reflect emotional maturity, acceptance of reality and self-restraint.

Adjustment 3: Change Self

We must stop calling for a better partner and start bettering ourselves. Many people will claim to already know this. We know, for example, that we must tolerate partners' shortcomings and we may believe that we change self by cutting a partner some slack. Changing self, however, means continually addressing personal shortcomings.

Twenty-first century psychology knows that changing behavior means changing brains. There is nothing science-fiction about becoming expert users of our own brains. The brain is and always has been an "organ of adaptation,"[9] wiring and rewiring itself minute by minute. (Much more on how to constructively rewire your brain in part 4.)

It's All About You—In a Good Way

The struggles of a few thousand clients and the realities of their constraints are respectfully reflected in these pages. Although conventional wisdom insists that the right way to save marriages is for couples to work conjointly, this notion is, for most, an unrealistic ideal. Disenchanted spouses often have partners who refuse joint therapy. The reasons behind this range from psychological (i.e., passive-aggressiveness) to financial (i.e., health insurance does not cover joint marital therapy). Most clients not only lack, at least initially, the cooperation of their partners, but also the time, energy and patience for complicated marriage improvement formulas.

Critical to credibility of the new paradigm is evidence that significant marriage improvement can result from individuals focusing on themselves. Mark A. Whisman, Ph.D., Lauren M. Weinstock, M.S., and Lisa A. Uebelacker, Ph.D., present a study of individual anxiety and depression as it relates to marital satisfaction in the *Journal of Consulting and Clinical Psychology*. Two findings:

- "Each spouse's level of anxiety and depression predicted not only their own marital satisfaction but their spouse's as well."
- "The more anxious and/or depressed either spouse was, the more dissatisfied he or she was with the marriage."[10]

Regardless of whether we're depressed and anxious because we are unhappy with our spouses or vice versa, optimizing individual mental health is essential for maintaining marital satisfaction.

Everybody Marries the Wrong Person explores:

- Conventional wisdom's myths about marriage
- *Dis*satisfaction-guaranteed expectations
- Biology and psychology of infatuation and disenchantment
- Psychological incompatibility
- Real-life anecdotes and psychotherapy excerpts
- Essentials of mature love and healthy behaviors of self-responsible partners

Chapter 2

I May Be Dumb...

From childhood, our minds are saturated with the traditions of conventional wisdom. For most of us, conventional wisdom about romantic relationships remains unquestioned, perpetuating misconceptions and myths that guarantee marital dissatisfaction. Although we behave as if myths are truth, many of us also sense that truth lies elsewhere.

As one twenty-something client, Amanda, said about her search for Prince Charming and the white picket fence, "It sounds so ridiculous, but I want it. Why?" Simply put, she wants what conventional wisdom and fairy tale movies taught her to want. Conventional wisdom maps marital futures because we take it for granted. We follow conventional guideposts because everyone else is following them and we do so without asking, *Where exactly is this leading*?

In order to avoid following the well-intentioned crowd toward marital dissatisfaction and divorce, we must know which conventional guideposts to ignore. We also need to know which path to follow instead. *Everybody Marries the Wrong Person* details both. Twenty myths and misconceptions to ignore, divided into three categories, are detailed and discussed.

I Need Somebody

1. There's one right person for everyone.

This fairytale notion, straight out of *Sleeping Beauty* and *Cinderella,* sets up everyone for disappointment. The "one right person" myth dies hard, because everyone deeply wishes for life to be easy, as it could be with that one right person. The harsh reality that every couple (opposite sex and same sex) experiences psychological incompatibility soon undermines our certainty about a partner's rightness. Questioning partners' rightness, however, leads to nowhere constructive. *Everybody Marries the Wrong Person* encourages questioning the rightness of the myth and entertaining a new conclusion: there are no *right* people. (More discussion of the concept of no *right* people in part 3.)

The notion that there is only one person with whom each person can share a happy, long-term relationship has theological roots, too—a concept called predestination. If you believe, as some do, that God chose your mate for you at the same time He chose you for salvation, you believe in predestination. If you do not claim predestination, don't apply this concept to your search for a life partner.

2. It's better to be unhappy with someone than to be alone.

This powerful belief explains why many unhappy couples stay together. These partners essentially think, *Being alone would probably be worse, so I might as well stick it out.* At the root of this attitude is the universal fear of scarcity. We fear loss of companionship and loneliness. We fear having no one to turn to in times of overwhelming trouble or financial ruin. Though these fears are understandable, they are, for most, unfounded.

Thinking this way also typifies resignation: *I've tried and tried to change my spouse for the better and it made no difference. I might as well give up and be glad I have someone.* Self-responsible spouses recognize that changing their spouses never is a realistic option and get busy changing themselves instead.

Additionally, this myth perpetuates the belief that being alone is something to be avoided. Relationship experts, however, point out key ideas:

- Better to be unhappy alone than unhappy with someone.
- Romantic love is not the only joy in life.
- Personal happiness does not depend upon being coupled.
- Many people are uncoupled for significant periods of time and are perfectly satisfied and happy.

Some even agree with Meryl Streep's character in the movie *Plenty*, who said, "The only dignified way to live is single."

3. Spouses are supposed to fulfill each other's wants and needs.
Seems harmless enough, but this myth can never be separated from its roots—the one-sided tradition of wives being expected to fulfill husbands' wants and needs—or its history of providing justification for abuse of women. Even today, some societies criminalize wives refusing sex to husbands, tolerate public floggings and honor killings of women. Evidence that one-sidedness continues can also be found among my clients. In the mid-1990s, for example, a young wife and mother of four whose husband emotionally, physically and sexually abused her went to her father-in-law for help. Her father-in-law's advice? "Submit to your husband and he won't be forced to abuse you." In 2004, a self-described biker chick told me, "I am my man's property. I do as he says."

Sometimes those who place the man at the head of the household give a nod to equality by pointing out the husband's responsibility to at least consider his wife's wants and needs. That's only fair, right? This approach not only perpetuates the myth but also fosters unhealthy emotional dependence in both spouses. (Part 4 explores emotional dependence in more detail.)

Key concept: Do not make the mistake of holding your spouse responsible for meeting your wants and needs. Emotionally mature adults take responsibility for meeting their own needs. If you practice generosity and voluntarily work to meet your spouse's needs, do not expect reciprocation. Give to your spouse in a no-strings-attached manner or don't bother.

But what about cooperative need fulfillment, otherwise known as teamwork? Partners are at their best when working together toward common goals. Not on a quid pro quo (I will, if you will) basis, but in a self-responsible manner with each individual contributing to the absolute best of his or her ability. (More on partner contribution in part 4.)

According to comedian Johnny Carson, "Married men live longer than single men. But married men are a lot more willing to die." This is amusing, because we all see that reality does not match the myth that married people should not only meet each other's needs but also guarantee each other's happiness. Psychological research agrees with Carson: Although marriage does correlate with longer life expectancy, especially for men,[1] married people are not significantly "happier" than single people.[2] As much as we wish it could be so, we cannot expect partners to meet our needs and make us happy.

4. If I love, I will be equally loved in return.

Talk about a romantic notion with spouse-devaluing potential! Because many of us end up thinking that we are the ones who love more, this myth guarantees my-spouse-should-love-me-more ruminations and impossible to fulfill expectations. Although everyone learns from experience that this belief has no basis in fact, many of us cling to the delusion that we *deserve* this degree of love. We then feel justified in blaming the spouse who does not seem to love us as much as he or she should. Eventually, we may leave a partner whom we once thought was the right person, believing that the myth can be true if we find the *real* right person.

Thornton Wilder describes the busting of this myth as "that secret from which one never quite recovers." Further, he writes:

> …even in the most perfect love one person loves less profoundly than the other. There may be two equally good, equally gifted, equally beautiful, but there may never be two that love one another equally well.[3]

5. Love cures loneliness.

Opportunities for companionship are a chief benefit of love and marriage. Our expectations mislead us, however, if we believe that the love of a partner will banish loneliness. Married clients (both men and women) have puzzled over the experience of feeling lonely while in the same room with their partners. Many times people blame their spouses:

- He doesn't connect emotionally.
- She doesn't pay enough attention to me.
- He doesn't sympathize with my concerns.

The problem, though, is not with the spouse. It is with the lonely one's expectations.

Men often express an ideal of a partner who is like a teammate, participating with them in sports, games and other activities of mutual interest. They are disappointed when their women lose interest in camping, detailing show cars or going to the shooting range. Women often wish for a partner who, like a girlfriend, joins them in empathic conversation. They are dismayed when their men fail to hold up their end of the conversation at dinner, on the way home from a movie or during a road trip.

Unmet expectations leave us feeling disconnected from our spouses. Given that individuals often have different first-choice preferences for getting companionship needs met, disappointment is inevitable. *The self-responsible approach*: Make the absolute most of every moment that your spouse voluntarily engages with you in your preferred manner. (Part 4 examines coping with loneliness in more detail.)

6. Jealousy is a sign of love.

Jealousy, worst-case scenario, is a symptom of paranoid delusions or personality disorder, both of which are unhealthy mental states. In most cases, it is a sign of insecurity. Though it may be human to feel jealous, it is never healthy to behave jealously.

Sometimes, if we believe this mainstay of conventional wisdom, we intentionally elicit jealousy as a test of our love's commitment to us. Does he or she care for me enough that talking to another attractive person arouses jealousy? What exactly will and will not be discovered from this time-honored test? First, you will discover nothing about your love interest's level of commitment. If she shows jealousy, this only tells you that she is reactive, controlling, doesn't manage her negative emotions, is willing to vent on you and is emotionally immature. Good information to have, but you may have known these things already. If he doesn't show jealousy, you may misinterpret emotional maturity as lack of commitment. Think about it. How does stirring up trouble demonstrate anything other than your own lack of emotional maturity?

Although we usually take offense at harmless flirtatiousness, we sometimes feel jealous because we accurately perceive mal-intent on the part of a spouse. Although many spouses are blindsided by marital infidelity, intuition alerts most of us. When this is the case, there is no better guideline than Clare Boothe Luce's famous quip, "It's matrimonial suicide to be jealous when you have a really good reason."

Jealousy is not a sign of love. It is all about the individual's negative interpretations of and emotional reactions to a spouse's behavior. When we feel and act jealous, we betray our insecurities. If we expect a partner to change his or her interactions with others, we behave badly, whether we whine or intimidate. Choosing benign interpretations and reactions are the better signs of love.

It's Not My Fault

7. *It takes a lot of years to train a spouse.*

This myth keeps alive the hope that every wrong person is trainable and will eventually transform into the right person. Sophisticated people claim to know this is unrealistic; but, sooner or later, we succumb to wishful thinking. At the time we commit to a relationship, we are infatuated and believe that we have found the one person who will never need to change—at least not in any significant way. In the unlikely event that minor change is necessary, we expect our partner to happily transform because of the deep love we inspire. This is an example of one myth based on two more myths (see myths eight and fifteen in chapter 2).

The major problem here is that this myth is based on a model—the parent/child model—that cannot appropriately be applied to romantically involved adults. Even if your partner behaves like a child, it is imperative that you understand *the formative years are over.* The idea that you will [need to] parent your spouse ruins a romantic relationship. Natalie Wood got it right when she said, "The only time a woman really succeeds in changing a man is when he's a baby."

For marriage, the appropriate model is adult/adult, which assumes that spouses are self-responsible grown-ups who do not require parenting. It's not unreasonable to think about how your spouse might change for the better. It is, however, unrealistic to imagine your spouse changing because you think he or she ought to do so. Expecting change in your partner based on any rationale other than your partner realizing some benefit to self is an intellectually lackadaisical mistake.

You may disagree. "If I make my partner's life a living hell until he changes, he is forced to do so," some may argue. Okay, if you pitch a fit, your guy may wipe up the crumbs on the counter because you've made him angry and, thereby, put the issue foremost in his mind. You must notice, though, how quickly he goes back to forgetting to wipe up the crumbs. What you inspired was momentary concession, not significant change.

8. If you love me, you will change.

The misconception here is that people change out of love for one another. People are capable of change. This truth is the reason for religion, psychotherapy and the self-improvement industry. But people change out of self-interest, not for the benefit of others. When we become depressed enough, anxious enough, battered enough, etc., we begin to see that our quality of life and, sometimes, our survival depends upon our commitment to change. Ultimately, capability and intention combine, creating the teachable moment and we learn whatever is essential for improving our lives.

The "if you love me, you will change" misconception has an equally relationship-threatening counterpart: If s/he *doesn't* change, s/he *doesn't* love me. No matter how many times you remind her, she never wipes up the crumbs on the counter. She hasn't changed for you, so she must not love you. This is the wrong conclusion.

9. Fighting is healthy.

This figment of the conservative imagination and its two equally misguided variations—fighting *fair* is healthy and it's *un*healthy to "hold in" anger—are decades-old pieces of conventional wisdom and pop psychology. The fighting is healthy myth gets endless play. In 2009, for example, the pastor of a local fundamentalist church put up a Web site offering to teach couples the art of "godly fighting." I hope that this latest variation doesn't catch on. Fighting is drama and drama is for soap operas, talk shows and emotional adolescents.

There is nothing healthy about slugging, intimidating, criticizing or punishing your spouse. Fighting *fair* is a contradiction in terms (unless you're in a boxing ring) and the notion that we harm our own physical and mental health by "holding in" anger is incorrect. To succeed at relationships, we must learn *not* to fight and to constructively manage our angry feelings (chapter 12 explains the basics of anger management).

As Julia Seton wrote in 1914:

> We have no more right to put our discordant state of mind into the lives of those around us and rob them of their sunshine and brightness than we have to enter their houses and steal their silverware.[4]

10. Our problem is, we don't communicate.

One of my more articulate professors taught me a basic truth about communication: "We cannot *not* communicate." Communication is unavoidable. Every word, gesture and expression communicates. When we withhold them, we still communicate. For example, the so-called "poker face" translates to, *I don't want others to know what I'm thinking or feeling.*

Again, conventional wisdom equals intellectual laziness or believing and saying things just because everyone else does. When disgruntled couples say that they don't communicate, they are also NOT saying a few much more telling things. Some meanings that ride tandem with "we don't communicate" are:

- My partner doesn't talk as much as I'd like.
- My partner doesn't listen when I speak.
- My partner doesn't answer when I speak.
- My partner doesn't care about my feelings.
- My partner doesn't follow through with our agreements.
- My partner doesn't give equal weight to my preferences.

Believing that you'll be more satisfied in your marriage if your partner improves his or her communication skills is an uninformed and unproductive conclusion. (Part 4 details how you can improve your own communication skills.)

11. He or she made me do it.

In *Feeling Good Together*, David D. Burns, M.D., reports research aimed at identifying attitudes that lead to happy and unhappy marriages. Although he and his University of Pennsylvania medical school colleagues hypothesized scores of variables, they found one mindset was by far the most important predictor of marital success: "The only thing that really seems to matter is this: Do you blame your partner for the problems in your relationship?"[5] Dr. Burns concludes that the prognosis for successful relationships is extremely positive for those who are willing to stop blaming partners and start examining their own roles in the problems.

In the extreme, blaming the other person is the classic mindset of batterers, verbal and emotional abusers. In fact, abusers abuse not because their victims bring it on themselves, but because abusers choose to abuse. (More about abusers in chapter 3.)

12. Trust is earned.

We hear this myth everywhere. Parents say it. Teachers and preachers say it. An old-fashioned investment firm said it. This, too, is conventional wisdom with limited constructive application.

Trust is, in fact, a choice. Think about it. Everyone makes their own choices about whom to trust and under what circumstances to do so. Occasionally, we trust the completely undeserving and fail to trust the truly sincere. We all know individuals with whom we have had both experiences. Perhaps your spouse is 100 percent trustworthy to bring home every dime of her paycheck but disconcertingly untrustworthy when it comes to curbing her sarcasm.

Because humans are intractably self-interested, everyone is untrustworthy to some degree. We tell lies, for example, in order to avoid consequences of our actions or to make ourselves look better. We also prove ourselves less than trustworthy by taking small liberties and stealing other people's time, energy and good moods. A few of us have no scruples. If you happen to be married to someone who lies, cheats and steals without regard for the effect on others, choosing not to trust is likely in your best interest.

13. Once a cheater, always a cheater.

Discovery of sexual infidelity almost always triggers a marital crisis. Whether fidelity is renewed depends on the unfaithful spouse, who must end the affair and repair his or her damaged marriage. Whether trust is regained depends on the spouse who's been cheated on. As unfair as this seems, it is not up to cheaters to prove themselves trustworthy. It is up to the spouse who's been cheated on to decide whether to hold fast to the myth or choose to trust again.

During twenty-eight years of practice, I have counseled the cheater, the cheated and the "other" woman or man. Sometimes, I've counseled two or more parties to the same incident of marital infidelity. *Sinking feeling* describes the sensation associated with suddenly realizing the love interest about whom a client is speaking is another client or the spouse of another client. This is when psychologists' training in ethics informs an unwavering commitment to maintaining confidentiality.

My advice to spouses is always the same. To the cheater: Decide whether or not you want to preserve your marriage and make your behavior reflect your goal. If you want to save your marriage, stop the affair and focus on becoming a self-responsible spouse. If your changes are viewed as too little too late, accept the fact that you are facing the unhappy consequences of your behavior. Cooperate with your spouse, even if he or she is seeking separation or divorce. Failing to cooperate only confirms your spouse's feeling that you do not deserve compassion.

To the cheated: Decide whether or not you want to preserve your marriage and make your behavior reflect your goal. If you want the marriage, forgive the affair and choose to trust again. If you choose not to forgive and not to trust again, end the marriage. Above all, do not diminish yourself and everyone around you by demanding details of the affair and/or seeking revenge.

To the "other" man or woman: If you are married, see advice to the cheater. If you're not married, face the fact that you are in a no-win situation. If your love interest has children, he or she will most likely not leave the marriage for you. If he or she ends the marriage, you must choose to trust someone who has a history of marital infidelity. It is also important to know that most observers will see you as the seducer and treat you accordingly. In this situation, you will soon discern your true friends.

One last concept (which will be further discussed in part 3): People do not have affairs because their spouses neglect them or treat them badly. People have affairs because they choose to do so.

14. If I have to tell my spouse what pleases me, it's not as special.

There are probably more irrational beliefs about relationships than this myth, but there are few more self-defeating. Ask yourself: Am I insincere when I am told about and then start practicing a new way of pleasing my spouse? Which is more narcissistic: believing I deserve special treatment or expecting my spouse to continuously search for ways to make me feel special?

If you tell your partner what pleases you and s/he permanently adopts this behavior, you have made an exciting discovery. You have found what psychologists call a one-trial learner. If you nag your spouse, you are parenting, which you now know is a ruinous mistake.

We'll Stay Like This Forever

15. My spouse will never treat me badly.

If you have seen your partner behave badly toward anyone, know that your turn is coming. Yes, the day will come when your beloved will intentionally hurt you. You, too, will someday intentionally hurt your beloved. Humans, like other mammals, act out of instinct and learning. Additionally, humans are capable of forming intent and choosing behavior. Loved ones inevitably choose to subject us to their feelings of anger, jealousy and mean-spiritedness.

Part 4, "Mature Love," discusses how partners can react constructively and go on loving after being treated badly. A key part of this is forgiveness. In *Minding the Body, Mending the Mind*, Joan Borysenko, Ph.D., writes, "Forgiveness means accepting the core of every human being as the same as yourself and giving them the gift of not judging them."[6]

16. Love is selfless.

Love is self-interest. We behave lovingly because it feels good or because we get something we want in return. This is not to say that no one is capable of choosing to behave selflessly. We've all heard about or witnessed selfless acts or been recipients of someone else's generosity. So-called selfless acts, however, are not purely altruistic. In other words, love is not all about the love object. It is self-centered.

Conventional wisdom extols the selflessness of acts of compassion and heroism. In fact, behaving humanely is not selfless at all. Many people assume that cruel acts are self-centered and motivated by destructive impulses, greed, hatred and revenge-seeking. Compassionate and heroic acts are also self-centered, though motivated by individual commitment to constructive personal values (e.g., need for approval, need to do the right thing, need to be loved, need to be admired). We want to be thought of as compassionate or heroic, so we behave accordingly.

Romantic love is the most self-centered love of all. Conventional expectations demand that spouses be cherished, honored and treated like royalty. As will be made clear throughout *Everybody Marries the Wrong Person*, it is crucial to marital satisfaction for individuals to avoid irrational expectations. Expecting partners to demonstrate love by consistently putting our needs ahead of their own is one of the most irrational.

A note to those who are thinking that parents' love for their children is surely an exception: Although it can be argued that producing children is a self-centered act, the closest that humans ever come to selfless love is in the parent/child relationship. The legendary selflessness of mothers is not in any way abstract. It has always been, in most cases, around-the-clock observable behavior. Now, neuroscience tells us that this selflessness is the result of brain chemistry, which is permanently altered by motherhood.[7] These alterations, in fact, are what make it possible for a mother to distinguish her baby's cry from all other cries in a nursery. Fathers can also learn to recognize their babies' cries, but associated brain activity patterns of fathers and mothers are significantly different.[8]

17. No matter how I behave, my spouse knows I care.

This one might be called the "love story" myth, "love is never having to say you're sorry" myth or "it's the thought that counts" myth. Although thoughts regulate behaviors, our spouses do not know our every thought. Behaviors are all that matter.

This myth is based on at least three faulty and dangerous assumptions:

- **My spouse expects the best.** On the outset, spouses may expect the best or, at least, reserve judgment. Too often, though, things are bullish only as long as partners manage not to seriously offend each other. Once offense is taken, spouses, like anyone else, exhibit both photographic memory of downturns and faulty recall of upswings. Some spouses, due to bad experiences with members of their families of origin or other boyfriends and girlfriends, actually expect the worst. The safest assumption: Marital satisfaction is like a bear market; your stock is more likely to go down than up.

- **My spouse is emotionally evolved.** Generally, this belief corresponds with infatuation and is equally as short-lived. If this actually is the case, you are most fortunate and must ask yourself: Am I equally evolved? If you are not, you also must ask yourself: How long is my spouse going to tolerate that reality?
- **My gestures of love and care are interpreted as such by my spouse.** This is often not the case. Among my clients, a common complaint is that they feel their spouses take them for granted. More than one female client has said that the care with which she folds her partner's laundry is an expression of caring. As she smoothes the fabric and handles each garment, she thinks lovingly of the one who will wear the T-shirt or socks. More than one male client has described maintenance of his spouse's vehicle as a gesture of love. As he changes the oil, checks tire pressures and tops off the fuel tank, he thinks protectively of the one who will get behind the steering wheel. Poignantly, spouses feel disappointed and unloved when wrinkle-free clothes and full fuel tanks are not interpreted as valentines.

Aren't you thrilled and touched by a gift that is exactly what *you* want rather than what the giver wants for you? Such a gift is evidence that the giver listens to what you say, notices what you like and gives you enough thought to choose something meaningful. It's the kind of heartfelt consideration we all dream of receiving from our loved ones.

To successfully communicate love and care, you must provide your spouse *his* or *her* dreamed-of level of consideration. Or as Dr. Martin Seligman put it in *Authentic Happiness*, "You must never scrimp on the attention you pay to the person you love."[9]

18. True love conquers all.

If we believe this myth, we harm relationships by imposing impossible standards. When spouses' shortcomings or the onslaught of life's problems seem impossible to conquer, we fall back on the "right person" fantasy and devalue the trueness of our partners' love. Or we question the trueness of our love for our spouses. Instead of questioning the myth, we question love.

As everyone knows, loving thoughts and actions have power to uplift and transform. However, these heartfelt sentiments are not magic wands to be waved over a less than perfect spouse. Only those practicing loving thoughts and actions can expect transformation—of themselves.

Love positively shapes children's lives. Kids, however, are not in need of psychological transformation unless they have been heinously mistreated by caregivers or by the larger society.

19. Find your soul mate and marry him or her.

Although soul mates may exist, calling a romantic partner a soul mate is just another way of declaring him or her the "right" person. Only someone who has experienced both a romantic partner and a soul mate knows the differences and unique satisfactions of each. In statistical terms, people married to soul mates are outliers, rare examples that lie outside the bell curve of normal.

A soul mate is a special kind of dream come true. From Dioscuri (Castor and Pollux) of Greek and Roman mythology to African soul twins, cultures idealize soul mates. In short, a soul mate is your psychological clone, the one with whom everything is easy because you share beliefs and values, likes and dislikes, perceptions, instincts, intuitions, dreams and approaches to daily life. Unless outsiders intrude and introduce conflict, there are no misunderstandings, disagreements, criticisms or wrongs. Though feelings of love, physical affection and tender gestures are characteristic between soul mates, romantic involvement is less likely. Classic soul mates are friends, cousins, siblings, gay/straight best friends forever. The harmony of a soul mate relationship is threatened only when romance enters the life of one of the soul mates.

20. Great sex is the key to marital success.

Mutual attraction brings couples together; when sex is great for both, marriages benefit. That is, until sex is not so great anymore. Conventional wisdom undermines couples' satisfaction with their sexual relationships, because it is fraught with misinformation, lack of respect for female sexuality and male-centric wishful thinking.

Counter to depictions by popular media (sex sells!), legitimate sexologists tell us that any human couple has a limited window of opportunity during which sexual activity peaks—somewhere between three months[10] and almost four years.[11] Published in 1994 by a group of legitimate sex researchers who compiled the first methodologically-sound findings, *Sex in America* by Robert T. Michael, et. al., presented information such as: Americans have sex relatively infrequently and frequency of partnered sex declines with age—starting in the late twenties![12]

For a whole array of psychological (sexual interest) and hormonal (sexual desire) reasons, both men and women are capable of saying they no longer have interest in the relationship. Evolutionary psychologists hypothesize that decline in sexual desire is the natural companion of decline in capacity to produce offspring. Biopsychologists hypothesize it is the inevitable effect of disenchantment hardwiring: the biological imperative to procreate and move on. (More about this in part 3.)

Depending on a couple's timing, sexual decline can occur before or after the wedding. Whenever the shift occurs, it is in direct opposition to spouses' plans for a lifetime of electrifying sex. If sex is great at times and mediocre at others or is an area of concern or conflict, you're not alone. If your marital satisfaction is jeopardized by sexual realities, add this to your list of problems to work on. Sexual satisfaction in any long-term relationship is the result of successful adaptation. (Parts 2 and 4 explore more about marital sex.)

If sex is abusive, the abuser will say that you are at fault. If you are raped, coerced into sexual acts that you abhor or intentionally humiliated by your partner, the abuser has broken the marriage. The self-responsible course of action is to leave the abuser and never look back.

Beyond Myths and Misconceptions

Even if we agree that conventional thinking is obsolete, we may feel upset at the loss of all those long-held beliefs. And, in order to move beyond a lifetime of wishful thinking, we will need more than steely resolve. When we decide to rescue ourselves from failed marriage paradigms, we need more than a new paradigm and guaranteed tools of implementation. We need evidence that a new paradigm is relevant.

This is the point at which my clients sometimes raise their eyebrows and say, "That's okay, I trust you." What they're essentially saying is, "You don't have to tell me how the new road is built. I'll be perfectly satisfied if you just point me toward it." Although going where others point is expedient, it is exactly how we headed down the old road in the first place.

Road-Building

In order to make one's own way in a self-responsible manner, one must question old assumptions, gather new information and draw informed conclusions. Knowing how the new road is built offers broader perspective and increases confidence to apply new insights and practice new behaviors. In the twenty-first century, studying anything related to the mind requires a look at cutting-edge findings from the exciting and relatively new field of neuroscience. If marriage improvement depends upon changing expectations and reactions, it depends upon changing our minds. And changing our minds means changing our brains.

In any scientific field, before conclusions are drawn, new data must be critically evaluated. The goal of every legitimate scientist is to make a contribution whether data support or fail to support particular hypotheses. Interpretation of results, though, can prove controversial.

Example 1: In the seventeenth century, Galileo wrote that data pointed to heliocentrism (the Earth revolves around the sun instead of vice versa). Because his interpretation of data conflicted with that of the Roman Catholic Church, he was ordered to stand trial in 1633. His eventual sentence was commuted to house arrest, which lasted until his death in 1642. History showed that his interpretation of the data was correct.

Example 2: Arkansas birdwatchers and Cornell University ornithologists announced in 2005 that a four-second video proved the existence of the ivory-billed woodpecker, thought to be extinct for sixty years. As expected, skeptics and scoffers sounded the call for indisputable proof. John Fitzpatrick, head of the Ornithology lab at Cornell, commented:

> Well, there are people who looked at the video and they're basically scoffing at us…But the fact is, there's information in that video. And, as you know, you can actually learn a ton from just a few frames of video.[13]

In the 1970s, science began questioning the long-held belief that adults cannot generate new brain cells. Since then, increasingly sophisticated studies of the nervous systems of sea slugs, rats, birds, primates and humans laid the groundwork for "what is quickly becoming a new Golden Age of neuroscience."[14] In *Brain Rules,* John Medina summarizes twenty-first century thinking about plasticity of adult brains:

> We do lose synaptic connections with age (some estimates of neural loss are close to 30,000 neurons per day). But the adult brain also continues creating neurons within the regions normally involved in learning. These new neurons show the same plasticity as those of newborns. The adult brain throughout life retains the ability to change its structure and function in response to experience.[15]

Two particular fields of study, neural plasticity and neurogenesis, document that our brains not only expand and rearrange interconnections[16] but also replace lost cells.[17] *Neural plasticity* means potential for modification in patterns of neural connectivity (i.e., emotion, memory, the connection of sensory and motor systems in new ways, mal-connecting and disconnecting). Alvaro Pascual-Leone and colleagues at the Harvard Medical School published data in 2005 that reveal expansion of neural connections in the motor cortex after subjects practiced a new skill (five-finger piano exercises). They also established that just thinking about practicing the new skill (same piano exercises, different subjects) expands the same cortical territory.[18] *Neurogenesis* is a special type of plasticity in which neural stem cells (cells that can take on functions of destroyed cells) integrate into existing neural circuitry. Compare neurogenesis to finding a bridge washed out one day and repaired the next.

Although behavioral neuroscience has only begun to fill in the details, it is indisputable that changing our behaviors means altering our brains and vice versa. When it comes to improving marital satisfaction, what used to be referred to as experiencing a change of heart is now more articulately described as rewiring one's neural circuitry. Transforming your marriage means transforming your mind. Start by abandoning myths and misconceptions.

Chapter 3

Red Flags

Adhering to the twenty myths and misconceptions outlined in chapter 2 is not the only misstep made by infatuated individuals. Sometimes, we ignore our own misgivings. Or, we claim that no one knows our beloved as we do and fail to heed outsiders' sound warnings. Ultimately, we reach critical mass in errors of judgment and not only marry the wrong person but also set our course toward a great mistake.

A girlfriend of mine had been divorced a couple of years before we met. She often talked about her ex-husband and ex-mother-in-law and their inexplicable disregard for her feelings. One day, she showed me her wedding album so that I could put faces with names.

Although I have never seen a more stern-looking, mother of the groom, it was another photo that stopped me. My beautiful girlfriend with her huge dark eyes, upswept brunette hair and a snow white, beaded gown stood alone at her wedding reception. "Oh, look," I said. "Look at the expression on your face! You knew! You knew *then* you'd made a mistake."

"Actually," she admitted, "I knew before the wedding."

Just as my friend did, many clients have confided that they went ahead with weddings despite nagging doubts. They convinced themselves it was prenuptial jitters, counted on post-matrimonial behavior improvements or, as anyone can well understand, feared the fallout of calling the wedding off. In hindsight, prenuptial jitters seem prophetic and obstacles to canceling seem all too surmountable. For most, relying on the wisdom of convention seems like the best alternative.

Jessica's Story

Happily, some individuals, like the client discussed next, honor intuitions and act on their own behalves. One of my first inpatient clients as a hospital psychologist was Jessica, a fourteen-year-old who had attempted suicide. She presented quite defiantly and made it clear that she had no interest in trusting me. After her release from the hospital, however, she elected to return for regular outpatient psychotherapy sessions. By the time she graduated high school, she had confided a life-altering secret, overcome some prominent issues and looked ready to take on the world.

Nearly ten years after she went away to college, she tracked me down at my private practice. She was about four weeks from marrying a man whom she had met while attending graduate school. Jessica said that although she and everyone else thought her fiancé was a great guy, she no longer felt sure about marrying him. She asked me the age-old question, "How do I know if he's the right person?"

During our first session, she made up her mind to call off the wedding. We scheduled two more appointments that week and she carried out, as gracefully as anyone could, everything that must be done to cancel a church ceremony and reception to which 200 guests had been invited. A few years later, Jess wrote to tell me that she had taken a job in another state, met and married a man whom she loved and was doing well.

Avoiding Great Mistakes

Though we are bound to marry the wrong person, there are two kinds of wrong people. Wrong people with whom a happy life can be made and wrong people who become great mistakes. Across twenty-eight years of clinical practice, scores of regretful clients have talked about ignoring intuitions or, worse, refusing to acknowledge one or more of the big six red flags. Red flags mean **stop**! Test your misgivings against this list: substance abuse and dependence, mental cruelty, battery, inappropriate venting of anger, controlling behavior/jealousy/paranoia and under-functioning or under-responsibility.

The Big Six Red Flags

1. Substance Abuse/Dependence

Substance dependence is defined two ways: medically (with physiological dependence) and psychosocially (without physiological dependence). The medical definition hinges on *tolerance* (the need for markedly increased amounts of one's substance of choice to achieve the desired effect) and *withdrawal* (development of the substance-specific syndrome due to cessation of use including significant distress or impairment in important areas of functioning). The psychosocial definition applies to people who may not yet meet criteria for the medical definition but abuse substances despite having experienced significant negative consequences.[1] These are individuals who continue to abuse alcohol and other substances despite warning signs:

- Bar fights
- Citations for operating a vehicle while under the influence
- Complaints by loved ones of mistreatment or neglect
- Mandatory drug testing as a condition of employment
- Significant physical and psychological symptoms (whether the direct result of or exacerbated by substance abuse)

Unchecked, almost all who are psychosocially dependent eventually become physically dependent.

One year of sobriety is a good guideline when considering romantic involvement or re-involvement with a recovering substance abuser. If you succumb to manipulation and intimately involve yourself with someone who has limited sobriety, you are likely to become a casualty of his/her relapse. You are also enabling or protecting your loved one from experiencing the natural consequences of his or her self-destructive behaviors. Enabling is a key concept, whether partnered with a substance abuser or not, and will be discussed in part 4.

2. Mental Cruelty

Most of us know someone who never misses an opportunity to harshly criticize, sadistically humiliate or gleefully slander others. Anyone who is sufficiently frustrated may occasionally resort to acts of mental cruelty. If, however, you are involved with someone who is persistently mean- spirited, do not make the additional mistake of believing that your "in love" status exempts you from becoming the target of that mean-spiritedness (see myth six in chapter 2).

Marsha's Story

One newlywed woman who became a victim of extreme mental cruelty told me that her husband threatened to divorce her unless she found a way to correct the fact that her vagina was not tight enough to suit him. She tearfully talked about humiliating visits to her family physician and gynecologist to seek advice about fixing her problem. The problem was never hers. Whether her husband suffered from inexperience, unrealistic expectations, obsessive-compulsive disorder or physical limitations remains unknown. Perpetrators of mental cruelty typically blame others for their behaviors or claim special-case status that exempts them from rules of civil conduct. For example, they may have been abused and hurt by others in prior relationships. Regardless, no adult can realistically expect to achieve marital success without accepting responsibility for managing his or her own negative emotions.

3. Battery

Physical and/or sexual abuse in any relationship is unacceptable. Perception of abuse varies, however, between men and women and among couples.[2] Those who study violence in intimate relationships tell us, for example, that men are less likely than women to perceive aggressive behavior directed towards them as domestic abuse. And, while some couples have fun with a bit of roughhousing, others are appalled by it.

Although many individuals say that they would immediately end physically and/or sexually abusive relationships, this is easier said than done. Self-doubts plague victims. Threats of escalation of violence—"I'll kill you if you leave me"—immobilize them. Assurances of financial ruin—"I'll make sure you get nothing"—stymie them. And the batterer's trump card: "I'll take the kids from you," unhinges them.

Unfathomable as it may be to outsiders, victims follow their own timetables for ending abusive relationships, often vacillating for months, even years. Early in my career, it became clear that domestic abuse victims succumb to pressure not only from manipulative abusers but also from well-meaning friends, family and therapists.

Behaviorally, this means that they stay with batterers out of fear of retribution, leave batterers out of fear of disapproval from supporters who encourage them to leave and give in to manipulation by their batterers and resume abusive relationships. When a victim returns to a batterer, an already bad situation worsens. Batterers who succeed in recapturing their victims learn that unwanted consequences for their abusive behavior are only *temporary*.

What happens next in abusive relationships exemplifies a behavioral principle known as intermittent reinforcement. Decades ago, animal experiments (now deemed unethical) demonstrated that when rodents and primates were exposed to electric shocks *every time* they touched their food dishes, they stopped feeding. Conversely, subjects randomly exposed to shocks continued feeding. In other words, guaranteed shocks discouraged feeding, while random shocks did not. The experience of sometimes feeding *without* being shocked (intermittent reinforcement) overrode the experience of being shocked, encouraging subjects to take their chances.

Both batterers and their victims experience intermittent reinforcement. Victims who stay with or go back to batterers do so hoping that fondly remembered good times will become the rule rather than the exception. Batterers continue to abuse on the strength of their experience that victims do not make consequences stick. Just when it seems that the batterer will pay for his crimes by losing access to his victim, contact is restored. Just when it looks like the batterer will spend a night in jail, charges are dropped. In order to extinguish unwanted behavior, consequences must be consistently delivered.

The prescription for ending violence in relationships is complex. Outcomes vary in studies about psychological treatment for batterers. Experts disagree about the effectiveness of addressing abuse within the context of joint therapy. Some victim advocates condone tolerating "one strike" while others advocate zero tolerance. All are adamant about seeking psychotherapeutic intervention (jointly or separately) and separating or divorcing if there are repeated incidents of abuse.

The universally shared perspective? If you have been maliciously pushed, struck, injured or subjected to unwanted sexual domination, you have been victimized. An abusive relationship ends only when adult victims act on their own behalves. To do so, victims typically need the help and protection of supporters, sometimes including law enforcement officers and the courts. Refer to the chapter notes for resources for battered partners.[3]

4. Inappropriate Venting of Anger

All human beings are innately aggressive and destructive. We not only harm other human beings but also destroy plants and animals and damage the environment. Even those who aspire to tread lightly on the earth thrive at the expense of other living things.

Since understanding and managing natural aggressiveness is essential to success in all types of relationships, many theories about aggression and methods to teach anger management have emerged. Not all theories and methods, however, make constructive contributions. During the 1970s, for example, the theory was that it is unhealthy to "bottle up" or "stuff" negative emotions and healthy to "get out" angry feelings. Unfortunately, the lingo caught on and became part of conventional wisdom (see myth nine in chapter 2). Forty years later, people still think and speak in these terms.

When I was a doctoral student, I encountered one of the silliest and least enlightened methods consistent with this theory: bataka bats. Bataka bats are foam noodles that group therapists and joint marital therapists encouraged clients to hit each other with as a "safe" expression of anger. Rest assured, the vast majority of psychologists, even if trained during this era, never subject clients to this lunacy.

Since the 1970s, psychobiologists have found in studies that physical acting out of anger (everything from shouting to throwing things to striking people) increases levels of agitating "fight or flight" hormones. This means that acting out behaviors are contraindicated. Additionally, behavioral medicine researchers sought to predict heart attacks based upon personality factors. They hypothesized several predictors including drive to achieve and time urgency. Researchers found, however, that only one personality factor predicted heart disease: hostility or persistently acting out angry feelings.

Inappropriate expressions of anger intended to manipulate, intimidate, punish or demoralize signal an individual's inability to empathize, delay gratification and control destructive impulses—all undesirable characteristics in a life partner. The trick is to select someone who has examined his or her natural aggressiveness and chosen to be less destructive than average. (Part 4 addresses appropriate management of angry feelings.)

5. Controlling Behavior/Jealousy/Paranoia

If your love interest commands you to do anything and seriously expects you to obey, he or she is exhibiting a narcissistic sense of entitlement and is attempting to control you. At worst, controlling behavior manifests as mental cruelty, battery and inappropriate venting of anger. More commonly, controlling behavior takes less aggressive (though no less telltale) forms. Clients have talked about partners who tell them when to go to bed and when to get up, insist that they wear certain clothing or hairstyles, impose curfews, exercise regimens or church attendance or forbid certain friends, expenditures or leisure activities. And what is a "honey-do" list but a bid to control a partner's free time?

Narcissists and other emotional adolescents can never be sexy enough or rich enough to make it all worthwhile. For example, "the cock who thinks the sun rises to hear him crow," as George Eliot put it, is unskilled at and disinterested in contributing to others' emotional well-being. The woman who brags about keeping her man walking on eggshells has every intention of being the taker not the giver. Relationships with controlling adults can psychologically damage partners as well as children in these unions.

Jealousy is not about loving. It is about possessing and controlling. It is a gateway behavior, an early indicator of eventual escalation to mental cruelty and/or battery. Paranoia can be a sign of serious mental illness including personality disorder and psychosis.

6. Under-Functioning/Under-Responsibility

People who under-function are chronological adults who do not show histories of financial independence or who do not take full responsibility for their own physical welfares and/or activities of daily living. They typically have no meaningful history of success. They may be unemployed or underemployed and dependent upon one or more over-functioners who provide financial safety nets. If they earn reasonable incomes, they may frivolously spend money or forget to pay bills.

Under-functioners are often thoughtless, careless and reckless with their own property, personal health and safety as well as the property and well-being of others (e.g., a partner who scoffs at the hazards of second-hand smoke and puffs away around whomever he or she chooses). They may expect to be waited on, catered to, picked up after and entertained. They may expect their partners to plan all social outings, celebrations and vacations. Under-functioners may fail to help with household chores and childcare or may help, if asked, but rarely volunteer. Almost always, family members, friends or coworkers will hint at or complain of feeling used by your charming but under-responsible love interest.

The importance of this red flag is a matter of degree. It can signal a lifetime of minor annoyances or serious grief. It may require you to adjust your expectations or to eliminate the individual as a potential partner. Either way, this is where knowledge of myths seven and eight in chapter 2 can be invaluable.

Miranda's Story

Miranda is a thirty-something never-married woman with limited dating experience until the past year or so. She recently ended a relationship with a divorced, rather stuffy businessman who discouraged public displays of affection and often put work before their relationship. Now, she's dating a new man.

On a recent Tuesday morning, I found a message on my office voicemail:

> Hi, Dr. Meinecke. This is Miranda. I just wanted to call and thank you for last Friday's session, especially our talk about the six red flags. The reason I kind of got quiet and lost was that Earl had five of the six. When I got back to the office, my girlfriends had been researching him and they found that he has a record of multiple assault charges, OWIs and court-ordered mental

> health and drug and alcohol treatment—which obviously hasn't helped because he's still drinking. So, I broke up with him this weekend and so far, so good. He also has several no-contact orders from other women, but he's leaving me alone. So, thanks again and I'll see you at our next appointment.

Miranda was sexually attracted to Earl and liked his ability to "work the room" in social situations. They shared many interests and had been going out several nights a week. When we discussed the six red flags, she acknowledged that he abused alcohol. Also, he worked part-time in retail and lived in a seedy residential hotel. Though she recognized possible signs of under-functioning, she didn't want to act the snob or judge him too harshly. Finally, she described an incident in which she was talking with him by cell phone as he was "freaking out" while driving to meet relatives for dinner. He reportedly felt angry that he had been asked to drive during rush hour to a restaurant across town. She said that she had essentially told him to "cut it out" and succeeded in calming him down.

Miranda's decision to swiftly end this relationship is an encouraging sign. What remains to be seen is whether she may be stalked by Earl or manipulated into resuming the relationship.

Blaming the Victim?

Maybe you are thinking that expecting infatuated individuals to recognize and evaluate red flags is dangerously close to blaming the victim for the great mistake. If so, remember the central premise of *Everybody Marries the Wrong Person*: self-responsibility. Spouses are responsible for meeting their own wants and needs and managing their own fears and dark moods. *Everybody Marries the Wrong Person* refutes old thinking that fosters drama and assigns blame and instead details a new paradigm that accepts consequences of actions and chooses rational thoughts and constructive behaviors.

Too Late Now?

When people are infatuated, they ignore red flags. If you are among those who did so, you may be wondering, *Is it too late now*? Do not despair. There was never a possibility of your partner changing out of love, anyway. Yet, it is never too late to change yourself, to learn how to think and behave self-responsibly and to practice mature love.

Yellow Flags

Yellow flags are observations that make us go, *Hmmm*. Unlike red flags, yellow flags are not ignore-at-your-own-risk signals to wise up about questionable behavior on your love interest's part. We may feel concern about behaviors that are essentially neutral. We may feel concern when we *don't* see behaviors that we believe to be reliable measures of rightness.

Yellow flags may or may not be deal breakers. What must be acknowledged is the possibility that we feel concern not because our love interest is behaving inappropriately, but because we believe in drama-fostering, conventional wisdom, stereotypes and myths. Yellow flags make good material for psychotherapy sessions, because clients are required to examine the legitimacy of their own expectations and reactions. Nine concerns regularly voiced by clients typically result in conversations more about practicing discernment than about proceeding with caution.

1. Rebound Relationships

Here we go again with the right person notion. This basketball reference compares couples to guards and forwards scrambling in the paint. What this conventional idea means, in my opinion, is that anyone in the post-breakup state of mind can't be the right person or won't find the right person because he or she is vulnerable, prone to making bad decisions, attracting the unsuitable or diving toward whatever bounces in his or her direction.

Clients who tell me that their friends say they need to watch out for rebound relationships usually wear a sheepish expression. "A rebound relationship is a waste of time, right? It'll never work out, because it's too soon." Despite the tenacity of this conventional wisdom, no one actually knows anyone who ended a relationship strictly because it was a "rebound." Yet, we let this one worry us.

Although occasionally individuals jump quickly into new relationships after a breakup, this is neither the waste of time nor the potential disaster that such conventional silliness predicts. The more we practice relationships, the better. Under non-red flag conditions, we learn how patterns of interaction increase or decrease intimacy and commitment. Under red flag conditions, we learn discernment, limit-setting and the primary importance of taking responsibility for our own welfares. Worrying that "rebound" might be a factor lowers estimations and raises defenses. Trying to prove that "rebound" can work out leads to ignoring or rationalizing red flags.

Lucky timing plays a key role in many love stories. This does not, however, validate the "rebound" myth. No matter what the timing of a new relationship, nothing is more predictive of success than the emotional maturity of the individuals.

2. Chivalry

Conventional wisdom leans heavily in the direction of judging the rightness of a man by his level of chivalry and the classiness of a woman by how much chivalry she expects. Unfortunately, what looks like a handy measuring stick can also deliver a nasty poke in the eye. Ladies, if your modern day Sir Walter Raleigh throws his cloak over a mud puddle, watch out! Gentlemen, if your Queen Elizabeth wanna-be stands by the passenger side door waiting for you to open it for her, ditto! While old school manners are charming, conventional wisdom, again, leads us astray.

Granted, courtesy and kindness cannot be overrated. And extreme lack of chivalry or bad manners signal red flags. Men and women who don't know how to behave politely may be under-functioners. Those who are intentionally rude may be inappropriately venting anger or showing mental cruelty.

Over-solicitousness, however, can also indicate two big red flags: under-functioning and controlling behavior. The over-solicitous can be manipulative and lack authenticity. Examples are sweet talkers who borrow your car and never refill the gas tank and a person who wines and dines you and expects sexual favors in return.

When women are the object of chivalry, reactions vary. In the not too distant past, people actually debated whether a man holding the door for a woman was sexist behavior. Some still see getting out of the way and letting a woman open her own door as a sign of respect.

Most women react positively to chivalrous behavior, but this may or may not bode well for partners. Some women associate chivalrous acts with childhood relationships in which they played the princesses while their fathers, grandfathers or big brothers played the heroes. These idealized memories can create impossible-to-live-up-to expectations, causing love interests to end up losers in a contest they didn't know they entered.

Women who exploit conventional wisdom's consensus that they deserve the royal treatment may be signaling red flags: underfunctioning, inappropriate venting of anger or controlling behavior. Whether endorsed by society or merely tolerated, a sense of entitlement signals unhealthy narcissism. Chivalrous behavior or expectations thereof are poor predictors of how hard someone will try in a marriage.

3. Getting Serious Too Quickly

This conventional wisdom is another time-honored guideline about proper pacing of romantic relationships. What exactly it means depends on the couple. Getting serious may mean making the bid for exclusivity, traveling together, sharing an apartment or declaring mutual love.

So, how soon is too soon to say, "I love you"? First date? First kiss? First overnight? This is what my brother calls trying to discern the indiscernible. No matter when love is declared, if feelings are not reciprocated, it is "too soon." If we hear "I love you, too," it's perfect timing. Everyone knows someone who took a risk and said, "I love you," on the third date, got engaged, married within a year and stayed with his or her beloved forever. Everyone also knows someone about whom others are saying, "She's just not that into him" or worse, "Why buy the cow when you get the milk for free?"

If getting serious quickly is about rushing to stake a claim, it signals the red flag triad of controlling behavior/jealousy/paranoia. On the other hand, moving quickly could be about honoring keen intuition or recognizing a mentally healthy, self-responsible single person when you encounter one. Marital success is never dependent upon skillful timing. It depends upon the partners' emotional maturity.

4. Too Many Outside Interests

Here we have yet another conventional wisdom about trying to determine whether someone is the right person. To clarify, in this context, outside interest does not mean outside *love* interest. That's a whole other issue. Also, outside interests do not include substance abuse and other compulsive behaviors such as gambling or shopping. These may be red flags.

Sometimes one partner feels deprived of attention when the other has lots of social, family and work commitments, hobbies, etc. The partner who declares that the other has too many outside interests must ask him or her self: *Am I feeling neglected by a partner who continues to engage in activities established before we met? Was I attracted in the first place partly because he or she lives a full and interesting life? Am I accepting responsibility for planning mutual activities that my partner enjoys? Are my negative reactions signaling a red flag—controlling behavior—to my partner?*

Gayle's Story

Gayle is a thirty-something recovering alcoholic who is active in Alcoholics Anonymous. She has disregarded the AA guideline to avoid romantic relationships for the first year of sobriety.

Gayle: I'm really questioning this relationship.

Dr. M.: What happened?

Gayle: There was this concert on Monday night and I wanted him to go with me, but he said no, as always, because he saves Monday nights for playing darts at the bar.

Dr. M.: He does that with his mother, right?

Gayle: Yeah, she's in the darts league.

Dr. M.: And he drinks a lot, too.

Gayle: Oh, yeah. I just don't get why he doesn't, at least, want me to come along.

Dr. M.: Maybe because it's a bar.

Gayle: Well, that's what he says, but I tell him not to worry, that I'm not going to drink. That I can drive my own car and leave anytime.

Dr. M.: Is the fact that he drinks becoming an issue?

Gayle: Probably.

Dr. M.: Do you think he's an alcoholic?

Gayle: My sponsor asked me that, too. For now, I'm saying no, but he definitely abuses alcohol.

Dr. M.: So, you're questioning the relationship because he won't give up playing darts and drinking and spending time with his mother to spend time with you.

Gayle: Pretty much. I'm just so disappointed. Tired of not feeling important enough. I guess I haven't made my needs known.

Dr. M.: From what you've told me, you've made your needs known—repeatedly. You just don't want to take no for an answer.

Gayle: He doesn't match my flow.

Dr. M.: Let's talk about your expectations and reactions.

Gayle: I know, I know. I'm high-maintenance.

Carl's Story

Carl is a forty-something accountant, married fifteen years with three children. He initiated sessions at his wife's urging, after the sudden death of one of his business partners.

Carl: I'm getting fed up. My wife is treating me like some kind of…afterthought.

Dr. M.: Say more.

Carl: I'm last, dead last, on her list. She's got time for her job, the kids, the flower garden, her family, her book club, volunteering at the homeless shelter, teaching Sunday school, you name it. Even pedicures come before me.

Dr. M.: Does she have time for sex with you?

Carl: Hell, no! She's always too tired. It's like, "Okay, got my kids. Don't need those sperm donations."

Dr. M.: Angry!

Carl: Yeah, sometimes. But, honestly, it's not just about sex. We used to do things together. Nothing all that spectacular, but we enjoyed ourselves. At least I thought we did.

Dr. M.: So, how would you know that you were no longer her last priority?

Carl: We'd spend time together…without the kids.

Dr. M.: When's the last time you offered to work beside her in the garden or at the homeless shelter?

Carl: Oh, those things aren't my idea of fun.

Dr. M.: When was the last time you made the plans for one of those things you used to enjoy doing together?
Carl: Honestly? (Pause.) She usually made the plans.

You may already have an idea of how the rest of this session went. The focus rarely stays very long on anything other than clients' responsibilities to make changes in their own expectations and reactions. Whether partners are busy high-functioners like this client's wife or just otherwise occupied, trying to get them to change themselves into the right person by eliminating a few outside interests is off-point.

5. Differences Regarding Children

This is a yellow flag that can signal trouble even though there is nothing about either viewpoint that is inherently inappropriate or associated with red flags. Conventional wisdom holds that right people must agree on this issue. Some of us claim to be ambivalent about raising children, some declare that we want nothing more than to be parents and some make it clear that children, though we may love other people's, are not in our life plans. Some of us already have children from prior relationships.

Problems arise not because we have differences but due to reacting negatively to these differences. We believe that someone who is so right for us, except for this one thing, must be persuaded into full "right" personhood. Then we start sounding like characters in a soap opera.

- **We try to change the other person's mind.**
  - "Not everyone is meant to have children. We're too spontaneous and free-spirited. We need to always be able to come and go as we please. Besides, neither one of us can keep a plant alive."
  - "Children are the main point of marriage. If we don't have them, we'll regret it forever. Besides, you can't want strangers taking care of us when we're old and senile."
- **We feel justified in going to extremes to make our case.**
  - "The world is chaotic, evil and will probably end soon. How can you even think about subjecting a child to a possible Armageddon?"

  - "Not wanting children is inhuman. What other kinds of inhumanity am I going to find out you're capable of?"
- **We blame the other person for the conflict.**
  - "You're selfish and oblivious. People like you need to start caring about the population explosion."
  - "You're selfish and unreasonable. You must think this way because you had such terrible parents."
- **We fail to acknowledge our own inflexibility.**
  - "If this becomes a deal breaker, it's all on you."

No matter how much a couple believes what they once decided, feelings, opinions, confidence levels and circumstances change. If we coerced a concession to our wishes, we told ourselves the lie that we succeeded in making someone the "right" person, thus compounding the errors of old thinking. How long is that false agreement going to last? If we based our "right" person assessment on what seemed to be the firmest of intentions, we likely underestimated the power of ticking biological clocks or maturing perspectives.

A nationally syndicated advice columnist responded to a woman who complains that after a year of marriage, her husband has decided he doesn't want kids at that time or maybe forever. She adds that she made her expectations explicit before they married and now feels "duped into believing he would come around." She closes by writing that engineering an "accident" may be her only hope and that this impasse is a deal-breaker for her.

The columnist's response starts out by indicating that an "accident" is a betrayal and that the woman is not entitled to choose parenthood for someone else. The columnist closes by encouraging the "duped" woman to approach the situation not as a lobbyist for children, but as a mate who is willing to set aside anger. I feel the important thing, though, is that the woman needs to have ideas about how to go about following this advice.[4]

I believe the columnist's assessment, that the relationship could only be saved if the woman forgives her husband's "horrible bait and switch", is not the advice I would give. Oh, how easily we join the chorus, parroting what conventional thinkers parroted before us. The "duped" woman squawks out the tune about her husband's blameworthiness; the columnist sings along.

I believe this woman and the advice columnist convey all kinds of old thinking. First, the woman and the columnist seem to agree that it is appropriate to label the husband's current viewpoint as a bait and switch. Second, the husband does not seem to have done anything for which he must be forgiven. Is forming a different viewpoint a malevolent act of betrayal? Third, a more constructive approach, I think, would require the woman to fully examine her angry assessment of her husband's viewpoint. Fourth, I believe the advice should concentrate on attempting to refocus the woman's outrage. Discouraging her impulse to stage an "accident" is only a start. Finally, the woman must focus entirely on her own disenchantment and lack of self-responsibility.

If this woman complaining about her husband were my client, alternate interpretations of her husband's so-called change of heart would be explored. Did the woman fully understand her husband's viewpoints about becoming a parent before they got married? Did she really listen to him or simply hear what she wanted to hear? Just how solid is their marital relationship? Might her husband's ambivalence about bringing children into their relationship signal trepidation about continuing their marriage? Is a wife who considers staging an "accident" emotionally mature enough to become a parent?

Indeed, deciding the future of existing or dreamed of children makes an excellent screening tool, but not in the way most of us think. What's at stake is too critical to be considered a closed subject after the check-mark is made on the "right" person checklist. When we address this issue with our partners, we learn very little about what the future might hold. If we pay attention, though, we can learn a lot about our love interest's level of emotional maturity. Emotionally mature individuals always keep in the forefront their responsibility to give highest priority to children's welfare.

6. Recovering Alcoholics and Drug Addicts

Eliminating any love interest from life-partner consideration who is recovering from chemical dependency presumes to eliminate wrong people and matrimonial slackers. This time, conventional wisdom gets it half right by waving a red flag around people with rampant substance abuse problems. The part conventional wisdom gets wrong is the suspicion that the chemically dependent (including the "recovering") are villains, losers or throwaway people, who are unlikely to put forth their best efforts in marriage. Villains and losers can be chemically dependent, but this is covered under red flags. Recovering substance abusers deserve a more nuanced appraisal.

Like so many of us, there are alcoholics and substance abusers among my friends and on both sides of my family. On a professional level, my postdoctoral fellowship with Johns Hopkins University School of Medicine was served as Clinical Supervisor of a substance abuse treatment program with both inpatient and outpatient components. My experience with chemically dependent individuals poignantly reminds me that it is wrong to go along with conventional wisdom's tendency to slander the character of people with a chemical dependency.

My first long-term, serious boyfriend was a substance abuser: marijuana, hashish, methaqualone, cocaine. In the beginning, it was easy to tell myself that he was young and would grow out of his druggie phase. He was a sweet, funny, sexy and articulate artist who gave me original oil paintings. My family and friends loved him and he always seemed to have my best interests at heart. Back then, he seemed like a potential "right" person.

Occasionally, he said things like, "I'm not good enough for you. You will find someone better." To which I replied, "You are good enough for me. I don't want to find someone else." Then he responded, "You're going to be a doctor and I'm going to be a derelict artist living in an abandoned warehouse." The accuracy of his predictions still amazes me.

Then there are my high school girlfriends. Six of us reunited to celebrate turning forty. It was a pretty wild weekend—much of it spent drinking in a lounge, a rented limousine and a hotel suite. It didn't take long to recognize that two of my dear friends had serious drinking problems. The key interaction went like this:

> **Girlfriends:** Okay, Chrissie, you're the doctor. Are we all alcoholics?
>
> **Me:** Yes.
>
> **Girlfriends:** That's what we thought you'd say.

Me: I'm serious.

Girlfriends: When we're sober, we want to talk more about this.

And we did talk more about it. Unfortunately, one of them has since died due to alcoholism.

We all know and love chemically dependent people, some of whom never recover. Others, however, do learn to abstain from substances. Too often, despite maintaining sobriety, recovering individuals are negatively affected by biases of conventional wisdom. Even recovering substance abusers have a bias against recovering substance abusers.

Chemical Dependency 101

So, apparently, the majority of us need more information about why this one may be a yellow flag rather than a red flag. Although recovering from chemical dependency requires steely determination and one-day-at-a-time persistence, chemical dependency never has been and never will be a matter of character. It is about DNA, environmental factors and gene expression. It is about activation of the brain's reward systems and, most probably, another brain region called the insula.

Until recently, the silver dollar-sized insula, found on both sides of the brain between the temporal and parietal lobes, had not inspired much research. Brain experts generally thought of this area as a part of the limbic system. Now, some think it merits designation as the brain's fifth lobe.

Taken together, the known functions of the insula suggest that this region is crucial to what may best be described as knowing what it feels like to be human.[5] The insula processes sensations on the skin and from internal organs. It also links into the complex circuitry of social emotions such as empathy and fear of rejection. The insula integrates body and mind and allows us to anticipate how events will feel before they happen, which is central to understanding why we buy concert tickets, avoid chainsaws, seek to experience the feelings associated with infatuation and crave substances.

Recent data document a key finding about the insula and chemical dependency: strokes and other types of damage to this area disrupt smoking addiction.[6] Subjects quit smoking less than a day after the lesion occurred and reported freedom from urges to smoke. Alert readers may wonder whether experiencing the awful realities of having a stroke offer an alternative explanation for subjects' decision never to pick up another cigarette.

Researchers wonder about alternative explanations, too, and employ controls and perform statistical analyses that allow them reasonable degrees of confidence about their findings. In this study, researchers found that the likelihood of disruption of smoking was significantly higher after a right or left insular lesion than after non-insular legions. In other words, confidence is high that the insula plays a role in addictions.

In light of scientific findings such as these, we can free ourselves of conventional wisdom's tendency to question the character of chemically dependent individuals. Most recovering alcoholics and drug addicts are comparable to those who successfully managed life-threatening illnesses, severe depression or anxiety. Again, while substance abuse can be a clear red flag, romantic interests who achieve "recovering" status are often working hard to advance themselves toward emotional maturity.

7. Codependency

While we're on the subject of chemical dependency, let's address codependency, another concept well-established in conventional wisdom. Those who write books, appear on talk shows and put up Web sites on the subject generally define codependency as "relationship addiction." Over the years, many clients have described themselves as codependent, which afforded opportunity for myth-busting discussions.

The concept of codependency is actually quite controversial. The term evolved, it seems, as an elaboration of the legitimately important Alcoholics Anonymous concept of enabling. Soon, however, it took on a life of its own.

In the 1980s, books like Robin Norwood's *Women Who Love Too Much* and Melody Beattie's *Codependent No More* gained popularity. At the time, the term *codependency* was primarily applied to women who were involved with chemically dependent men. In response to widespread adoption of the concept, the committee of medical and mental health professionals that revises the *Diagnostic and Statistical Manual of*

Mental Disorders considered adding codependency as a new diagnosis of psychological pathology.

Clear-thinking advocates for elevating rather than degrading the status of women argued that it would be a disservice to assign this psychiatric diagnosis to individuals solely on the basis of their relationship to chemically dependent partners. The committee decided against adding a codependency diagnosis.

Today, Web sites galore explore and discuss the topic. The controversy boils down to this: Well-established groups such as Co-Dependents Anonymous advise us to guard against being too *un*selfish and, thereby, destructive to self and others. Contrarians claim that the codependency movement is ruining marriages by prescribing equally destructive selfishness as the antidote for pathological unselfishness. What is missing from both sides of the debate is attention to the constructive concept: self-responsibility.

Potential partners who voice concerns about codependency—their own or yours—are assessing "right" person status and verging on two kinds of wrong. Feel free to discard codependency criteria along with the fantasy of one "right" person. Instead, think about levels of self-responsibility and emotional maturity.

8. Fear of Commitment

Conventional wisdom loves this one as a measure of rightness and as a way of predicting the likelihood of matrimonial slacking. What it means, I guess, is that the love interests' timetables for agreeing to exclusivity or to someday getting married aren't synchronized. Too many lengthy delays occur to suit the one who points out the other's fear of commitment.

Bonnie's Story

A thirty-something registered nurse, Bonnie has never married and recently reconnected with a guy she dated in high school.

> **Bonnie:** I think he has a fear of commitment. He's always been like this. Other guys used to steal his girlfriends all the time in high school.
>
> **Dr. M.:** Did you get stolen away from him in high school?

Bonnie: Not really. We didn't even go to the same school. We mostly just met up at hockey games, if you know what I mean.

Dr. M.: Mostly sex?

Bonnie: Yeah. Kids experimenting. But now we're not kids. I want commitment.

Dr. M.: Marriage?

Bonnie: Oh, I don't know. I guess I just want him to *want* to marry me.

Dr. M.: Marriage hasn't been mentioned?

Bonnie: He talks around it. Mostly about what disasters his two marriages were and how he never wants to go there again.

Dr. M.: Meaning?

Bonnie: I assume he means he doesn't want a *bad* marriage again.

Dr. M.: Might be worth clarifying.

Bonnie: Well, if he wanted marriage, I guess I'd know it. What I really want is that settled feeling you get when you're committed.

Dr. M.: Now, we're getting somewhere. Let's talk specifics.

Bonnie: Sure. He sets too many limits around our time together. He wouldn't even go with me to my parents' for dinner on Sunday. He said it was too soon and he would feel uncomfortable.

Dr. M.: But he's met your parents.

Bonnie: Exactly my point.

Dr. M.: Wait a minute. Sunday was Father's Day! Is his dad still living?

Bonnie: Yeah.

Dr. M.: Does his dad live nearby?

Bonnie: (Starting to smile.) In town.

Dr. M.: Was this a test? Would spending Father's Day with your dad instead of his own have been a sign of commitment?

Bonnie: (Laughs.) Oh, I know where this is going: "Look at your own expectations. Look at your own reactions."

Dr. M.: Exactly.

I doubt that my client's love interest is having fun failing tests and being labeled commitment-phobic. By pushing for a made-to-suit timetable for commitment, my client is signaling a red flag: controlling behavior. Her love interest could be signaling a red flag, too: under-functioning.

Ultimately, this yellow flag indicates the importance of discernment. We may, in fact, be engaging in wishful thinking by staying with love interests who do not share our visions of the future. On the other hand, when we label our love interests as commitment phobic, we may be failing to address within ourselves whatever is causing any lack of that "settled feeling" in a relationship. (We'll discuss this further in part 4.)

9. Refusal to Consider Premarital Counseling

This is one of conventional wisdom's ideas about how to insure against matrimonial slacking. If a not-quite-right love interest refuses your suggestion that premarital counseling might provide insight into how he or she might improve himself or herself, don't be surprised.

Those who show determination not to be influenced may be exhibiting what psychologists call counterdependence, which may be an indicator of red flags: controlling behavior/paranoia or under-functioning. Counterdependence is acting like a rebellious adolescent, masking emotional dependence with over-the-top and unsustainable shows of independence. Know this, though: If you are seriously involved with an acting-out, emotional adolescent, no amount of premarital counseling is going to save the relationship.

If you phrase it as a joint endeavor since you both have things to work on and are still refused, don't overreact. There are many legitimate reasons that partners object to premarital counseling. Most commonly, a love interest is likely to be unenthusiastic about counseling if he or she believes that an effort is being made to change him or her into a "right" person. People rarely agree to be the one to get "fixed." If you are willing to commit, instead, to examining how you might change for the better, arrange individual counseling for yourself.

Part 2

Infatuation

Chapter 4

Nature's Cruel Joke

Everybody marries the wrong person means that infatuation is temporary. What starts out so right eventually seems all wrong. No matter how much in love we are or perfect the match, most of us wind up looking at our spouses and asking, "Who *is* this person? How can it be that she doesn't watch sports with me anymore? Why doesn't he even look up when I walk into the room?"

Things are just not the same. What initially seems like profound compatibility becomes unsustainable, the result of individuals' putting their best feet forward, otherwise known as playacting. The problem with playacting is that, as actress Elizabeth Ashley put it, we "play a part that the other really likes," encouraging expectations that are impossible to live up to for a lifetime.

Crazy In Love

Although infatuation is a normal experience, it is not a normal state of being. Thanks to temporarily enhanced neurochemistry, people in love feel that they are the "right" ones, that their romance is special and that they are bound for marital success. Infatuated couples (of any age) engage in behaviors that, absent infatuation, would be seen as delusional, obsessive-compulsive and manic.

Brain scans of infatuated individuals show neuronal activity that is similar to cocaine intoxication. In *Change Your Brain, Change Your Life,*

Daniel Amen, M.D., points out that romantic love has cocaine-like effects on the brain, robustly releasing dopamine in the basal ganglia. (The basal ganglia are a set of structures near the center of the brain, a part of the limbic system. Known as the anxiety center, the basal ganglia also mediates pleasure.) He features a scan of a male subject's "love-affected" brain and states:

> The activity in both the right and left basal ganglia was very intense, almost to the point of resembling seizure activity. Love has real effects on the brain, as powerful as addictive drugs.[1]

Thoughts and behaviors of the infatuated also resemble the narcissism of adolescence. Poet Jim Harrison offers this definition of narcissism: "in Mexico the poor say/ that when there's lightning the rich/ think that God is taking their picture."[2] Christopher Lasch, who has written about the subject for thirty years, explains that narcissism is "a difficult idea that looks easy—a good recipe for confusion."[3] In most cases, the narcissism of the in-love is not the hopelessly unhealthy narcissism of the psychopath but garden variety narcissism, defined by Lasch as "self-absorption and delusions of grandeur."[4] Although society harshly judges narcissistic behaviors under other circumstances, most everyone indulges in-love individuals' sense that they are the center of their universe.

Nature's Cruel Joke

If you've been there, you know:

- You feel insanely happy and sexy in the presence of Mr. Wonderful.
- You feel insanely let down after Hot Girl goes home.
- You lose your appetite.
- You feel energetic even though you're not getting enough sleep.

Nothing interests you as much as he or she does. In fact, you can't stop thinking about your love object. It's exhilarating, irresistible, incomparable and it does not last.

It cannot last because our bodies seek homeostasis, a relatively stable state of equilibrium or evenness. It's only a matter of time until brain chemistry stabilizes and infatuation cedes to reality. Seemingly overnight, perceptions change. Mr. Wonderful begins to resemble a channel-surfing ingrate and enchanting Hot Girl seems disturbingly like (or unlike) dear old Mom.

Post-Infatuation Frustration

Diabolically, infatuation runs its course within three months to four years,[5] landing us in a whole lot of post-infatuation frustration. At this point, couples begin to suspect that they are not unique after all, to worry that their partners are not the "right" people and to question whether their partners are trying hard enough. Then they do what comes naturally to adolescent narcissists: They "make extravagant demands on each other and experience irrational rage and hatred when their demands are not met."[6]

Frustrated men echo Sigmund Freud's famous question, "What do women want?" Equally frustrated women want answers, too, perhaps to the question, "Why does he make me the enemy?" We stop thinking happily-ever-after and start wondering whether the cynics we know could be right—that marriage offers little but intermittent, if not everlasting, suffering.

Perpetuation of the Species

So, what earthly purpose might a temporary, delusional state serve? Remember the jump rope rhyme?

Ben and Crystal,
sittin' in a tree,
k-i-s-s-i-n-g,
First comes love,
then comes marriage,
then comes pushin' a baby carriage.

Did you ever notice there's no second verse? "Pushin' a baby carriage"—end of story. Just as Nature intended.

Biologists call it pair-bonding. For most species, pair-bonds last for one mating season. Psychologist Dr. Martin Seligman argues that marriage (the longer-lived, human equivalent of pair-bonding) was "invented by natural selection, not by culture" because "humans are born big-brained and immature, a state that necessitates a vast amount of learning from parents. Those of our ancestors, therefore, who were inclined to make a deep commitment to each other were more likely to have viable children and thereby pass on their genes."[7]

Our instincts for mating stem from pathways deep within the brain including the basal ganglia and the limbic system. The limbic system is a network of structures deep in the brain's center with direct connections to the prefrontal cortex. Limbic system neurotransmitters regulate mood, sex drive, appetite and sleep and also inhibit aggression and pain. Also imbedded in the limbic system is the neurocircuitry of reward-seeking, which produces pleasurable sensations and drives humans to explore in search of novel experiences. You need look no further than a toddler tearing through a toy box or an adult exploring what *else* is on television to see curiosity and reward-seeking in action.

When the drive for new experiences intersects with the drive to reproduce, people search for new people with whom to pair-bond. These drives predispose us (yes, women, too[8]) to search—and keep searching—for multiple partners with whom pair-bonding is possible. *Though not ideal for marital satisfaction, humans are hardwired to become disenchanted with a mate and move on.*

Pulitzer Prize-winning science writer Deborah Blum notes that while 90 percent of birds are monogamous, 97 percent of mammals "live by the rules of promiscuity." Among primates, "perhaps, twelve percent are monogamous—if you include borderline cases such as humans."[9] Procreate and move on is Mother Nature's way of promoting healthy diversity in the gene pool.

The merging of dissimilar DNA produces genetic improvements. Think of hybrid fruit trees or Knockout and Double Knockout roses, developed to improve hardiness and disease resistance. Likewise, the chances of human survival increase as diverse DNA strands blend, producing handsomer specimens, broader immunity to disease, richer abilities and diversified talents. Celebrity examples include Raquel Welch, Martin Sheen, Halle Berry, Greg Louganis, Tiger Woods and Barack Obama.

The Gift and Curse of Complexity

Love is more complex than genetic drives. All human behavior involves instincts, as well as emotions (emanating from the deep center and various sites around the brain) and cognitions (generated in the frontal lobes or neocortex, an area of the brain unique to mammals.) The neocortex or the prefrontal cortex (PFC) is the most evolved part of the human brain, representing 30 percent of the entire cortex. In *Making a Good Brain Great*, Daniel Amen calls the PFC "the boss in your head, supervising your life."[10]

Such complexity, however, is both a gift and a curse. The gift is the capacity of the brain to override destructive instincts and inhibit powerful negative emotions. The curse is the never-ending battle of the devil on one shoulder and the angel on the other, representing the struggle between what we want to do and what we ought to do, the push and pull between our destructive sides and our constructive sides, the tension between instinctual drives and higher cortical powers.

Pair-Bonding Versus Marriage

This same internal battle rages over the urge to merge. Animal instincts define coupling as one thing and human cognitions define it as another. It is the age-old battle of pair-bonding versus marriage.

Pair-bonding	Marriage
Instinct	Cognition
Procreation	Love
One mating season	Until death do us part
Natural law	Divine/civil laws
Survival of the species	Quality of life

The basic plot of pair-bonding: attraction leads to procreation leads to instinct-based abandonment of one family to start another. The basic plot of marriage is something else: attraction leads to settling down leads to living out any of the multitude of possibilities imagined by the human neocortex—everything from decades of heartfelt Valentine's Day celebrations to incidents of murder of spouses. Though outcomes determined by the indifference of Nature can be cruel, nothing is crueler than behaviors generated by human emotions such as blame and bitterness.

Logical question: If human brains got us into this mess, can our brains also get us out? Nihilists say not a chance. From Kurt Vonnegut's *Galapagos*:

> To the credit of humanity as it used to be: More and more people were saying that their brains were irresponsible, unreliable, hideously dangerous, wholly unrealistic—were simply no damn good.[11]

Optimists such as the fourteenth-century Sufi poet Hafiz, on the other hand, say otherwise:

Even
After
All this time
The Sun never says
To the Earth,
"You owe me."
Look
What happens
With a love like that.
It lights the
Whole
Sky.

Perpetual-Infatuation Fantasy

Conventional wisdom embraces the perpetual-infatuation fantasy. This is the belief that only the inept let infatuation die and that expired pair-bonds can be revived by resuscitating crazy-in-love sensations. This fantasy is kept alive not only by couples' wishful thinking, but also by advertisers' promises.

Think about it: You can't pick up a magazine, log on to the Internet or turn on the television without seeing pitches for guaranteed romance re-kindlers: diamonds, lingerie, penis enlargement, sex-improvement guides. In reality, the biochemical state of infatuation is, for any given couple, a one-time-only opportunity. The super-charged state of infatuation can be experienced only with a new partner.

What's Love Got to Do with It?

Humans have long sensed that deliverance from the grim realities of Nature depends upon the practice of giving and receiving love. Not to be confused with lust and infatuation, love promises long-term enhancement of human lives. Love and healthy bonds between parent and child, siblings, friends and spouses are experienced as feelings and, also, manifested as behaviors. Mature love is constructive, careful, empathic and learned through practice. It is the outcome of all the "hard work" that older and wiser people keep talking about. Though most of us think we know what this means, marital satisfaction surveys and divorce statistics document that we do not.

According to data collected by University of Iowa researchers, two adages about romance, birds of a feather flock together and love is blind, are, in fact, true. The studies draw these conclusions:

1. Romantic interest causes positive comparisons to self.
2. Such comparisons to self cast love objects in a favorable light and also blind us to their shortcomings.
3. Romantic interest leads to overestimation of similarities.[12]

Compatibility

Despite the seemingly false start of infatuation, areas of genuine compatibility exist for many couples. During the getting-to-know-you phase of any relationship, we test the limits of compatibility in three areas:

- Physical/sexual compatibility or **mutual attraction**
- Emotional compatibility or **mutual admiration**
- Cognitive compatibility or **shared values, beliefs and interests**

The next three chapters explore mutuality, the meeting of minds and the uniting of souls that motivate couples to sustain marriage beyond infatuation.

Chapter 5

Hot Sex Here

Mutual Attraction

Mutual attraction both fuels and outlasts infatuation. Physical/sexual compatibility is the fulfillment of two people's idiosyncratic preferences regarding physical appearance and much more. It has been called erotic love, passion and, long before twenty-first century science revealed the accuracy of the term, people called it chemistry. Now, we know that neurotransmitters and hormones associated with sex drive, fertility, mood, motivation, immune factors and pair-bonding are the essence of mutual attraction.[1]

Psychoneuroendocrinology researchers conduct studies about the interdependence of behavior and body chemistry. They collect data about the effects of various biochemical compounds on brain function and psychological states and vice versa. Some of the compounds studied are known as ectohormones and are believed to work *between* individuals. Other compounds, known as endohormones, work *within* individuals.

Ectohormones may ultimately explain why we feel a connection with one person and not with another. Most everyone has noted a lack of sexual attraction to an indisputably attractive acquaintance or encountered a complete stranger, experienced a rush of arousal and felt that something more was at work than simple appreciation of appearance. Though a somewhat controversial subject, many scientists think that these experiences are due to a type of ectohormone found in mammals.

These ectohormones, called pheromones, broadcast sexual compatibility and influence reproductive systems. Found on the skin, these substances are perceived via the sense of smell yet can be essentially odorless. Scientists also hypothesize that a previously understudied pair of cranial nerves (called nerve zero to avoid renumbering the established twelve pairs of cranial nerves) routes pheromone messages through the brain to reproductive systems.[2]

Many researchers believe that, like other animals, humans "communicate" or influence levels of sex hormones via pheromones. This phenomenon reveals itself not only in "that old black magic called love," but also in nonromantic circumstances. For example, male spectators at sporting events escalate one another's testosterone levels. Even non-beer-drinking male fans are more likely than their female counterparts to scuffle in the stands or storm the field after a game. Women who live or work together affect each other's hormones, too, as evidenced in the synchronization of menstrual cycles. Martha McClintock, Ph.D., who has investigated pheromones for more than thirty years, summarizes her rationale:

> The field of physiological or bio-psychology typically looks at how biology causes changes in behavior. What we're trying to do is say that that's a very reductionist approach, and what is really important is to realize that psychology and social interaction also regulate biology.[3]

Endohormones

Endohormones, such as reproductive and stress hormones and limbic system neurotransmitters, also play a role in sexual attraction and the biochemical state of infatuation. Scientists have documented that hormone levels in men and women who are in love vary from normal in fascinating and unexpected ways. For example:

- Levels of testosterone (the reproductive hormone associated with sex drive and aggression) *drop* in men.
- Levels of testosterone *rise* in women.
- Cortisol levels rise in both sexes, indicating that stress hormones are flowing.[4]

One-Sided or Short-Lived Sexual Attraction

One-sided attraction equals unrequited love. One-sided or short-lived attraction in marriage equals marriages without "spark" and spouses who say, "I guess I thought sexual attraction would develop over time." Though I rarely hear this statement from husbands, I occasionally hear it from wives. This is a sad, some would say tragic, situation for both partners.

Clients have also told me what happens to physical compatibility when abuse occurs. Sometimes, revulsion is the result of abuse at the hands of a partner. Other times, sexual attraction is the primary factor that draws a victim back into an abusive relationship.

Essential as it is, mutual attraction alone is not a basis on which to launch a life-partnership.

In the late 1980s, an Iowa judge ordered a couple to be evaluated by a psychologist before he would grant their divorce. Presumably, the judge did not accept the couple's assertion that their four-month marriage was a mistake. So, the couple called the psychology department of the hospital for which I worked and they ended up on my schedule. My role was to determine whether their marriage could be saved. If I agreed with the couple, I was to supply a letter indicating this to the judge. If I agreed with the judge, the couple was to try marital therapy.

Both partners were in their mid-twenties, exceptionally attractive (think young Hollywood meets serious athlete), college-educated and employed. They met at a health club.

While speaking with them jointly, they agreed that they had chosen each other strictly on the basis of appearance and had gotten married because they thought their babies would be the world's most beautiful.

While speaking with them individually, the husband claimed that his wife was annoyingly disinterested in domestic pursuits and overly interested in going to bars with her girlfriends. The wife complained that her husband was boring, sexually inept and only interested in bodybuilding. Both asserted that they had nothing in common beyond their obsession with physical attractiveness and now realized that they were far from perfect for each other.

When I asked the husband whether he loved his wife, he looked at me blankly then shook his head. The wife's response? She rolled her eyes and laughed. My letter indicating this couple's marriage was unsalvageable went out to the judge the same day.

Incompatibility

No matter how intense an initial attraction, long-term relationships are all but guaranteed to encounter some degree of sexual incompatibility: the most talked about, least understood and most volatile area of any romantic relationship. Sexual incompatibility in opposite-sex couples stems, in part, from "very fundamental sex differences between arousal patterns in men and women."[51]

Regardless of sexual orientation, couples experience libido differences, mood mismatches, major and minor sexual dysfunctions, idiosyncratic pleasure fixations and rational and irrational fears. The spontaneity of both men and women can be dampened by concerns about pregnancy, infertility or sexually transmitted diseases. Women experience diminished interest in and reduced enjoyment of sex as hormones fluctuate (either naturally or when ovulation is suppressed by use of oral/injection contraceptives), if intercourse proves painful and if chronic vaginal and urinary tract infections occur.

Straight, gay and lesbian clients talk a lot about sexual incompatibility, describing multitudes of conflicts:

- He said he'd get a vasectomy but now refuses, which leaves me 100 percent responsible for birth control.
- She refuses anal intercourse.
- He compulsively masturbates.
- She won't talk dirty.
- He's obsessed with pornography.
- She's always too tired.
- He says I'm fussy. I call it basic hygiene.
- She's inhibited; she worries about the kids walking in on us.

The Gift and Curse of Testosterone

While most romantically involved men have gotten the message that "no means no," nobody likes to be told no. When partners balk, men, it seems, think a penalty is in order. It's as if they can hear an umpire yelling, "Take a base!" Men who believe that the rules of the game have been violated tend to react badly. Women who detect irritation or anger or who are subjected to coercion also tend to react badly.

If men get angry over a partner's sexual reluctance, they make what was initially *not* a personal rejection into a personal rejection. When men apply pressure in seeking sexual gratification, women, at minimum, lose desire. Most clients tell me that they also end up feeling guilty if they don't have sex and angry if they do. Whether women claim their right to refuse or go through the motions to avoid further conflict, they label what transpires as "having sex," never as "making love."

So, why do men find it difficult to dispassionately accept a partner's lack of desire for sex? Dismayed wives are not the only ones to ponder this question. Mary Catherine Bateson (daughter of anthropologist Margaret Mead and psychologist Gregory Bateson) refers to the inexorable link between the testosterone-regulated drives for sex and aggression as the male drive for dominance.[5] Elizabeth Wurtzel calls the same phenomenon the "dark stuff":

> If feminism could snuff all the dark stuff out of sex and we could all enjoy the edenic love that has the family entertainment feel of a trip to Disney World, then sexism will be completely eradicated. But not until then. So it's basically never.[6]

The husband and wife authors of *Heroes, Rogues, and Lovers: Testosterone and Behavior* also discuss the testosterone-dominance link and suggest that low testosterone people (both men and women) "tend to prefer the kinder, gentler approach."[7] The holistic view is represented by Robert Sapolsky in *The Trouble with Testosterone*: "This is critical: Testosterone isn't *causing* aggression, it's *exaggerating* the aggression that's already there."[8] In other words, testosterone exaggerates the instinctual, aggressive response to encountering an obstacle to getting a need met.

It's not just biology. Social factors and individual attitudes affect behavior, too. For example, many female clients and even a few male clients have said, "If you really think about it, sex is weird!" Some other viewpoints clients express about sex:

- "You push paper all day, pick up the kids on the way home... then do *that* at night? It's bizarre. And what's even more bizarre is that people you work with and curse on the freeway do the same thing." (Married man)

- "I don't want anybody goin' down on me. What if I smell bad?" (Lesbian)
- "After a few years, sex is kind of like when you say the same word over and over until it loses its meaning. Is that just crazy?" (Married woman)
- "Can you even imagine this? He'd rather jerk off in front of a computer screen than have sex with me. I find the nasty tissues in the trashcan by the desk." (Gay man)
- "How can I freely *do* all this kinky stuff in bed then be embarrassed to *talk* about it?" (Nonmarried woman)

Why Can't We All Just Get Along?

Sexual incompatibility (biological or attitudinal) is not well understood because legitimate sex research has not flourished. As the authors of *Sex in America* state, "the history of attempts to study sexual behavior is almost a tragi-comedy."[9] This is true for two reasons:

- Funding for research is limited by societal taboos and related socio-political climate[10]
- Quality of research is limited by unreliable data on sexual behavior[11]

Early sex researchers such as Alfred Kinsey and others at the Kinsey Institute compromised the generalizability of their findings by conducting non-random surveys.[12] Masters and Johnson acknowledged in *The Human Sexual Response* that various factors, such as paid volunteers, biased their results.[13] Even in studies that are methodologically sound—only available since the 1990s—it is impossible to be 100 percent certain about the veracity of what subjects tell researchers.

Since *untrue* self-reports contaminate data, all legitimate, survey-based studies include what are known as "controls" for the effects of social desirability. There are just some things about which people fib. Ask yourself: Does the weight on my driver's license reflect reality or something more socially acceptable? When I used those sick days, had I really hurt my back? For many reasons, research subjects just might tell a sex researcher that they have intercourse seven days a week rather than seven times a year.

Regrettably, in ultra-competitive and/or politically-driven arenas, unethical researchers have been known to change, omit and embellish facts to reflect particular viewpoints. Also, in the make-it-sexy infotainment business, supposedly unbiased journalists sometimes get caught up in the *zeitgeist* and over-interpret data. Taking seriously any talk show or pop media claims about the latest information on what is sexually normal, from frequency to positions to levels of enjoyment, is not likely to enhance your life.

Generally speaking, a culture's most powerful people heavily influence what is socially taboo and socially acceptable. This is true not only because the most powerful tend to impose their beliefs on the less powerful, but also because the less powerful tend to imitate the most powerful in an attempt to gain power. Since males continue to exert greater power than females, cultural expectations regarding sex continue to be shaped by males. Despite the efforts of contemporary spokeswomen from Dr. Ruth to Eve Ensler to Gail Sheehy,[14] female perspectives on sexuality continue to be less well-known and less well-respected, doing disservice to both sexes.

In the race to shape the public's expectations regarding sexuality, pop culture leaves scientific research in the dust. When was the last time you heard a friend quote one of the thousands of sexologists and other trained professionals who conduct research, publish peer-reviewed journals and participate in organizations that attempt to advance legitimate knowledge about sexuality? If you're like most people, you're not spending your leisure time at the library or bookstore digging into scientific texts and scholarly essays on sexuality. The majority of people prefer images, sound bites and entertainment. As Karl Rove said to campaign finance chief Don Evans, "It's all visuals. You campaign as if America was watching TV with the sound turned down."[15]

Most of us get our information or, more precisely, our misinformation about sex from the following outlets:

- Tall tales spun by adolescent peers or standup comics
- The fiction of television, movies, popular music and romance novels
- Pornography
- Advertisements for everything from automobiles and alcohol to cosmetic surgery and male enhancement supplements

A reliable source, *Sex in America,* reveals:

- "America has a message about sex, and that message is none too subtle. It says that almost everyone *but you* is having endless, fascinating, varied sex."
- "Americans, we find, are not having much partnered sex at all—at least not much compared to what we are told is a normal or optimal amount."
- "Only one third of Americans aged eighteen to fifty-nine have sex with a partner as often as twice a week."
- "Although most people don't do it very often, many say they are perfectly happy with the sex when it happens."[16]

For the most part, pop culture's images reflect what pleases most men or what most women believe pleases most men. For a classic example of these phenomena, refer to Marabel Morgan's *The Total Woman,* the book to which the now iconic husband-pleasing housewife is attributed.[17] Today, the female perspective on sex comes from various vantage points.

From female and male researchers:

- "An unfortunate stereotype in our culture [is] that women, much more so than men, are somehow sexually flawed."
- "If half of the women in the country have a [sexual] problem, it's not a problem by definition."
- "Orgasm is not the pinnacle for many women."[18]

From female writers:

- "I'm pro-pornography."[19]
- "It can be difficult, even painful, to be sexual in a sexist, violent society. We have blamed ourselves and been blamed if sex didn't go well. We have accepted cruel labels such as 'frigid,' 'cold,' 'dysfunctional,' 'cockteaser' or 'insatiable.' Yet when we talk with other women, we learn that many others have had the same problems we suffered over in the privacy of our bedrooms."[20]
- "Some experts have argued that natural selection has given women a lower sex drive than men, and that such inhibition

makes sense: We shouldn't be out there screwing around and taking the chance of being impregnated by a genetic second-rater. The theory is rank nonsense. Sex is too important on too many social and emotional counts for us to be indifferent about it. Women display abundant evidence of a robust sex drive."[21]

Gradually, what women have to say about female sexuality is becoming more widely known. Healthcare professionals (obstetricians/gynecologists, family physicians, psychologists and marital and sex therapists) are now disseminating information such as:

- Although men tend to prefer sexual activity as a form of stress-relief, women do not.
- Women tend to prefer other forms of stress relief and prefer sexual activity under lower stress conditions.
- Sexual interest and sexual desire are distinct concepts, especially for women.
- Sexual interest depends upon a simple wish to be physically close to a partner.
- Female sexual desire depends upon a complex interplay of reproductive hormone levels and intrapersonal, interpersonal and situational factors.
- Men's testosterone levels peak daily (highest in the early morning) and in the autumn, while women's testosterone levels peak once a month at ovulation.[22]

Now, before you start saying things like, "My partner and I really do have a *lot* of sex," remember the non-psychotic, delusional state called infatuation. The biochemistry of the in-love brain can and does override (for three months to four years) what is typically true. And, post-infatuation, harmonic convergence of all variables can occur and provide inspiration to make the most of an opportunity.

A common topic with female clients is their desire to meet their partners' sexual needs without feeling used and objectified in the process. To address this, we first explore the fact that *feeling* used and objectified may or may not be the same as *being* used and objectified. Then, we focus on playing to two of women's strong suits: tending and befriending. (Part 4 expands on this.)

Male clients routinely confirm the dearth of understanding about female sexuality. Sometimes, they display stunningly dismissive attitudes regarding their female partners' perspectives. Other times, they seem touchingly genuine in seeking mutually-satisfying solutions to sexual stalemates.

Josh's Story

Though few of my male clients shed tears as copiously as some female clients do, no client has ever spontaneously cried harder than Josh. He asked for my help after his wife threatened to divorce him, saying that sex with him frightened her. She did not like being held down or handcuffed and balked at fun-and-games like being tied to bedposts. Josh acknowledged that his attitude had been dismissive of her complaints and that his goal was to discover ways to get his wife to lighten up.

According to Josh, his wife had no history of being sexually assaulted and had never been physically injured as a result of his antics. His reaction to my question about why he didn't simply give up coaxing his reluctant wife into his sadomasochistic fantasies was unenthusiastic. "I don't know why she doesn't trust me. She has to know I'd never hurt her. I love her."

"You know," I said, "allowing men to get in our beds requires women to override messages from primitive parts of our brains that warn us this could be unsafe."

Josh's face wore an expression of interest and puzzlement.

"Any woman," I continued, "who has been physically restrained by a man, knows all she ever wants to know about men's superior upper body strength. To you, it feels like harmless erotic role-playing. To your wife, it must feel like being defenseless against an attacker."

This is where my client burst into tears. "Ohhh, I never thought of that. If I'd thought of that..."

Reactions like this—breakthroughs, epiphanies—sometimes catch me off guard. Therapeutically-speaking, I was just getting started, laying groundwork. Josh's wife had undoubtedly tried many times to tell him the same thing. Yet, at that moment, this man's resistance yielded. As

Thornton Wilder wrote in *The Bridge of San Luis Rey*, "Now learn, learn at last that anywhere you may expect grace."[23]

Melissa's Story

Occasionally, in the small city where I practice, I become the psychologist of choice within a loosely connected network of family, friends, co-workers and acquaintances. It is sometimes necessary to send a newly referred client elsewhere because his or her connection to another client is potentially problematic and doing this without breaking a current or former patient's confidentiality requires creativity.

Women can also be the demanding ones in sexual relationships. A divorced client referred her ex-husband to me. This couple had no children and amicably ended their marriage. The former wife told me she ended the relationship because her husband was "a player" who had repeatedly cheated on her. The former husband was a charming, intense, obsessive-compulsive transplant from a cosmopolitan city whose psychotherapy goal was to discuss why he couldn't seem to settle down.

Melissa, an intense, divorced mother in her early thirties, came to me because she and her children had recently moved to town and she wanted some input about adjustment problems her children seemed to be having. One day, she mentioned Jim, a new man in her life. You guessed it: the "player." Confidentiality prohibited me from acknowledging that this man was also a client, but knowing him enhanced my perspective.

> **Melissa:** People say he's got a playboy reputation, but he doesn't seem that interested in sex to me.
>
> **Dr. M.:** Oh? What gives you that impression?
>
> **Melissa:** Well, he must not be that interested, if he won't work for it.
>
> **Dr. M.:** Work for it?
>
> **Melissa:** Yeah! With me, a man doesn't get something for nothing. He has to invest time and money. He has to hustle. Put on the full court press.
>
> **Dr. M.:** (Smiles.)
>
> **Melissa:** Okay, maybe I'm a bit high-maintenance.

Rachel's Story

At times, experienced women are partnered with inexperienced men. Rachel, a single woman in her late twenties, asked my opinion regarding what might be done about her new boyfriend's limited imagination regarding sex.

Rachel: It's always the same. He has to turn on music, light candles, get in bed and have foreplay for at least an hour.

Dr. M.: Well, some women…

Rachel: I know! Would be envious. It just seems…

Dr. M.: Formulaic.

Rachel: Exactly. And he always wants me on top. It's like he read a book about how to please women.

Dr. M.: And got the one woman who isn't pleased.

Rachel: Well, it was okay in the beginning, but I like spontaneity.

Dr. M.: Any other reasons that you're not pleased?

Rachel: Well, being on top *is* usually painful.

Dr. M.: But you haven't told him.

Rachel: Oh, he's trying so hard to make it good for me that I haven't had the heart to say anything.

Dr. M.: Okay, let me get this straight. Being on top hurts you and you want variety but you haven't suggested another position because it might hurt his feelings.

Rachel: That sounds really stupid.

Dr. M.: I wouldn't call it stupid. I'd call it taking responsibility for his needs and not your own.

Rachel: That's exactly why I didn't think of this before. All I have to do is tell him it hurts me to be on top and I'll get variety without criticizing his technique.

Lifelong Mutual Attraction

Whether a relationship thrives or fails, mutual attraction can last a lifetime. Just ask anyone who has encountered an old flame and felt the heartbeat quicken. Even better is the couple that ignores stereotypes and infotainment and instead finesses mutual attraction into a long-term, custom-tailored sexual relationship.

Chapter 6

Mutual Admiration Society

Human beings are hardwired to experience feelings and express emotions and our early years are full of fearful howls and joyful squeals. Over time we sort out which feelings to keep private and which emotions to make known; we experience emotional compatibility with those who choose similar parameters. Automatically, we form mutual admiration societies with kindred spirits who get goose bumps at flyovers and teary-eyed at symphony concerts. And if we're lucky, mutual admiration and mutual attraction converge, leading us to romantic love.

One fine model of mutual admiration can be found in the fifty-year relationship of existentialists Simone De Beauvoir (1908-1986) and Jean-Paul Sartre (1905-1980), who never married. De Beauvoir authored one of the twentieth century's most significant feminist works, *The Second Sex*.[1] Sartre said, "Hell is other people" and is known as the only writer ever to refuse the Nobel Prize for literature. Although they approached their relationship with relative rationality and maintained separate residences in Paris, they unmistakably shared emotional connection. In De Beauvoir's words, "The greatest success of my life is Sartre."

Emotional Attachment

Mutual admiration depends not only upon making favorable assessments of one another but also upon experiencing the emotions of attachment.

For the majority, emotional attachment to numerous others is inevitable. Scientists assert, based on neural connections between the brain's sensory pathways, emotion centers and our facial muscles, that humans are capable from birth (via the gaze-monitoring instinct) of "reading" others' emotional states.[2] Anyone who has gazed back at an infant while feeding her a bottle knows the power of this instinct. It is via this well-documented phenomenon along with the first smile (also believed to be an instinct) that infants endear themselves to caregivers, thereby helping to insure survival.

As our brains mature, gazing behavior facilitates our innate ability to "read" others' eyes; reading eyes enables us to "read" minds and build theories about others' emotional states. Accurate interpretation of others' emotional states allows us to adapt our behavior accordingly, which is fundamental to surviving and forming emotional bonds. Also known as social intelligence,[3] "mind reading" abilities vary among individuals.

Undoubtedly related to genetics, females generally possess greater abilities in this realm than males. Studies documenting female predisposition to emotional sensitivity and social interaction are myriad. For example, a University of Barcelona study used the Brazelton Neonatal Behavioral Assessment Scale with neonates ranging from forty-eight to eighty hours old and documented newborn girls' higher functioning, especially in the social interaction organization cluster. Baby boys scored higher on irritability.[4] Some men possess social intelligence equal to women's, but at the other end of the continuum, males are approximately ten times more likely to be diagnosed with autism, a disorder characterized by significant deficits in social intelligence.[5]

Attachment Styles

Twentieth century researchers John Bowlby and Mary Ainsworth identified four attachment styles that effect behavior from the cradle to the grave. Researchers devised experiments in which a one-year-old child played with toys in his mother's presence. Then the mother left the room and a stranger entered but did not interact with the baby. Finally, the baby was reunited with his mother. Patterns of behavior between different babies and their mothers were observed and four attachment styles identified: secure, avoidant, anxious-ambivalent and disorganized.

Approximately 70 percent of children exhibited secure attachment. By briefly running to their mothers for comfort then returning to play, secure children indicated confidence in their mothers as soothing, safe havens and were comfortable with playing independently. Avoidant types essentially ignored their mothers' return, showing lack of confidence in them as a source of comfort. Anxious-ambivalent types sought solace from their mothers but engaged in over-the-top demands for attention, indicating that the mothers' presence actually escalated the children's anxiety. Heartbreakingly, disorganized types reacted to their mothers as if they were dangerous to be around.

It is generally accepted that we attach to romantic relationships in the same style that we attached to our mothers. This means that automatic assumptions and emotional reactions transfer. If we are fortunate enough to have bonded in the secure style, romantic attachment can also feel secure. If we bonded in another style, romantic attachment will feel, to greater or lesser degree, anxiety-producing. Fortunately, it is never too late to recognize unhealthy patterns of thought and behavior and work toward change. Refer to the chapter notes for resources on the subject of attachment styles.[6]

The Same Only Different

Individuals who express strong positive emotions about the same things experience emotional compatibility. Research also tells us that people who express negative emotions[7] or shed tears[8] about similar things experience emotional compatibility. Whether outraged by politicians' abuse of power or moved to tears by the death of a loved one, we bond with those who suffer and grieve as we do.

Even when couples feel emotionally compatible, individuals do not experience emotions identically. In the 1950s, psychologist Olga Campos asked her artist friends Frida Kahlo and Diego Rivera to represent a series of emotions in drawings. Her stated purpose was "to determine the differences between Frida Kahlo's and Diego Rivera's response in paint to various human emotions." The results of Campos' experiment record the profound uniqueness of two individuals' visual descriptions of the same emotions.[9]

When I saw an exhibit of these drawings,[10] I expected to see similarities in the works of these spouses. Both artists created abstract drawings of twelve emotions including love, anger, sorrow, fear, jealousy, peace and joy. Not one pair of drawings was similar in any way. Not in placement on the page, use of color, form or even direction of brushstroke. The net effect was renewal of my appreciation of the wisdom of making no assumptions about the particulars of anyone's feelings or emotions.

Neurochemistry Made Me Do It

In *Mind Wide Open,* Steven Johnson writes, "Our felt emotions are the sum total of dozens of physiological and chemical changes in our body."[11] The elation of infatuation, for example, is produced by brain chemicals, summarized by Barbara and Allan Pease: "Dopamine gives the feeling of well-being, phenylethylamine increases excitement levels, serotonin creates a sense of emotional stability, and norepinephrine induces the feeling that you can achieve anything."[12] Here are some facts men and women should know about the chemistry of the emotions of romantic love:[13]

- During infatuation, both men and women experience increased levels of serotonin, dopamine and norepinephrine.
- In both men and women, increased serotonin levels reduce sensitivity to rejection, lessen feelings of depression and anxiety and heighten feelings of fascination.
- In both men and women, increased levels of dopamine, oxytocin and endorphins produce pleasure sensations.
- Increased oxytocin levels reduce social phobia and potentiate bonding.
- Both sexes release oxytocin during orgasm.
- Estrogen potentiates oxytocin and oxytocin levels are negatively correlated with testosterone levels. In other words, the more estrogen, the more oxytocin and the more testosterone, the less oxytocin.
- Males also release vasopressin (the male "bonding" hormone) at orgasm.

If we accept that positive emotions of love boil down to brain chemistry, can we assume that the same is true of negative emotions? Since we're supposed to stop blaming spouses for our bad behavior, can we start blaming neurotransmitters? Can we vent negative emotions then blame our negative actions on something other than ourselves?

Unlike toddlers, adults cannot reasonably blame meltdowns on missed naps or too much birthday cake. Practicing self-restraint is central to the self-responsible marriage paradigm. (More about managing negative emotions in part 4.)

What I Did Caused My Neurochemistry

Just as neurochemistry affects behavior, behavior affects neurochemistry. *Think and act the way you want to feel* is the central premise of the gold standard of psychotherapy: cognitive behavioral therapy. As Pierce J. Howard, Ph.D., observes, "emotions can last for less than a second or for a lifetime, partly depending on whether we decide to will the cognitive part of the reaction to subdue the emotional part."[14]

For example, ranting and raving at poor customer service or running for a plane increase adrenaline levels. Aerobic exercise, yoga, laughter and social interaction increase levels of "feel good" hormones. Less active behaviors, such as thinking dark thoughts, listening to music or receiving a massage, also alter neurochemistry.

In *Two Aspirins and a Comedy*, Metta Spencer points out that professional actresses and actors, while *acting* emotions, experience "meta-emotions"—positive and negative mood changes that carry over into their personal lives. She reports that whether an actor is "up or down" depends upon the emotional content of the role he or she is performing and cites a study by Nicholas Hall that documents corresponding changes in actors' immune function. Whether one is performing on a stage or living daily life, behaviors affect emotions and biochemistry.[15]

For some, it may seem an impossible oversimplification to attribute the perplexing emotions of love to the ebb and flow of brain chemicals. After all, conventional wisdom's expectations about romance are based on millennia of poetic metaphor. Although it may be difficult to accept, the new Golden Age of neuroscience will expand the lexicon of love to include terms such as neurons, glia and brain waves.[16]

Consider for a moment the inspiring last line of Annie Proulx's National Book Award-winning novel *Shipping News*: "And it may be that love sometimes occurs without pain or misery."[17] Even if this is counter to one's experience to date, it seems profoundly true. Love *can* be free of pain and misery. Free, at least, of the pain partners make for themselves and each other. Free, too, of the misery caused by our unwavering devotion to the biggest home wrecker of all time: the belief that we cannot or should not be expected to manage our negative emotions.

Chapter 7

So Much in Common

Shared belief in impossible things can be the basis of any couple's "you and me against the world" solidarity. For example, here are six impossible things my husband and I believe:

1. Less is more.
2. Some animals are more equal than others.[1]
3. Good people must not obey laws too well.
4. No good deed goes unpunished.
5. Common sense is not so common.
6. Give peace a chance.

Cognitive (mind and brain) compatibility including shared values, beliefs and interests is the third essential area of mutuality.

At one level, pointing out the importance of cognitive compatibility might seem like stating the obvious. It is the stuff of personal advertisements, computer match services and singles' must-have lists. Shared likes and dislikes validate our idiosyncrasies and instill confidence in our ability to get along. Everyone's enthusiasm peaks around the like-minded:

- You were a Deaniac, too?
- You've read *Galapagos*?
- You avoid onions?

In addition, cognitive compatibility affects the other two essential areas of mutuality. Without shared beliefs about the sensual and the sexual, mutual attraction loses its charge. Without harmoniously blending beliefs about emotional expression, mutual admiration societies lose their fascination.

Cognitive compatibility extends well beyond shared values, beliefs and interests or *what* we think. Thinking styles or *how* we think can vary, too. Optimism/pessimism, introversion/extraversion and flexibility/rigidity, for example, all of which are associated with thinking style, appear to be influenced by individual brain architecture and neurochemistry. Hemisphere dominance also affects thinking style.

Biology of Mind

From time to time my clients ask, "What exactly is the difference between the mind and the brain?" The Greeks asked this question and concluded that the invisible mind was imprisoned in the body (brain). Rene Descartes (1596-1650) reflected upon this question and concluded that the brain's pineal gland was the site at which the nonmaterial mind interacted with the material body. Modern neuroscience offers a more complete answer. In the words of Nobel Prize winner Dr. Eric R. Kandel, "Mind and brain are inseparable. … mind is a set of operations carried out by the brain, much as walking is a set of operations carried out by the legs, except dramatically more complex."[2]

Neuroscientists who seek links between cellular/molecular neuroscience and cognitive neuroscience no longer think in terms of "*the* mind," which implies a single brain location for mental operations. To keep unity and complexity foremost in everyone's thoughts, the phrase "biology of mind" has been coined.[3]

And what exactly does biology of mind have to do with marital satisfaction?

- Marital satisfaction is a product of our minds.
- Our minds and our brains are one and the same.
- In order to improve marital satisfaction, spouses must change their minds.

Changing minds, changes brains and vice versa.

Fortunately, despite sex and personality differences, couples can experience satisfying like-mindedness when they discover thinking style compatibility. When couples encounter thinking style *in*compatibility, knowledge that such differences are more about brain chemistry than contrariness provides enlightened perspective, a foundation for acceptance and tolerance. Blaming a partner for thinking differently than you do is like blaming him or her for being taller than you.

Hemisphere Dominance and Thinking Style

Before addressing the effect that hemisphere dominance has on thinking style, it must be established that oversimplification has occurred in describing the functions of the two hemispheres. For example, there is the popular generalization (now known to be inadequate) that the right hemisphere is the creative side of the brain and the left hemisphere is the logical side. In the burgeoning field of neuroscience, the only safe generalization about our brains is: Every human brain is both similar to other human brains and unique unto itself.

The uniqueness of each human brain is well established. Although everyone marvels at stories about similarities between identical twins raised apart, studies of identical twins raised together reveal that even identical twins' brains are not identical. Another source of reliable data is pre-surgical brain mapping. Before neurosurgeons cut into brain tissue, they must establish what functions are located adjacent to a surgical site. Neurosurgeons never assume that common functions (from movement of limbs to recognition of faces) are carried out in exactly the same location in any two patients' brains.

Scientific data points away from inferences of "better or worse" with regard to myriad inherent characteristics. This includes hemisphere dominance and handedness. Now, let us consider possible implications for romantic couples of brain differences and similarities.

Individual brains tend toward right-hemisphere dominance, left-hemisphere dominance or more equal utilization. Though women's brains appear to be particularly well-wired for cross-utilization, men's brains also engage in what Diane Ackerman describes as "collaboration, an open exchange" between hemispheres.[4] As is the case in eye dominance and hand dominance, both sides continuously contribute to activities of daily living and unless an individual's brain is damaged, differences attributed to hemisphere dominance are counted among the "multiple expressions of normality."[5]

A note to left-handers: 10 percent of women and 14 percent of men are left-handed. In left-handers, brain organization is often different than right-handers: While about 90 percent of right-handers are typical in their cerebral organization, only 66 percent of lefties are typical. There are three types of left-hander differences:

1. those whose brains are similar to right-handers;
2. those whose hemispheric organization is reversed;
3. those who have language and spatial abilities in both hemispheres.[6]

Brains also can be designated as male-differentiated, female-differentiated or combination. Though clearly an oversimplification, the left-brain repertoire of thoughts and behaviors (outcome-oriented and analytic) are often characterized as "male." Right-brain thoughts and behaviors (process-oriented and intuitive) are often characterized as "female."

At our city's state-of-the-art science center, the curious are invited to determine whether a "male" brain, "female" brain or "combination" brain occupies his or her skull. Having experienced various measures of hemisphere dominance during our training as psychologists, my husband and I (both right-handed) were curious about our results on this six-question measure. Despite my best efforts to outwit the test, my outcome was the same as always. My brain is decidedly "female," as are 90 percent of women's brains. My husband, however, again achieved indicators of what I believe to be a natural advantage: a "combination" brain, found in 20 percent of men and 10 percent of women.[7]

Hemisphere Dominance and Self-Esteem

When correlated with scores on various psychological measures, data gathered from twenty-first century scans of living brains reveal certain trends. For example, left-hemisphere dominance corresponds with better self-image while right-hemisphere dominance correlates with feeling worse about one's self.[8] Related studies show right prefrontal cortex activity associated with avoidance behaviors and negative emotions, while left prefrontal cortex activity is associated with approach behaviors and positive emotions.[9] It has also been shown that the right frontal lobe houses only negative emotional processes and the left frontal lobe houses both positive and negative emotional processes.[10]

As is often true in new areas of scientific investigation, studies produce findings that both corroborate and refute one another. Therefore, it is inappropriate to draw "better than" or "worse than" conclusions about complex constructs such as self-esteem. Right hemisphere dominance, for example, does not doom one to low self-esteem, just as left hemisphere dominance does not guarantee high self-esteem.

I once heard football great Terry Bradshaw say, "Nobody had self-esteem when I was growing up, and we turned out okay." Conventional wisdom, a witch's brew of old wives' tales, sitcom one-liners and pop psychology, overemphasizes self-esteem's relevance to almost everything. Professional psychology overcomplicates the concept.

Simply defined as one's reputation with one's self, self-esteem ceases to mystify. Reputation with self dips and soars. Depending upon the circumstances and our self-talk, spinach in the teeth or an open barn door can trigger a momentary dip in self-confidence or an episode of agoraphobia. (More on how self esteem improves as self-responsibility increases in part 4.)

Thinking Style and Decision Making

In *The Executive Brain,* Elkhonon Goldberg reports research findings on another thinking style continuum: context-dependent and context-independent decision making. He defines context-dependent decision making as the "attempt to capture the unique properties of the situation and 'custom-tailor' responses" and indicates that males show a subtle preference for this style. He defines context-independent decision making as the "attempt to formulate all-purpose 'best' responses" and indicates that females show a subtle preference for this style. He also states that optimal decision making reflects a "dynamic balance" of the two cognitive styles.[11]

Dr. Goldberg offers some behavioral examples of the influence of thinking style on decision making:

> Jane Blane and Joe Blow are self-employed consultants whose incomes fluctuate from month to month. Jane Blane practices a context-independent approach to life. She always saves 5 percent of her income, never buys clothes costing more than $500 per item and always takes her vacation in August. By contrast, Joe Blow's approach to life is context-dependent. When his monthly income is below $5000, he saves nothing, when it is between $5000 and $7000 he saves 5 percent and he tends not to buy clothes costing more than $500, except when his monthly income is particularly high. He takes a vacation whenever his workload permits.[12]

Thinking About Past Emotional Events

Dr. Larry Cahill, a neuroscientist at the University of California, Irvine, studies neural mechanisms of emotionally-influenced memory and has proposed another thinking style difference: "Our work is showing that sex and cerebral hemisphere constitute twin, interacting influences on brain mechanisms of emotion and memory that can no longer be ignored."[13] He documented subjects' brain activity while watching horror films and found that women's left amygdalas were effected and men's right amygdalas activated.

The thinking style difference became apparent when he tested subjects' memories of the traumatic event a week later. Women tended to recall emotional details while men tended to recall the emotional "gist." Subsequent research by other scientists has documented similar memory differences in men and women for both stressful and positive events.

The Cognitive Match Game

All aspects of cognitive compatibility play a part in marital satisfaction. When seeking a life partner, the economy of effort promised by a cognitive match appeals to everyone. We believe, quite correctly, that synchronicity can happen where there are shared preferences about big things and little things.

Big Things	**Little Things**	
Sex	Health Behaviors	Sense of Humor
Money	Household Chores	City v. Country
Children	Decorating	Owl v. Lark
In-Laws	Food/Diet	Spontaneous v. Planned
Religion	Fashion/Grooming	Active v. Sedentary
Politics	Music	Economy v. Luxury
	Entertainment/Hobbies	Tidy v. Lived-In
	Friends/Sociability	Pets v. No Pets
	Climate/Temperature	

Mutual Wish Fulfillment

Being on the same side of big issues and little issues increases couples' satisfaction by reducing conflict and eliminating the need for compromise. Compromise requires spouses to be mental contortionists, attempting to achieve a degree of cognitive compatibility that does not come naturally. Although everyone pays homage to the concept, compromise (a euphemism for sacrifice) is nobody's first choice. Most of us prefer immediate, non-negotiated agreement and mutual wish fulfillment.

During my clinical practice, I've observed what appears to be a sex difference regarding compromise. For reasons about which we can only speculate, men seem to experience compromise as demotion to a one-down position. Women, on the other hand, seem to experience compromise as elevation to a one-up position, as in, "Oh, at least I get part of what I want." Tellingly, I have never mentioned this to a woman who didn't laugh and say, "Oh, how true!"

The reaction among men has been more measured. Even if male psychotherapy clients who live in the Midwest (the population to which my observation might be generalized) do not share my opinion, a British study concluded something similar. British researchers identified married couples that rated themselves as good compromisers. Interviewers then gleaned the details of the couples' "compromises." Significant numbers of husbands and wives independently acknowledged that "compromises" had, in fact, amounted to the husband getting his way. Wives tended to perceive simply *discussing* situations as "compromising." Although the study did not address partners' underlying expectations, it appears that there are wives who value having their desires heard as much as actually getting their ways.

Though not achieving actual compromise, the couples in this study successfully resolved conflict. One partner dominated, the other gave in. There is nothing inherently unsatisfactory in this. Sometimes, one partner sees a situation more clearly, has greater experience and wisdom or has a better idea. Mentally healthy individuals, regardless of gender, concede under these circumstances. (Much more about resolving conflict in part 4.)

In addition to those who simply wish to be heard are those who strive to change the world's persistent elevation of men's needs above women's. A non-profit group called Dads and Daughters is interested in increasing women's comfort with "taking up half the space on the planet." One Dads and Daughters project called "See Jane" seeks gender equity in children's television programming. For the launch of this project, actress Geena Davis designed a T-shirt logo: a hand-drawn Earth and the words, "Women. We'll Settle for Half."[14]

Incompatibility Feels Threatening

Since incompatibility and disagreement feel threatening, "fight or flight" reactions and associated emotions can be triggered. The emotions associated with "fight" reactions are anger and frustration. Fighters take action to *oppose* threat. Fighters go against reality. When we fight, we think, "No way, no how. Not in my lifetime."

The emotions associated with "flight" reactions are fear and anxiety. Those who flee take action to *escape* threat. Fleers expect the worst from reality. When we flee, we think, "I can't handle this!"

The way that partners manage automatic reactions highlights another area of potential cognitive compatibility. Fight or flight reactions are triggered by sensory input. Escalation or de-escalation is determined in the cingulate cortex and neocortex. Brain-imaging studies have actually pinpointed the spot in the brain—the rostral anterior cingulate—where inhibition of negative emotion takes place. One such study published in the journal *Neuron* in 2006 concluded that the function of this area of the brain is not merely to monitor conflict between emotion and cognition but to actively resolve such conflict.[15] This, then, is the area of the brain activated when we take a second look at what startled us and realize, "Oh, that's a stick not a snake."

If you unexpectedly encounter your spouse lurking in a dark corner of your bedroom, you may freeze or scream, but kneejerk reaction is quickly followed by rational choice. Do you escalate threatening situations into high drama or de-escalate into no big deal? Which direction does your partner take things?

Consider another example: the scenario of being fired from your job. One person might think, *This is awful, horrible. What if no one else hires me?* Another person may think, *At last. Motivation to find a better job.* Yet another person may lose it and become violent.

Significantly different reactions are the product of unique biology and psychology, the interplay of impulses, emotions, memories, values and beliefs. The degree to which individuals inhibit emotional responses varies. Therefore, the effects of like-mindedness in this realm can be significant.

Internal Values Conflicts

Sometimes we experience values conflicts not only with others but also within ourselves. For women, a common *intra*personal values conflict is the one about wanting both career and children. These are the mothers who feel unfulfilled when they stay at home and guilty when they hold full-time jobs. For men, a common *intra*personal values conflict is wanting to spend time pursuing personal interests, which preempts time with family. These are fathers who enjoy regular visits to the gym or golf course yet worry that their wives and children will feel neglected.

David's Story

David is in his twenties, married seven years and has no children. He examined several intrapersonal values conflicts before finding resolution. David believed that his values of open communication about emotions and an upbeat and energetic home atmosphere were compatible and that his wife shared these values. It was not until his wife experienced clinical depression that these values came into conflict.

Although David valued open expression of emotions, his spouse's dark moods and bitter complaints that he was not empathetic enough ran counter to his desire for an upbeat home life. Short of his wife's depression remitting, resolution of internal conflict depended upon his willingness to sacrifice one value in service of the other. Which of the conflicting values was more important? Would another value, such as pursuit of personal happiness or loyalty to marriage partner, ultimately take priority?

To clarify his priorities and generate potential cognitive reframes, we focused on the fact that he had been aware prior to marriage that his beautiful, talented and charming wife, Darla, struggled with depression. In other words, David was not naïve to the possibility that coping with episodes of depression might be an aspect of being her partner. Initially, he conceded that his need for an upbeat home life could not be reliably met and honored the shared value of emotional expression. David also shifted focus to another important value: loyalty to his marriage partner.

In this case, as in most, complications continued to mount. In part due to her depression, my client's wife, Darla, was unemployed for four years, which led to depletion of the couple's savings. David's sense of urgency about his wife returning to work intensified over time. Darla, however, maintained that their finances were not as bad as he feared and that his request that she return to work showed lack of empathy. Ultimately, he concluded that another value, personal happiness, trumped all and he ended the marriage.

Susan's Story

Susan is a forty-something, stay-at-home mother and community activist, married thirteen years. She and her husband share many progressive political values and take seriously their commitment to gender equality. From time to time, this client conveyed to me her husband's appreciation after psychotherapy resulted in a concession on her part. Susan frequently found her intrapersonal values of upholding gender equality and behaving compassionately pitted against each other.

> **Susan:** Vic's promotion is taking a toll. He's home less than ever and not as helpful with chores.
>
> **Dr. M.:** You're doing everything?

Susan: My sons help. They're so good about picking up, vacuuming, setting the table. But Vic either channel surfs or works from home. I don't like the example that sets for the boys. I don't want them thinking that when they're grown, they won't have to do housework.

Dr. M.: Vic does nothing?

Susan: Well, he still cooks sometimes and he does dishes…and yard work.

Dr. M.: What have you told the boys about the change in routine?

Susan: That Dad's learning a new job and things will eventually get back to normal.

Dr. M.: So, what do *you* need to take a look at here?

Susan: This is going to be one of those times Vic thanks you, isn't it? (Pause.) I just don't want to be a downtrodden, caretaking female like my mother. I guess I'm fighting for my own self-esteem.

Dr. M.: And how will your sons become better men or your self-esteem improve or the cause of women be elevated if your already better-than-average husband does more chores?

Susan: Oh. Good point. (Silence.) Okay, this is me, shifting my focus. I need to focus on being compassionate…and to remember that there's power in compromise.

Assessing Cognitive Compatibility

So, how can we accurately assess the authenticity of someone else's values? Simply watch their actions. Your beloved can claim whatever values he or she thinks the situation requires, but the truth lies in how he or she spends time and money. Is there any doubt about the values, beliefs and interests of the individual who regularly practices yoga? Restores a fixer-upper in an historic neighborhood? Auditions for community theatre? Spends evenings and weekends shopping online or bellying up to the bar?

Although mutual attraction and mutual admiration are equally important factors in partner selection, marital success is unlikely without cognitive compatibility. As infatuation neurochemistry normalizes, cognitive incompatibility becomes apparent. Although inevitable, incompatibility can be mediated and compatibility can be optimized. It's, in my professional opinion, all a matter of changing our minds.

Part 3

Disenchantment

Chapter 8

Bait and Switch

Everybody marries the wrong person means that disenchantment is inevitable. Even when we experience sexual, emotional and cognitive compatibility, incompatibilities crop up, giving rise to post-infatuation frustration. As sex differences, gender and other socialization differences along with unmet expectations steal focus, post-infatuation frustration turns to disenchantment.

After neurochemistry normalizes, our "right" person seems less pleasing. Conventional wisdom, safely removed from the cutting edge of science, naively suggests that the negative feelings and emotions of disenchantment are due to *someone* "not trying hard enough." We feel disappointment and blame our spouses; our equally disenchanted spouses blame us. We vent frustration and the relationship is strained.

Expectations adopted during the chemically-enhanced state of infatuation set the bar impossibly high. We overestimate compatibility and expect to be endlessly pampered, praised and cherished. Most likely to contribute to our disenchantment is the self-serving belief that a spouse is duty bound to please us. Inevitably, the focus shifts from likenesses, real and imagined, to differences, real and imagined.

Sex Differences and Gender Differences

The ongoing Human Genome Project has determined the sequence of three billion genetic "letters" of the human genome and reported that the DNA of any two humans is about 99.9 percent identical.[1] Included in the 0.1 percent of bio-uniqueness are components of variation in realms such as disease predisposition and immunity, special talents and abilities and sex differences including male-differentiated, female-differentiated or so-called combination brains. Sex differences, accounted for by variation in genetic codes, brain structures and baseline bio-chemistry, are, as Pierce J. Howard, Ph.D., puts it, "immutable except for surgical or pharmaceutical interventions."[2]

Unlike sex differences, gender differences are "heavily influenced by one's cultural environment."[3] Taken together, sex differences and gender differences foster the incompatibility that is the basis of the proverbial battle between the sexes. From Aristophanes (c.448-385BCE) to Edward Albee (1928-), playwrights have imagined the all-too-familiar battlefields of *Lysistrata* and *Who's Afraid of Virginia Woolf?* Some real-life couples turn homes into combat zones, permanently scarring each other's memory-scapes as well as their children's. Perpetuated by anachronistic misogy-nists, man-haters and the sirens' call of conventional wisdom, it seems this battle of the sexes will go on indefinitely.

Today, it is understood that we are who we are because of the inter-action of genetic and environmental/social factors. Insights into male-female incompatibility are no longer sought in the nature versus nurture debate. It is not either/or. It is both.

In the perhaps not-too-distant future, a complete catalog of the millions of single nucleotide polymorphisms (SNPs, called "snips") that account for the 0.1 percent of human genetic variation will reveal genetic components of the sexes' incompatibility. These bits of data will then inform enlightened expectations. In the meantime, research findings lend support to old and new theories about male-female brain and behavior differences. Among long-held theories are those that describe male brains as "specialized" and hardwired for spatial abilities and "sys-temizing" and female brains as "plastic" and hardwired for verbal abilities and "empathizing."[4] In scientific jargon, *plastic* means flexible, adaptable.

Also, the debate rages on about the accuracy and, yes, the political cor-rectness of voicing theories that differentiate capabilities based on sex. Leader of the National Economic Council and former Harvard President

Lawrence H. Summers is very familiar with the negative consequences of making a comment attributing men's overrepresentation in science and math (systemizing) careers to natural brain advantage.[5] As Susan Pinker puts it, "the idea that there are inherent differences is a sensitive issue in the present because it provided cover for abuses in the past."[6] Another voice of reason, psychologist Dr. Sandra Bem, offered this viewpoint insight:

> No matter how many sex differences are someday shown to have a biological component, that knowledge will thus add little or nothing to our understanding of why women and men have universally played such different—and unequal—roles in virtually every society on earth…So yes, women might turn out to be more biologically nurturant than men on the average, but that should make them psychiatrists, not secretaries. And yes, men might also turn out to have a higher aptitude for mathematics than women on the average, but that would not explain why so many more women have a high aptitude for mathematics than have careers requiring one.[7]

Sex-Differentiated Brains

Chromosomal makeup (XX or XY) combined with in utero hormones determine whether individuals possess so-called male-differentiated or female-differentiated brains. An estimated 20 percent of men and 10 percent of women possess so-called combination brains.[8] Pierce J. Howard compiled many male/female brain differences in *The Owner's Manual for The Brain*:[9]

Male	**Female**
15 percent larger, heavier	Smaller, lighter
Thinner corpus callosum	Thicker corpus callosum
Vocabulary work engages front and back of left hemisphere	Vocabulary work engages front and back of both hemispheres
Emotions activate right hemisphere	Emotions activate both hemispheres
Visual/spatial perception engages right hemisphere	Visual/spatial perception engages both hemispheres

Although on average males and females have equivalent general intelligence, it is believed that brain differences account for some behavior differences.

It is important to note that in certain areas of neuroscience correlations between structure and function are not fully established. Also, as in all areas of scientific inquiry, data is sometimes contradictory or initially appears to be contradictory. For example, structural differences have been observed in proportions of gray matter and white matter in male and female brains. Gray matter, comprised of neuronal cell bodies and dendrites (receiving), makes up the information processing centers of the brain. White matter, comprised of axons (sending), provides the networking between information processing centers.

In 1999, Ruben Gur, Ph.D., and other University of Pennsylvania researchers pointed out that the female brain, being more densely packed with gray matter, provides concentrated processing power and more thought-linking capability and that the male brain, having more white matter, allows greater potential for inhibition of "information spread," which may account for the single-mindedness men apply to difficult spatial problems. Dr. Gur also suggested that the female's (on average) larger corpus callosum (which is made of white matter) allows more global neural participation (plasticity) in difficult verbal tasks.[10] Later, functional MRI studies "cloud the issue" with evidence of larger corpus callosa (female-differentiated brains) in some males as well.[11]

Richard Haier of the University of California-Irvine and Rex Jung of the University of New Mexico reported what might, at first glance, be interpreted as a reversal of earlier conclusions. Their 2005 data show that women have more white matter and males have more gray matter. Close examination of the data reveal, however, that this seeming reversal relates only to *intellectual skills.* Haier and Jung suggest that these data help explain why men tend to excel in tasks that require local processing (like math) and women tend to excel in tasks that require integrating and assimilating information from various gray matter regions around the brain (language facility).[12]

Regarding hemisphere specialization versus hemisphere intercommunication, Dr. Howard states:

> The male separation of language...and emotional specialization helps to explain his traditional ineptness at talking about feelings; the neural basis of his feelings has far fewer connections with his language production. The female, with her emotions seated in both hemispheres and (perhaps) a thicker *corpus callosum*, has greater access to her own feelings and the feelings of others as she produces her language.[13]

For more than three decades, researchers have systematically assessed behavioral differences among neonates. Data from these studies support the belief that innate differences exist not only among individuals but also between male and female newborns. For example, significant sex differences have been documented in infants forty-eight to seventy-two hours of age on measures of behaviors associated with social interactivity and self-quieting.[14] Refer to the chapter notes for titles by several authors who discuss interesting sex differences and gender differences from a brain science perspective.[15]

Hunters and Gatherers

Anthropologists and evolutionary psychologists also study sex and gender differences.[16] They point out complementary sets of survival skills inherited from ancestral hunters and gatherers, typically males and females, respectively. Ancient hunters' survival, as well as survival of those whom they fed and protected, depended upon their ability to spot prey before the prey spotted them; hence, modern men's superior long-distance vision[17] and ability to shut out distractions. Ancient gatherers' survival, as well as that of their children, depended upon their ability to perform several tasks (seemingly) simultaneously. Ancient women scanned for and harvested edible grains and berries, watched for and eluded potentially dangerous critters, tended to toddlers and infants and kept an eye on older children; hence, modern women's superior peripheral vision[18] and ability to see detail.

Like so many mainstays of conventional wisdom, multitasking is being exposed as a misleading concept. The ability of many people, especially women, to simultaneously perform two or more tasks is more accurately described as fast, sequential tasking. As John Medina states in *Brain Rules*: "To put it bluntly, research shows that *we can't multitask.* We are biologically incapable of processing attention-rich inputs simultaneously."[19]

Another hunter-gatherer difference is hypothesized. Though group cooperation among hunters improved the odds of successful kills, individual prowess was even more critical. Superior strength and sharper aim not only directly improved the individual's immediate likelihood of survival but also indirectly improved, by raising his status in the group, the likelihood that his genes would survive. "Every man for himself" was the rule when the prey turned on the hunting party. It is safe to assume that the man who unselfishly allowed fellow hunters to escape ahead of him was not the man who survived.

Ancient hunters willed personal survival and throughout history, humans have battled the natural world and each other. Today, "survival of the fittest" is still the rule, resulting in "win at any cost" politics and wars, competition for power and resources and emotional detachment at the workplace and athletic field. Everyone knows and loves many fine men who are indisputably first in their competitions of choice and lacking in emotional availability. Everyone also knows exceptions to the rule: the husband who seems sweeter and more touchy-feely than the wife, the guy who cries at chick flicks and the steaming athlete who says, "Hi, Mom," to the sideline camera.

In contrast, among gatherers, group cooperation was more crucial than individual prowess. Females' emotional investment increased everyone's willingness to share resources and extend protection to one another's children. Associated tendencies in modern women are *tending and befriending* behaviors exhibited even in the most competitive settings. Everyone knows and loves many fine women who are indisputably first in their competitions of choice and also agree with George Eliot who said, "What do we live for, if not to make life less difficult for each other?" Everyone also knows exceptions to the rule: hard-as-nails mothers, me-first wives and sooner-kill-you-than-help-you female co-workers and bosses.

Other Socialization Differences and Unmet Expectations

In addition to sex and gender differences, myriad non-sex-specific differences that we failed to notice or deemed insignificant feed romantic disenchantment. Although we claim not to expect continuous compatibility, we dearly hope that we will prove luckier than most, which leaves us vulnerable to feeling caught off guard. We feel chagrined over unmet expectations and begin to suspect bait and switch. Next, we panic and mentally grasp for explanations and solutions. The majority of us settle for what is readily available in the tenets of conventional wisdom:

- Disenchantment is the result of my spouse's incompatible behavior.
- The answer to disenchantment is persuading my spouse to change.
- The answer to disenchantment is finding a new, more compatible spouse.

Disenchantment is sustained by our persistent focus on differences and negative reactions to unmet expectations. Unless partners are abusive, blaming spouses for our one-of-a-kind interpretations of reality is a mistake.

Junk In, Junk Out

So, why do spouses follow a path that leads from bad to worse? Is it because we do not try hard enough? No, it is, in my opinion, because "junk in, junk out" is the way our brains work. Minds full of conventional, self-serving thoughts churn out ill-considered, partner-annoying behaviors.

Freedom of Association

Early in the twentieth century, well before twenty-first century neuroscientists glimpsed neuronal activity, the Freudian psychoanalytic technique of free association provided insight into the brain's operation. Though no longer a mainstay of psychotherapy, free association demonstrates the existence of associative networks: neurons that fired together and wired together, connecting ideas, images, memories and emotions. At any time, sensory input or a random thought can trigger electrochemical impulses that activate neural networks.

Notice the chains of association triggered in your brain when you read this data: At a zoo in Bloemfontein, South Africa, Charlie, a chimpanzee, smokes cigarettes. In "monkey-see, monkey-do" fashion, Charlie learned the habit by watching visitors smoke then picking up discarded butts and mimicking what he'd seen. Now, zoo-goers toss him lighted cigarettes to watch him puff away.[20]

First reactions are pretty much always feelings. When I first saw the photo of Charlie, I felt flip-flopping emotions: amusement and chagrin. Then, I thought, *That is just wrong.* Then a conclusion, *Yet another ugly exploitation of animals.* Next, my one-of-a-kind network branched toward experiences that made me smile: memories of trips to the zoo with my nephews and niece and one particular image of the stunned expression on my six-year-old nephew's face when a chimpanzee started slinging feces at zoo-goers. Then images of an outing to a different zoo with undergraduate friends, one of whom later became a boyfriend. Next came memories of college boyfriends and on and on.

What emotions, images, thoughts and memories are triggered by Charlie's actions for you? Maybe you laughed or criticized the jokester who tossed the cigarette. Maybe the chain reaction in your brain branched toward insights about a golden marketing opportunity or support for the theory of evolution. Maybe your associations included images of smokers' lungs or oral lesions or opinions about tobacco subsidies or class action lawsuits.

The advantages and disadvantages of the brain's associative networks are evident in all relationships. Advantageously, a spouse may benefit from positive associations. Your partner opens the car door for you, triggering associations to your father's gentlemanly ways and your love for your father. Disadvantageously, a spouse can suffer the unhappy consequences of negative associations. Your partner raises her voice, triggering emotions and thoughts associated with intimidation, manipulation or abuse by a parent, sibling, ex-lover or former spouse. Even if unrelated to present circumstances, chains of association create the context or frame of mind out of which we respond.

Unless a marriage qualifies as a great mistake, marital satisfaction depends upon each individual's level of expertise at managing his or her frame of mind. As I've previously mentioned, our marital satisfaction is what we think it to be. Although chains of association get us started, we are free, at any point, to change direction.

In his book *Emotional Intelligence,* Daniel Goleman writes that psychotherapy brings about emotional relearning and that "while we cannot decide *when* we have our emotional outbursts, we have more control over *how long* they last."[21] We can either follow unhappy emotions and memories down the disenchantment path or create new sets of association, wiring around neural pathways mined with explosive junk. (Details about how this can be accomplished are in part 4.)

Chapter 9

Soap Operas

Sustaining disenchantment is simple: embrace drama and dysfunction. Keep communicating the same destructive thoughts, words and deeds. If we feel something needs to change, conventional wisdom encourages us to let our partners know what they should do to better suit us. This only leads to more drama and dysfunction.

Mara's Story

This thirty-something mother of two initially sought psychotherapy after experiencing constructive changes in her relationship with a close girlfriend who had been a client of mine. Mara's girlfriend's comments about self-responsibility piqued her interest and she wanted to examine her own lifelong patterns of emotional reactivity and controlling behavior. At the beginning of our therapist/client relationship, Mara focused on changing the way that she related to the girlfriend who referred her, as well as to co-workers and supervisors.

Early on, she found learning to think self-responsibly to be quite challenging. She kept applying herself and made significant changes not only in the way she handled herself at work but also with family members. Then her husband entered psychotherapy for depression and they had a few joint marital sessions.

Although Mara was now thinking and behaving self-responsibly, her husband, Clark, was not. He blamed his depression on Mara's controlling ways during their fifteen years of marriage and acted out dramatically, even threatening suicide. At his insistence, Mara moved to an apartment. Then Clark became involved with a female co-worker and asked for a divorce.

Many months later, Mara started dating. Her criteria for continuing a new relationship were stringent: sexual attraction, no red flags and proof of self-responsibility.

Mara: (Beaming.) I've met someone new.

Dr. M.: Tell me.

Mara: I think he's actually emotionally mature.

Dr. M.: Jackpot!

Mara: (Laughs.) Yeah, but I'm worried about something. Is it possible to be too easygoing?

Dr. M.: Say more.

Mara: Well, you know how I am now. As soon as I see drama, I'm, like, "See ya, wouldn't wanna be ya." But this guy is the definition of easygoing.

Dr. M.: That's a problem?

Mara: Oh, I don't know. Maybe I'm just thinking it's too good to be true.

Dr. M.: But you're feeling uneasy.

Mara: Okay, in the very beginning I told him that I'm recently divorced and not looking for anything serious. And he said that was fine. Now, we're getting serious, talking about making it exclusive and he's fine with that, too. Maybe I'm uneasy, because I'm so used to drama.

Dr. M.: Even though you don't want drama.

Mara: Right. Even though I don't want it, I kept finding it…meeting dysfunctional guys—until now.

Dr. M.: Maybe *you're* the one making drama. Getting back to old habits, telling yourself, "Oh, he's not dramatic. That's probably a sign of something bad."

Mara: (Raises eyebrows.) Ohhh…I know what you mean. Even though I'm consciously changing my approach, the past still effects my thinking—at least temporarily.

Communicating the Same Thing

Disenchanted couples universally complain of what they refer to as communication problems. Marital distress is not, however, a result of partners failing to communicate (see chapter 2, myth ten). It is, instead, the result of partners communicating that our not-trying-hard-enough spouses are failing to meet our completely reasonable expectations. Although most partners communicate this in good faith, it is neither helpful communication nor the way to improve a marriage. In order to improve communication, we must stop thoughtlessly taking the usual and customary approach. We must consciously choose new thoughts and establish constructive new patterns of interaction. Here are eleven mistakes of thought and behavior guaranteed to sustain disenchantment:

1. Expecting a fair world
2. Expecting quid pro quo
3. Misusing the parent/child model
4. Taking too much responsibility
5. Resorting to tit for tat
6. Giving free rein to negative emotions
7. Indulging in museum trips
8. Expecting too much happiness
9. Over-involving outsiders
10. Thinking like a victim
11. Expecting others to meet our needs

1. Expecting a Fair World

To some degree, everyone clings to the hope that life is fair. We want to see goodness rewarded, evil punished and success enjoyed by those who deserve it. As children, we are taught that if we behave, good things will happen to us. And who can blame our teachers? Can you imagine saying this to a child?

> Honey, no matter how much you want this thing, no matter how hard you work for it, this thing is never going to happen. Even though you totally deserve it, this thing will not be yours. In fact, it will be handed over to someone less deserving.

If you told a child that meritocracies do not exist, you would probably never be forgiven. If you leaked the demoralizing facts—life can be profoundly unfair and goodness often goes unrecognized—you would soon regret it.

Belief in the fair treatment ideal is so central to our worldviews that even after we know it's a fantasy we hear ourselves blurting out things like, "It's not fair! Why me? This can't be happening!" In romantic relationships, we look to our partners to be the people who never treat us unfairly, restoring our childlike faith in a fair world. The trouble with clinging to this hope is that disappointment is 100 percent guaranteed.

2. Expecting Quid Pro Quo

Translation: Something for something. I will, if you will. Pretty much everyone has tried this.

- I'll be sweet, if you will.
- I'll give you sex, if you give me affection.
- I'll stop watching sports, if you stop ordering off the Internet.

Quid pro quo seems so logical and fair. Our parents tried it on us, so we try it on our spouses. Even marital therapists (who have exhausted their repertoire of techniques) have recommended trying such arrangements. The reality is that quid pro quo does not lead to marital satisfaction.

The main reason this approach doesn't work is that it grows out of scorekeeping. If you feel the need for a quid pro quo arrangement, you have tallied up the score and decided to point out your spouse's failures to match your level of effort. You are the winner and your spouse is a loser. Then your spouse points out that you, too, are a loser, just a different kind. You might as well be matadors waving red capes at bulls.

3. Misusing the Parent/Child Model

The parent/child interaction is the first relationship that humans experience when our brains are packed with related neural networks. Within these neural networks are the origins of our associations to essential concepts like love, affection, trust, loyalty, power, control, generosity and forgiveness. These associations, both positive and negative, provide the

Yankton Community Library
515 Walnut St.
605-668-5275

Title: Ten stupid things couples do to mess up their relationships / Laura Schlessinger.

Barcode: 31600000844894

DueDate: 01/30/2015 at 11:59 PM

Title: A happy marriage : a novel / Rafael Yglesias.

Barcode: 31600001147313

DueDate: 01/30/2015 at 11:59 PM

Title: Everybody marries the wrong person : turning flawed into fulfilling relationships / by Christine Mei

Barcode: 31600001193341

DueDate: 01/30/2015 at 11:59 PM

Due dates for items checked out today are above. Return or renew items by due date. PLEASE KEEP THIS RECEIPT.

Thanks,

Circulation Department

standards by which all other relationships are measured. These associations also provide a template for behavior in other relationships. For example, your mother teaches you elegant table manners and you replicate what pleases your mother at relatives' and friends' dinner tables.

The main reason the parent/child template doesn't work for marriage is that a successful marriage is an intimate friendship between two adults, each taking responsibility for his/her own existence. The parent/child template is one in which the parent takes responsibility for the child's existence. Reenacting the parent/child template with a spouse portends disaster. If your spouse actually needs parenting, you have an under-responsible, emotional adolescent on your hands and your parenting will foster rebellion. If your spouse is an emotionally mature adult, your parenting will foster righteous indignation.

Witnessing adults engaged in parent/child relating can be downright comical. These kinds of interactions fulfill the basic requirements for comedy—unexpected and out of place. The television sitcom *Friends* provided laughs with adults delivering cranky parent lines to other adults:

> **Joey:** What did I just say?
> **Phoebe:** Don't make me come over there.
> **Monica:** If I am harsh with you, it's only because you're doing it wrong!

Adults do learn from other adults. My husband has encyclopedic knowledge of sports cars, post-impressionism, bicycling and Steely Dan, and I have chosen to learn a lot from him. The operative word here is *chosen*. Believing that you or your spouse has an obligation to instruct and/or obey the other person is applying the parent/child model. Believing that your spouse is emotionally mature and acts in good faith with the best interest of the relationship in mind is the adult/adult model.

4. Taking Too Much Responsibility

According to conventional wisdom, spouses are extensions of each other and are, at least partially, responsible for each other's behavior. Again, conventional wisdom misleads. We are not responsible for monitoring our spouses' behavior. We are responsible for monitoring our own behavior.

In order to stop taking responsibility for a spouse's behavior, we have to be willing to set limits. *Now, hold on*, you might think. *Isn't setting limits trying to change someone?* Setting limits *is* about changing someone. But not our partners. This is about setting limits with ourselves, reacting differently.

Jason's Story

Jason is in his forties and married over twenty years.

Jason: I know, now, why my wife acts strange all evening and never remembers what we talk about.

Dr. M.: Uh-oh.

Jason: She's only drinking a couple of beers, but she's drinking vodka, too. I found eight empty bottles at the bottom of our dumpster.

Dr. M.: Uh-oh.

Jason: I feel bad…like I caused this by harassing her about drinking too much beer.

Dr. M.: You're not responsible for her behavior.

Jason: But she never did this before.

Dr. M.: Still—you're not responsible for her behavior.

Jason: But if she's an alcoholic, I've got to do something. Should I threaten to leave?

Dr. M.: Do you want to leave?

Jason: No! I just want her to drink less.

Dr. M.: What has she said when you've told her that?

Jason: She says, "I know. I know. I'm a terrible person."

Dr. M.: She's distracting you…going for sympathy.

Jason: But what if she really thinks that?

Dr. M.: You're not responsible for what she thinks about herself.

Jason: So you say.

Dr. M.: Try talking to her about what *you're* going to do differently.

Jason: Like what?

Dr. M.: I'm a big fan of Al-Anon.

Jason: Oh, I don't know if I'm ready for that.

Dr. M.: Okay. Which of your reactions to her drinking are you dissatisfied with?

Jason: I don't like harassing her...but if I stop, she might think I'm okay with it.

Dr. M.: Just tell her that you're going to stop harassing her because you don't like that behavior in yourself.

Jason: Oh. (Pauses.) Okay, I could also stop counting how many drinks she's had...and stop looking for hidden bottles.

Dr. M.: Exactly.

Jason: I could stop drinking myself, I guess. Is that necessary?

Dr. M.: It sends a solidarity message.

Jason: I'm the one who buys the beer. I could stop doing that.

Dr. M.: This is definitely the way to start. Talk to her, without blaming, about what you've decided to change about your own behavior.

5. Resorting to Tit for Tat

The evil twin of trying to help is trying to bully a partner out of destructive and self-defeating behavior by behaving badly ourselves. Conventional wisdom encourages tit for tat. Your partner goes out dancing, so you go out drinking. Your partner wastes money playing poker, so you buy lottery tickets. Your partner is cranky, so you're crankier. This is NOT setting appropriate limits.

The main problem with this strategy is that it leads to endless cycles of aggression. Sadly, we all know more than we'd like about people trying to right one wrong with another wrong. From the profound to the petty, the world's battlefields to small claims courts, halting the frenzy of retaliation requires somebody to go first, to rise above base human impulses and to practice self-restraint and forgiveness (more information in part 4).

6. Giving Free Rein to Negative Emotions

Despite guaranteed damage to relationships, nearly everyone excuses his or her own emotional excesses. Belief that the end justifies the means is a mainstay of conventional wisdom. Is there anyone who hasn't tried to manipulate a partner with crying or pouting? *If he sees how much I'm hurting, he'll give in,* someone thinks. And many people have attempted to intimidate partners with anger: *If she thinks I could lose control, she'll relent.*

We all experience jealousy, envy, anger, resentment, frustration and irritation. It is okay to *feel* these feelings, but it is never productive to abandon rational thinking and succumb to negative emotions. Some readers might be having doubts about this and thinking, *I can't help how I feel! Isn't it unhealthy to hold in emotions? I think being honest about feelings is something partners owe one another.* These are all falsehoods based on conventional wisdom.

The reason expression of negative emotions fails to improve marriages is that it leads to escalation rather than resolution of conflict. Remember this: Acting on negative emotions is like running with your hair on fire. It *feels* like the thing to do, but decidedly is not. (More about managing emotions in part 4.)

7. Indulging in Museum Trips

Museum trips are when you point out to your spouse, like pointing out pictures at an exhibition, example after example of his or her offenses and failures.

- You let me down again. Just like the time you forgot my birthday and the time you let out my cat and she got run over.
- You say you care about the kids, but you've missed eight soccer games, three dance recitals and every parent-teacher conference.

The misconception here is that museum trips are about providing constructive criticism. Your spouse is neither likely to benefit from your account of his blunders nor likely to engage in reflection upon his shortcomings. Since museum trips are really about punishing—delivering verbal blows, inflicting emotional pain, doing unto others what has been done to you—your spouse is likely to become defensive, argumentative and resentful.

Some people may be thinking, *What am I supposed to do? Let him/her get away with everything?* No, but punishment is not the answer. Punishment is good for nothing except doing psychological damage to both punished and punisher. (More about constructive alternatives in part 4.)

8. Expecting Too Much Happiness

We make a lot of our own trouble in relationships by expecting too much happiness, marital and personal. As Eric Hoffer points out, "The search for happiness is one of the chief sources of unhappiness." We don't intend to doom ourselves into unhappiness by wanting the perfect marriage, but we do exactly that by holding onto unrealistic expectations.

The problem is that expectations based on misconceptions, formed during a period of altered neurochemistry (infatuation), invariably prove unrealistic. Then we feel disheartened. Rather than accepting that "happily ever after" is a fairytale, we devalue our marriages and harshly judge our partners' efforts.

According to Plato, poverty is not the absence of goods but, rather, the overabundance of desire. The same can be said about unhappiness. At this point, you may ask, "Could she actually be saying that if I *lower* my standards enough, I'll find happiness?" No psychologist would suggest lowering standards. This is about adjusting expectations to reflect reality.

For example, remember the tale of the bridezilla who fled before the wedding ceremony and claimed she had been kidnapped and sexually assaulted by a "Mexican"? Apparently, wedding plans more elaborate than Princess Diana's (over five hundred guests and twenty-eight attendants) did not make her happy.

It is not that she would have been happier if she had lowered her standards and planned a less elaborate wedding, but impossibly elaborate expectations (whatever the particulars) are the essence of refusing to acknowledge reality. Perhaps this bride's husband-to-be or his or her family disappointed her. Maybe she disappointed herself by overestimating her ability to meet the demands of staging the happiest day of her life. In the end, the unhappiness associated with unmet expectations led her on an elaborate flight from reality in a flurry of running and lying.

9. Over-Involving Outsiders

Arguing with spouses in the presence of friends and family members or talking too much to others about marital dissatisfaction are common mistakes. Conventional wisdom supports getting negative feelings out in the open. When we showcase our spouses' weaknesses, however, we risk alienating key people in our lives. Loved ones, understandably, find it difficult to integrate into their relationships with your spouse the fact that he or she called you an imbecile, doesn't pay bills on time or views pornography. More importantly, when we over-involve outsiders, we betray our promises to honor the marital relationship as our most important relationship.

For anyone who has been in psychotherapy, venting discontent and criticizing spouses in the context of the therapeutic relationship is the exception to this rule. Occasionally, clients are overly concerned about being disloyal by "badmouthing" their spouses. These clients actually err in the direction of downplaying their discontent or attempting to justify partners' behavior. In my experience, frank criticisms of partners' behavior provide excellent material and can be utilized to good effect. For example, Katy, one of my clients, set the stage for constructive discussion when she mentioned that she and her female co-workers spend every break and lunch hour trashing their partners.

Outside the psychotherapy office, trashing spouses with "I can top that" stories is costly. Broadcasting anecdotes that make our spouses sound like fools or villains (even if the facts are accurate) weakens marital solidarity. Scoring a few laughs because she snores like a bison or he naively believes he's a top chef loosens our commitment to persist in love and loyalty. People are loyal to alma maters, soft drink brands and political parties. How can we be any less loyal to life partners?

Successful marriages are ones in which partners keep their promises to honor each other above all others. Relationships with parents, siblings and friends become secondary. This is not a license to neglect loved ones, but rather encouragement to team up with spouses. When we find ourselves triangulated (around holiday plans, for example), self-responsible partners support spouses. Loyalty to spouses sets the right precedent for everyone involved.

Except in abuse situations, spouses do not need family and friends aligning with them against partners. Self-responsible spouses privately address conflicts and dissatisfactions. Then, if partners are unresponsive, self-responsible spouses cope by drawing on inner resources or seeking professional help. (More about how to fortify inner resources in part 4.)

10. Thinking Like a Victim

There is a crucial difference between thinking like a victim and being a victim. If you are, in fact, being abused by your partner, see chapter 3. Thinking like a victim involves assuming the one-down position and having thoughts like:

- This would not happen if you listened to me.
- I'm under-appreciated.
- I should be treated better.

In the minds of the conventionally wise, speaking out is rewarded and inspires free expression of righteous indignation and anger. In reality, only someone who is thinking like a victim points the finger of blame.

So, what's wrong with getting angry and blaming the culprit? For starters, an angry victim is no less a victim. Second, anger leads to victimization of those by whom we feel victimized. Finally, we shift responsibility for change onto the culprit. Thinking like a victim characterizes a denier of reality and shirker of self-responsibility. In romantic relationships, pointing out how partners are at fault is an attempt to shift responsibility for improving marital satisfaction.

Sometimes we go so far as to blame partners for not defending us against psychological or emotional abuse by others. A common example is a wife or husband who feels betrayed because a spouse stands mute while she or he is criticized. Perhaps your mother-in-law critiques your choice of a home in a transitional neighborhood or your spouse's stepfather makes a crack about working mothers or stay-at-home dads. Self-responsible spouses do not expect to be defended or rescued. Self-responsible spouses expect to handle situations themselves.

Elyn's Story

In her early twenties, Elyn is a newlywed.

> **Elyn:** My in-laws out-and-out said I was ruining their lives by taking a job in another town. And my husband said nothing! I feel so betrayed.
>
> **Dr. M.:** How did he betray you?
>
> **Elyn:** He should have stood up for me.

Dr. M.: Said something in your defense?

Elyn: Exactly. He never does that.

Dr. M.: Well, maybe he thinks of you as an adult who can speak for herself.

Elyn: (Frowns.)

Dr. M.: Not intervening could be a sign of respect.

Elyn: For his parents?

Dr. M.: (Laughs.) For you!

Elyn: (Raises eyebrows.) Oh, whoa! I never thought of that. This is what my girlfriend and I call a "whoa" moment.

Dr. M.: Did you accuse your husband of betraying you?

Elyn: No, luckily. He told me later that it's not worth arguing with his parents. That we're moving, regardless, and that's all there is to it.

Dr. M.: Sounds pretty respectful to me.

Elyn: (Nods.)

11. Expecting Others to Meet Our Needs

To some degree, everyone has a narcissistic sense of entitlement. As Jane Austen said, "I have been a selfish being all my life, in practice, though not in principle." Conventional wisdom supports fighting for our rights, even if it means getting our needs met at others' expense. Examples abound of those who feel entitled: superpowers, terrorists, celebrities and paparazzi.

Anyone who acts out anger is displaying a sense of entitlement. We tell ourselves we are entitled because we have been wronged. From the International Criminal Court to the sleaziest talk show, conventional wisdom endorses expression of so-called righteous anger. Images of the triumph of the archetypal, ninety-pound weakling justify the ranting and raving, and bursts of adrenaline fuel feelings of false empowerment. In order to relinquish our sense of entitlement, one must recognize that venting is self-indulgence and righteous indignation is self-deception.

Another lie we tell ourselves is that success entitles us to special treatment. A company owner believes she is entitled to employees' respect. A philanthropist believes he is entitled to invitations to join exclusive clubs. Star athletes and elected officials believe they are entitled to perks and exemptions. The primary income-generator believes he or she is entitled to final say in spending decisions.

Expecting a spouse to adapt to our needs rather than requiring ourselves to adapt to the realities of partnership shows a sense of entitlement. The degree to which sense of entitlement threatens the happiness of a union depends upon the degree to which expectations are shared. In any given situation, if spouses agree about whose needs come first, individual sense of entitlement will be tolerated and marital satisfaction unaffected. If spouses disagree about whose needs come first, marital satisfaction is threatened.

Bart's Story

Bart is in his thirties and is often left alone with his three children because his wife frequently travels on business. His primary treatment goal was to learn anger management.

Bart: It's not how I thought it would be.

Dr. M.: Did you expect to have children?

Bart: Oh, yes.

Dr. M.: Did you expect both you and your wife to be employed?

Bart: (Rolls eyes.) I just didn't think I'd be going it alone. It's exhausting to work all day and take care of kids at night.

Dr. M.: You cook?

Bart: Sure! And clean up after the kids, play games with them, help with homework, do baths and bedtime stories.

Dr. M.: And you're angry about it.

Bart: Yes! And I take it out on everybody. I yell at the kids and I accuse my wife of enjoying being away.

Dr. M.: Which shall we talk about first?

Bart: Yelling at the kids.

Dr. M.: What are you yelling about?

Bart: I yell at them to quit whining and fighting and stalling at bedtime.

Dr. M.: It feels like they're disrespecting you. Challenging your authority.

Bart: Bingo.

Dr. M.: So, you feel entitled, as their father, to respect.

Bart: (Hesitantly.) Yeah…

Dr. M.: And taking care of them gets in the way of your need for…

Bart: Relaxation. Peace and quiet. Downtime.

Dr. M.: Are you listening to yourself?

Bart: (Questioning expression.)

Dr. M.: It's all about what you feel entitled to. Respect. Downtime.

Bart: You sound like my wife.

Dr. M.: I think that if you work on your sense of entitlement, you'll feel less angry with your kids and your wife.

In fact, Bart, with my therapeutic help, did work on himself, his expectations and his reactions to his relationship. Thus, his marriage and life improved.

Part 4

Mature Love

Chapter 10

In with the New

Everybody marries the wrong person means that marriages cannot succeed without mature love. Since infatuation is temporary and disenchantment is inevitable, a couple's best hope for happily sustaining their "'til death parts us" union is to practice mature love. Although age and experience may foster mature love, chronological maturity is secondary.

The developmental period known as adolescence begins with the physical/biological changes associated with puberty and ends with full development of the brain's prefrontal cortex. Brain-imaging data show development continuing well into the twenties. Those under twenty-five can experience sexual attraction and the emotions of love. Late adolescents can be kind, thoughtful and self-sacrificing, but the majority of them are not fully prepared to succeed at practicing mature love.

These facts of brain development may be the best argument yet in favor of delaying marriage. The first years of life are dominated by development in brain regions associated with emotions, impulses and reward-seeking behaviors. Gradually, our brain develops capacities for self-regulation. Areas of the prefrontal cortex that are essential to the practice of mature love—judgment, inhibition of impulses, logic and understanding of consequences—are the last to develop.

Seeking mature love at any age is akin to looking for a miracle to occur. Not a miracle like winning a dream house, but something extraordinary, nonetheless. Seeking mature love means asking oneself to perform a near-miracle by rising above conventional wisdom, self-involvement and disenchantment.

Expecting Something Extraordinary

Romantic myths focus on the extraordinariness of our love objects:

- You make me want to be a better man.
- You are my true north.
- You complete me.

Successful marriages focus on less popular ideas:

- Do not expect your partner to change in any of the ways you want her or him to change.
- Work to be the best possible partner you can be.
- Expect to put more into it than you get out of it.

Ray's Story

Ray is in his late twenties and married six years.

Ray: Put more into it than I get out of it?
Dr. M.: Yes, if you want a better than average marriage.
Ray: Why has no one ever said this to me before?
Dr. M: It's not the way most people think.
Ray: Not very sexy.
Dr. M: It's the hard work we're always told about.
Ray: This is a whole other way of thinking.

Self-Proclaimed "Pro-Marriage" Counselors

As some readers may know from experience, self-proclaimed "pro-marriage" counselors have increased in numbers lately. Whether you listen to their radio talk shows or hear a former client's horror story, one doesn't have to listen long to understand what "pro-marriage" means. First, it means that the most appropriate, perhaps, the only appropriate outcome of counseling is staying married. Second, the label gives the none-too-subtle message that mental health professionals who do not claim to be "pro-marriage" may be anti-marriage, waiting to urge couples into the offices of their best friends, the anti-marriage divorce lawyers. Finally, "pro-marriage" counselors are just that—advocates for marriage. Many, in fact, are advocates for what they believe to be the Divine institution sanctioned by God. Be aware that "pro-marriage" counselors may not be advocates for you. Advocates for you consider your unique circumstances and stated goals, then, first and last, advocate for your psychological well-being and emotional maturity.

Practicing Mature Love

If your goal is to stay married and feel glad that you did so, you will want to learn all about practicing mature love. Two concepts are fundamental to mature love. First, spouses must understand that mature love is faithfully practiced and never fully achieved. Although experts at anything make it look easy, they always say their success is the result of practice, practice, practice. For example, it has been said for thousands of years that yogis and yoginis never *do* yoga. Rather, they *practice* yoga. The same is true for romantic relationships. Second, spouses who aspire to mature love must shoulder responsibility for their own existences and for their beliefs about the *quality* of their existences. Psychologists call this being self-responsible and view self-responsibility as a hallmark of emotional maturity.

Self-responsible partners honor commitments made at the altar and, more importantly, commit, as Sue Monk Kidd put it, "not just to love—but to persist in love."[1] We persist in love as we continue the seemingly endless work of making ourselves the best partners we can be. To become a self-responsible partner practicing mature love, cultivate eight skills:

1. Acceptance of spouse's weaknesses
2. Acknowledgment of personal weaknesses
3. Enlightenment regarding gender roles
4. Choosing to sacrifice
5. Management of reactivity/negative emotions
6. Understanding trust
7. Being proactive
8. Delaying gratification

1. Acceptance of Spouse's Weaknesses

Unless your choice of partner qualifies as a great mistake (see chapter 3), you must continue to overlook your beloved's imperfections. If you marry someone with a mullet or a penchant for spandex, get used to it. Precedent has been set. You focused on your beloved's strengths, not his or her fashion faux pas, before the ceremony and your spouse expects you to continue to do so. If you try to tweak your partner toward your idea of perfection, you are parenting (see chapter 10) and asking for trouble.

Even if you are a person who wants to be told that your pants are too short or that you smell like garlic, understand that spouses are not renovation projects. Self-responsible spouses do not suggest in any way that their partners become new-and-improved versions of themselves. The words, "Don't you think you should...," are never volunteered by a self-responsible spouse. If your partner requests constructive criticism, be as candid as you know he or she can tolerate. Then do not take offense or dwell on dashed hopes when your partner chooses, as he or she inevitably will, to ignore your input and stick with imperfect preferences and opinions.

2. Acknowledgment of Personal Weaknesses

Acknowledging our own weaknesses prepares us to behave constructively in provocative situations. If your partner's polished appearance attracted you in the first place, don't get upset when she keeps you waiting to go out. First, manage your own weaknesses. Impatience, for example, is a weakness you can manage. Harassing, pressuring and berating only give your partner reasons to be angry with you, blame you for her tardiness and make you still later. If it is *that* important to you to be on time, take responsibility for your need by doing everything you can to make it happen. Polish her shoes. Corral the children. Finish the kitchen cleanup. Adapting to reality is self-responsible behavior.

On the flipside, the spouse who needs two hours for grooming must take responsibility for making necessary allowances. Then, if best-laid plans go awry, manage your weaknesses. In this example, defensiveness is a weakness to manage. Don't raise objections when your spouse proposes leaving without you. Being inconvenienced is the consequence of not being ready on time. Saying, "I'm doing this for you. You don't appreciate me" or "If you'd help out, I'd have time to get ready" (even if true) is shirking responsibility. Presenting a polished appearance is *your* need.

3. Enlightenment Regarding Gender Roles

Three elements are essential to an enlightened view of gender roles: presumption of sexual equality, assimilation of scientific knowledge about biological sex differences and respect for individual preferences. Despite millennia of efforts toward parity, gender clichés persist, as do our attempts to justify the clichés. Some individuals go against convention, choosing not to subject their partners to anachronistic expectations.

When my nephew was three years old, I asked him to tell me about his preschool experience. "We ride trikes," he said. "The girls ride slooow and the boys ride *fast*." Around the same time, I interviewed Dr. Jerome Frank of Johns Hopkins University School of Medicine for a professional journal article. The world-famous and universally respected professor emeritus, who earned both a Ph.D. in psychology and an M.D. with a specialty in psychiatry, offered a professorial variation on the same theme:

> I'm very much for women's liberation, but part of it is delusionary. I'm convinced, you see, that biological differences are extremely important. You can't get away from the fact that the male sex hormones and chromosomes are related to aggressiveness and to assume that women can get their share of the same kinds of the world's goods that men are fighting for all the time, I think, is a delusion. Take the fight for equal pay for equal work. I'll bet there are always going to be differentials.[2]

People tend to have strong emotions associated with adherence to or divergence from traditional gender roles. Traditionalists and progressives alike support their viewpoints by citing biological imperatives, common sense and moral tenets. Our judgments about how well we live up to gender appropriate ideals affect self-confidence and our judgments about how well our spouses live up to these ideals affect marital satisfaction.

During my years of clinical practice, I have found there has been nothing over which clients agonize more. Some stay-at-home moms devalue their traditional role. Some dads shed tears over the breadwinner role limiting their time with children. Some gay men marry women and father children. Some single women worry about educating themselves out of marriage and motherhood. Some wives hold themselves to the Madonna-whore stereotype. Some husbands hold themselves to the head-of-household stereotype.

Some men and women make marital trouble by measuring their partners against gender role stereotypes. Some men fault fulltime employed wives for not putting home-cooked meals on the table. Some women fault husbands for not making enough money. Some wives devalue husbands who refuse to do yard work and some husbands devalue wives who balk at giving dinner parties. Stereotypes about gender-appropriate appearances also emerge, causing devaluation based on weight gain, baldness, descending breasts and aging skin.

As if we don't cause enough trouble by criticizing deviations from supposedly admirable, gender-role stereotypes, we make things even worse with additional criticism of adherence to supposedly undesirable stereotypes. Too many husbands are subjected to snide comments about refusing to learn to cook or dance or to fluff pillows. And too many wives are subjected to ridicule about chick flicks, PMS and navigation via landmarks.

To varying degrees throughout history, women assumed equal rights and freedoms and fought against being objectified, taken advantage of and disrespected. Twenty-first century women face the challenge of carrying forward the larger work and, at the same time, trusting the intentions of and expecting the best from their own romantic partners. If spouses are believers in equality, women owe them their due as exceptions to the overarching rule that humans devalue women. Just as eons of gender-role stereotypes and sins against women cannot be ignored, seeing devaluation where none exists spawns its own form of injustice.

4. Choosing to Sacrifice

The world has seen enough people who sacrifice everything for love or loved ones. If we satisfy our need for a life-partner, we are called upon to sacrifice the freedoms of single life and other important needs, too. For example, Person X has the need to be with Person Y and the need to live in a tropical climate. Person Y has the need to be with Person X and the need to live in a temperate climate. Too often we expect the one who fulfilled our need for a life-partner to meet our every need, to sacrifice for us rather than vice versa.

Chrissy's Story

A full-time employed mother of two, Chrissy is in her thirties and married for the second time.

Chrissy: My husband's family business is bankrupting us.

Dr. M.: Are you the only one who realizes this?

Chrissy: He's in denial.

Dr. M.: What, besides the obvious, doesn't he want to face?

Chrissy: Well, he needs to fire his alcoholic uncle who pads his expense account. He also needs to stop paying his uncle's full salary, leaving nothing for us.

Dr. M.: He'd rather go without than ask that of his uncle?

Chrissy: He doesn't exactly go without. First, we used my entire savings, about twenty thousand dollars. Now, he's charged tens of thousands to our credit cards.

Dr. M.: And you've talked with him directly about where you see this going?

Chrissy: He always says things will be fine as soon as he closes the next big deal.

Dr. M.: How long has he been saying that?

Chrissy: Three years. Ever since we got married.

Chrissy soon saw the futility of her original plan to use psychotherapy to learn ways to convince her husband to stop enabling his uncle or to find other employment. Effectively, she gave up her belief that she could make her "otherwise wonderful guy" even more to her liking and accepted the reality that sacrifice was unavoidable. Chrissy had to choose between her need to maintain a certain lifestyle and her need to stay married to the man whom she loved and approved of—except for the way he handled his business.

Her husband was behaving irresponsibly—jeopardizing their financial security and putting his relationship with his family-of-origin ahead of his marriage—but she was colluding. Did Chrissy value her marriage enough to endure the fallout of insisting upon separating business and personal accounts and living within their means? Or did she value a certain lifestyle enough to end her marriage to a mostly "wonderful" guy.

This story ended happily for my client and her husband. After Chrissy made clear her commitment to living within their means, her husband left the family business for a position in another state.

5. Management of Reactivity/Negative Emotions

A life oozing with negative emotions is a life saturated with fear of extinction and loss. While fears associated with physical threats (e.g., heights, immersion in water, loud noises, sudden movements) are innate, other fears are learned. Humans can learn to fear anything from the seemingly innocuous to the purely psychological: loss of dignity or threats to peace of mind, for example.

All negative emotions are reactions to perceived threats, and learning to manage fear-based reactivity is central to individual mental health as well as to marital success. Our skill at distinguishing life-threatening from non-life-threatening greatly affects our quality of life. If we ignore the life-threatening, we risk physical harm. If we overreact to the non-life-threatening, we risk our relationships and mental health; as most everyone knows, chronic overreaction to the non-life-threatening (stress) can jeopardize physical health, too.

Hypersensitivity rooted in prior experiences can lead us to perceive danger where presently there is none. The interpersonal dangers of acting on hypersensitivities are addressed in research conducted by Dr. John Gottman and colleagues. After interviewing hundreds of newlywed couples over fifteen years, they devised a mathematical model for predicting with 94 percent accuracy whether a relationship will fail within four years of observation. One important predictor of relationship failure was a pattern during an argument of positive statements made by one partner getting a negative response from the other partner.[3]

Lasting relationships were characterized, in part, by a factor related to self-responsibility—a pattern during an argument of positive statements from one partner producing a positive response from the other. Taking a self-responsible approach—responding constructively even during disagreements—contributes to marital success. Easier said than done, yet well worth learning to do.

6. Understanding Trust

As I discussed in part 1, trust is a choice to honor a social contract based on mutual self-interest. For example, customers order dinner at a restaurant trusting that cooks and wait staff practice appropriate food-handling hygiene. Restaurant employees do their jobs, trusting that customers pay their checks, tip appropriately and recommend the restaurant to friends. Everyone knows that food poisoning sometimes happens, even at the best restaurants, and that miserly tipping occurs, even after superior service. Nonetheless, customers keep ordering meals and restaurant employees keep serving customers. Most of us choose to trust the system.

In intimate relationships, we approach trust in one of two ways: unconditionally or requiring loved ones to prove themselves. Regardless of our approach, spouses, like everyone else, will eventually betray our trust. Once trust is broken, it is up to us to choose our reaction. If we see betrayal as evidence of a "great mistake", choosing *not* to trust may be the healthier option. If we want to stay married, forgiving betrayal and choosing to trust again are the healthy options.

Jennifer's Story

In her early twenties, Jennifer has been married fewer than two years and has no children. At initial evaluation, this gentle and articulate young woman told me that she was seriously considering ending her marriage. Jennifer reported that her husband, Nick, frequently demanded that she obey his commands (prime example of narcissistic sense of entitlement) and intimidated her into compliance by shouting, throwing things and punching walls. Although Nick, had not yet physically harmed her, he had recently made a threatening statement that motivated her to ask her family physician for a referral to a psychologist. Jennifer hoped to get a professional's opinion about whether she might be overreacting to her husband's threat.

Jennifer told me that one day she came home from work with a migraine headache and lay down to rest. Soon Nick began insisting that she get up to help him move a mattress up a flight of stairs. Jennifer explained she had a headache and didn't want to move the mattress, but he continued to demand her help. When Nick started kicking the bed on which she was resting, Jennifer decided that her best option was to get up and help him.

During the moving process, Nick yelled and criticized her efforts. After the job was done, Jennifer picked up her keys and started toward the door, intending to drive to her parents' house to rest. What her husband said then was the thing she thought could be the final threat. "If you leave," he said, "I'll kill your cat."

More important than my professional opinion about whether she might be overreacting was the fact that her trust in her husband had been irreparably broken. By our second session, Jennifer had filed for divorce. She had recognized her great mistake and made up her mind to rescue herself.

Steve's Story

In his late thirties, Steve is in the third year of his second marriage. He has a two-year-old son. This teacher and football coach sought counseling after an argument with his wife, Anna, escalated into a physical confrontation. He said that this was a first for them and that "things got out of hand" because they had both been drinking. Steve said that Anna had tried to slap him and he had grabbed her wrists and held them to her sides. His goal was to talk about how to better handle his wife's "controlling behavior." He cited, as an example, the fact that she imposed a curfew when he occasionally went to a sports bar with a group of fellow coaches. Although he resented the curfew, Steve also seemed to think he might be doing something to "deserve" her attempts to control his behavior.

First, we addressed Steve's self-responsibility quotient by evaluating his guys' night out behavior. Was he picking up women or having an extramarital affair? No. Was he drinking to excess and driving? No. Because of their positions in the community, the coaches took turns being the designated driver. Was he unable to go to work the day after? No. Was he directly or indirectly harming his wife with his behavior (e.g., waking her from sound sleep when he returned home)? No.

> **Dr. M.:** Then what do you think your wife is afraid of?
>
> **Steve:** (Long silence.) Well, this gets into the deep, dark secret of how we met.

Dr. M.: In a bar?
Steve: (Nods.)
Dr. M.: Were you both married?
Steve: She was.
Dr. M.: You were single.
Steve: Divorced.
Dr. M.: Then this is *her* issue. Not yours.
Steve: It is?
Dr. M.: Your wife's lack of trust is based on *her* lack of trustworthiness, not yours.
Steve: Tell me what you think of this: She wanted to go through my e-mails and cell phone records.

With one exception, the degree to which we trust others is a reflection of the degree to which we trust ourselves. If we know ourselves to be sufficiently self-disciplined, have a history of meeting life's difficulties with integrity and do not make false promises to ourselves, we know that we can be trusted.[4] If we tend to be reliable for ourselves and for others, we tend to trust that others will do the same for us.

Steve's wife, Anna, eventually joined him for a couple of sessions. She turned out to be very likeable, not only because she was intelligent and humorous, but also because she admitted to being paranoid about her husband. At first she claimed that her paranoia was justified because his good looks and extroversion attracted women of all ages to him. She proved willing to acknowledge, though, that her touchiness about guys' night out had to do with her own history of infidelity and that her desire to control her husband's behavior had to do with her lack of self-trust. Ultimately, an agreement was reached that it was *not* Steve's responsibility to "prove" his trustworthiness and that his attempts to do so were counterproductive.

The one exception: Some people are dangerous, like poisonous snakes. No matter how convincingly a poisonous snake promises not to bite, it would be foolish to put one in your pocket. When we are intellectually lazy or refuse to face reality, we collude with those who intend to use or abuse us. Broad examples:

- Cigarettes are not carcinogenic.
- Your retirement funds are secure.

Truth and Honesty

No discussion of trust is complete without addressing truth and honesty. Realistically, different relationships inspire greater or lesser degrees of honesty. If we are with like-minded people, with those who welcome diverse opinions or with those who view truth-telling as a high compliment, being honest is fun and freeing.

All too often, truth-telling triggers others' insecurities. In such cases, some thoughts are better kept to ourselves. Perhaps you believe that religious fundamentalists do more harm in the world than good, but choose not to mention this to your Southern Baptist in-laws. "Well," some may say, "that's just being phony. I want to be completely honest in my relationships. My spouse, in particular, deserves to know the complete truth about what I think and feel." This viewpoint wins style points, but under everyday wear and tear, it falls apart like a pair of cheap shoes.

We must also manage our responses when partners speak troublesome truths. Although our first reactions may be defensive or combative, acting out negative emotions discourages spouses' attempts to give us the very thing that we say we want. Self-responsible partners encourage truth and honesty by reacting constructively.

Passing Judgment

Interestingly, it is not simple disagreement that discourages honesty. We discourage others' honesty by passing judgment on whatever has been said and expressing disapproval of their opinions, preferences or decisions. For example:

> **He:** (Watching the evening news.) I'm so sick of stories about the evils of prostitution.
>
> **She:** (Thinks and says) Oh, for Pete's sake! You think men should get away with that?
>
> **He:** (Thinks and says) Oh, hell! Here we go again!
>
> *Stupid argument ensues.*

OR

He: I'm so sick of stories about the evils of prostitution.
She: (Thinks *You think men should get away with that?* but gives her man the benefit of the doubt.) How come?
He: (Thinks *Here we go again!* but gives his woman the benefit of the doubt.) It's a matter of civil liberties.
Interesting discussion ensues.

A self-responsible partner is concerned not only with his spouse's trustworthiness, truthfulness and honesty, but also with his own. A self-responsible partner recognizes her own insecurities and manages her negative reactions. Self-responsible partners view honesty as the ultimate gift of trust and truth as the ultimate vote of confidence.

7. Being Proactive

To be proactive means to act in anticipation of future problems, needs or changes that could come about in one's life. The use of motorcycle helmets and automobile seatbelts are hallmarks of proactive travelers. Setting alarm clocks and grabbing umbrellas are also good examples.

For models of proactive social behavior, look to activists of the civil rights movement. As Dr. Martin Luther King, Jr. said, "Darkness cannot drive out darkness; only light can do that." Activists transcended personal reactions to bigotry and abuse and chose behaviors that advanced the larger cause. Despite outrageous provocation, individuals exercised restraint and sought the rewards associated with achieving the ultimate goal.

Being proactive in relationships requires applying forethought and self-discipline to every interaction. It means reality-testing expectations and troubleshooting situations that invite destructive behavior, much as parents babyproof a room. Rather than dwelling on why our spouses care so little as to let us down, we put energy toward employing alternative means for meeting our needs. We handle disappointment without blaming those who fail to meet our expectations. We shift focus off others' failures and onto overarching goals. Although it does not mean walking on eggshells or resigning oneself to domination by an impossible-to-please tyrant, it does mean foregoing quick-draw reactions and employing a sense of finesse.

In marriage, we sometimes find ourselves reacting to a partner's outrageous provocation. Being proactive means assessing the degree to which potential reactions are consistent with a higher purpose. Snapping at your spouse with a wisecrack may do justice to a first reaction yet, at the same time, undermine the greater cause of marital success.

8. Delaying Gratification

Everyone's earliest years are all about instant gratification. Although we don't recall having our every need met on demand, most of us started life that way. Then, inexplicably, people started asking us to delay gratification: "Wait your turn. Share your toys. You can't always get what you want."

Delaying gratification means saying no to appetites and impulses or as Freud put it, using the superego to tame the id. If, for example, your goal is to lose weight, it means tolerating hunger and ignoring impulses to take a nap instead of work out. If your goal is to improve your marriage, it means tolerating annoying behaviors and ignoring impulses to give your spouse a piece of your mind.

A delay in gratification also means *not* doing what most of us do best: taking the path of least resistance. It takes effort to redirect destructive thoughts and impulses. Thinking or even saying, "Oh, what the hell" is so much easier.

Biologist Dr. Lewis Thomas points out in *Lives of a Cell* (for which he won a National Book Award) that the natural state of every living cell is rest.[5] What a revelation! No wonder life seems so difficult. Since our default setting is inertia, surviving and thriving require going against what every cell of our body is urging us to do. Hence the relief we feel when we stop expending energy, when we do what comes naturally rather than what requires effort.

Delaying gratification requires effort. It is a matter of choice and determination and it is a hallmark of emotional maturity. It is important to recognize, however, that this is just the sort of behavior that spouses tend to take for granted. "Good job with waiting your turn" are words rarely spoken to anyone older than age five.

Dale's Story

Dale is in his fifties, a recovering alcoholic with twelve years' sobriety and active in AA. Married over twenty years, Dale has three children. He is financially secure enough to take a year off after being "downsized" out of a company he helped start. Currently, he is in the process of orchestrating the family's move to a less expensive house.

Dale: I am fed up with waiting around.

Dr. M.: Haven't sold the house yet?

Dale: No! But that's just one of the loose ends I'm dealing with. I haven't heard about the job I applied for, my daughter hasn't heard from even one of the colleges she applied to and my wife hasn't made up her mind which weekend she wants to make the move.

Dr. M.: Frustrating.

Dale: Nerve-racking. It's the kind of stuff that used to be my perfect excuse to drink.

Dr. M.: Going to meetings?

Dale: (Nods.) No excuses.

Dr. M.: Sleeping okay?

Dale: Seven to nine hours.

Dr. M.: Good. So, waiting around to tie up loose ends gets you feeling anxious.

Dale: Yeah, I've done *my* part, everything possible from my end, and nothing's happening. Oh, man! You should see our yard. It's perfect.

Dr. M.: (Smiles.) So, what are you doing besides yard work to reduce your anxiety?

Dale: Like relaxation? (Shakes head.) I don't know if that really works for me.

Dr. M.: It works for everybody who gets good at it.

Dale: I think this is more a mental problem. It's me wanting what I want when I want it.

Dr. M.: Time to bring expectations in line with reality.

Dale: Definitely.

Even though delaying gratification usually leads to more delays, it eventually yields rewards. All of us have censored some comment or action and thanked our lucky stars that we chose the more considered approach. When we forego immediate gratification, we improve our reputation with ourselves. The better our reputation with ourselves, the more likely we are to believe that we can persist in practicing mature love.

Not as They Are, But as We Are

According to Anias Nin, "We don't see things as they are, we see them as we are." It also can be said that we don't see our spouses as they are, but rather as we are; that our marital satisfaction depends less upon our spouses' suitability than it does upon our own mental health. "It's all about me"—in a self-responsible way.

The preceding chapters have likely triggered a few "ah-ha" moments and an appreciation of the relevance of being a self-responsible spouse. The remaining chapters offer effective tools and strategies for transforming self, which can lead to improvement in one's marriage. Self-transformation starts with taking stock of our behavior repertoire. What healthy behaviors do we already practice? Do we make the most of our strengths? Also, we must take an ego-confronting look at unhealthy behaviors and make up our minds to change satisfaction-blocking thoughts, emotions and actions.

Whether we affect desired changes through self-help or psychotherapy, specific goals that describe psychological destinations are essential to success. In the next chapters, the general goal of improving marital satisfaction by becoming a self-responsible partner is addressed via four specific behavioral goals:

- Make the most of psychological strengths
- Manage psychological weaknesses by directing my own thoughts, emotions and actions, not my spouse's
- Increase emotional independence
- Redefine the marital relationship as often as necessary

I also present strategies for meeting these goals.

Chapter 11

Strengths and Virtues

Making the Most of Psychological Strengths

Making the most of your psychological strengths (assets of personality) is the first goal aimed at improving marital satisfaction. Although this may seem like an obvious goal, it is, for many, difficult to achieve. For most of us, others' strengths are more easily identified than our own and we need encouragement to claim and exercise our assets of personality.

When it comes to selecting a spouse, most of us choose someone whose personality inspires us. University of Iowa researchers published findings about the effects of personality on romantic attraction. According to both male and female subjects, the most attractive personality characteristic in a potential mate is compassion. The study, in 2003, also reports that we are attracted to people we perceive as:

- Secure
- Similar to ourselves
- Similar to our "ideal" selves (the person we want to be)

Additionally, researchers concluded that our *perceptions* drive attraction regardless of others' *actual* personality characteristics.[1]

In another investigation of romantic partners' perceptions of personality, Sandra Murray, Ph.D., and colleagues concluded that marital satisfaction is effected by *romantic illusions*, defined as the discrepancy between what subjects' partners believed about their mates' strengths and what their friends believed. Among the findings:

- Satisfied couples ascribe personality *assets* to partners that friends do not
- Dissatisfied couples ascribe fewer personality assets to partners than friends do
- Idealized partners actually try to live up to romantic illusions[2]

The effects of positive emotions on relationships also have been evaluated. For example, studies concluded that partners of optimists are positively affected by their partners' positive outlook,[3] that individuals whose achievements are enthusiastically supported by partners tend to report the highest levels of relationship satisfaction[4] and that sharing the joy at positive events better predicts relationship satisfaction than showing compassion at negative events.[5] Happy couples focus on personality strengths rather than weaknesses.

Personality 101

Personality fascinates almost everyone. We observe fellow humans and decide whom to like or dislike based on judgments about their psychological assets and liabilities. From time to time, we ponder our own "most mysterious of structures" and wonder whether we are sole architect or must share credit. And most of us like to be told we have a good personality unless we consider it an insult to our appearance.

But what exactly is personality? Where is it located? Through the centuries, many theorists attempted to form a definition. Proponents of each model groped in the dark, describing a proverbial ear, tusk or trunk of the elephant. Medicine, religion, Freudian psychoanalysis and twentieth century behaviorism offered unique insights and jargon. The ancients, for example, defined personality as related to four body fluids: blood, phlegm, yellow bile and black bile. Subsequent schools of thought defined personality less tangibly, choosing terms such as virtue and sinfulness, superego and id, adaptive and maladaptive behavior.

Today, psychologists subscribe to the biopsychosocial model that recognizes interaction of the biological/psychological (brain/mind) with the social (environment) and defines personality as temperament plus character. Temperament refers to inborn traits of personality. Character refers to factors of personality acquired through social interactions and life experiences.

Counter to conventional beliefs, scientists now believe that some 50 percent of the variations in human personality are associated with genetic factors.[6] Evidence affirming biological factors of personality began accumulating in the 1970s with findings of The Minnesota Twin Study, which studied identical twins raised apart. Today, behavior and genetics links continue to be identified by geneticists.

Anthropologist Dr. Helen Fisher described a neurotransmitter/hormone theory of personality in her 2009 book *Why Him? Why Her? Finding Real Love by Understanding Your Personality Type*. She identified four personality types associated with particular inherited genes in various biochemical systems:[7]

Personality Type	**Neurotransmitter/Hormone**
Explorers	Dopamine/Norepinephrine
Builders	Serotonin
Director	Testosterone
Negotiators	Oxytocin/Estrogen

She also hypothesized that personality type predicts partner selection. According to Dr. Fisher, Explorers mesh well with Explorers, Builders with Builders, Directors with Negotiators and Negotiators with Directors. *Why Him? Why Her*? includes a questionnaire designed to determine your type.

Positive Psychology

Most people accurately associate psychologists with the diagnosis and treatment of psychopathology. Most also understand that individuals seek psychotherapy for various reasons. While some patients are seriously mentally ill, many are stressed, anxious, mildly to moderately depressed, struggling to adjust to life events or experiencing unhappiness in relationships.

When it comes to imagining what actually goes on in psychotherapy sessions, television and movie depictions provide the standard. What everyone expects is the emphasis on identifying and correcting unhealthy behaviors. Less well-known, though equally integral, is the emphasis on making the most of personality strengths and engaging in health-enhancing behaviors.

Based on ample evidence that positive emotions not only correlate with good mental health but also predict future wellness, a specialty area known as positive psychology is gaining importance. Positive psychology researchers study character strengths, happiness and positive emotions in the present (mindfulness), about the past (gratitude) and about the future (hope and optimism). Ultimately, positive psychology seeks to expand established therapeutic options.

Positive psychology must not be confused with the phrase *positive thinking*, which suffers from overexposure. Positive thinking has become synonymous with conventional wisdom's happy talk and sappy platitudes. Even more concerning is its association with self-serving and dangerous, delusional thinking: for example, "Mission accomplished" and "Go ahead. Get that interest-only loan. This property is bound to appreciate."

Character Strengths

One of positive psychology's foremost researchers, Dr. Martin Seligman, and colleagues identified six overarching "virtues" and character strengths that almost every culture worldwide endorses:[8]

1. Wisdom and knowledge
   - Creativity
   - Curiosity
   - Open-mindedness
   - Love of learning
   - Perspective

2. Courage
   - Authenticity
   - Bravery

- Persistence
- Zest

3. Humanity
    - Kindness
    - Love
    - Social intelligence

4. Justice
    - Fairness
    - Leadership
    - Teamwork

5. Temperance
    - Forgiveness
    - Modesty
    - Prudence
    - Self-regulation

6. Transcendence
    - Appreciation of beauty and excellence
    - Gratitude
    - Hope
    - Humor
    - Religiousness

Marital satisfaction is, in part, dependent upon each spouse's ability in recognizing and generously sharing his or her positive traits. Look again at the list above, claim your character strengths and commit to freely exercising them. Choose one or two new ones to which you aspire and add to your repertoire of positive behaviors.

Happiness

Positive psychology seeks not only to study positive psychological traits but also to develop ways to improve individual happiness. Seligman and colleagues researched several strategies for improving happiness. Two exercises stood out as particularly effective in helping subjects improve their levels of happiness and maintain improvement for at least six months.

- **Three good things in life.** "Participants were asked to write down three things that went well each day and their causes every night for one week. In addition, they were asked to provide a causal explanation for each good thing." At the one-month follow-up, participants in this exercise were happier and less depressed than they had been at baseline and they stayed happier and less depressed at the three-month and six-month follow-ups.
- **Using signature strengths in a new way.** "Participants were asked to take [an] inventory of character strengths online … and to receive individualized feedback about their top five ('signature') strengths. They were then asked to use one of these top strengths in a new and different way every day for one week." Immediate effects were less pronounced than for the *three good things* condition, but at the one-month follow-up and beyond, participants in this condition were happier and less depressed than they had been at baseline.[9]

Also among the exercises tested was one associated with the so-called "gratitude movement." Subjects completing the gratitude exercise initially showed an increase in happiness, but positive effects wore off within thirty days. Not surprisingly, degree of efficacy of the two most helpful exercises depended upon whether participants actively continued their assigned exercises on their own and beyond the prescribed one-week period.[10]

Another thorough and thought-provoking examination of what scientists know about happiness can be found in psychologist Daniel Gilbert's national bestseller *Stumbling on Happiness.* Dr. Gilbert concludes: "There is no simple formula for finding happiness. But if our great big brains do not allow us to go surefootedly into our futures, they at least allow us to understand what makes us stumble."[11]

Hope

Positive psychologists Drs. Diane McDermott and C.R. Snyder of the University of Kansas, in their book, *Making Hope Happen*, describe "high hope" and "low hope" individuals and report that "high hopers" have better self-esteem, take better care of themselves and are better at meeting their own needs than "low hopers." Low hopers, as one might expect, are less satisfied with most aspects of their lives, including their relationships.[12] Clearly, practicing hopefulness is consistent with cultivating greater self-responsibility and, thus, improving relationships.

The Enneagram

One personality system compatible with the biopsychosocial model began taking shape in the 1970s. This system, called the Enneagram, offers descriptions of the strengths and weaknesses of nine basic personality types, each of which understands reality differently and develops unique ways of coping with the stress of being alive. The system also offers type-specific prescriptions for enhancing psychological health.

Taking its name from the Greek word *ennea,* meaning the number nine, this system designates personality types by numbers one through nine. It is important to note that the nine types are not rank-ordered. No type is better or worse than any other type. All types are potentially transcendent, depraved and everything in between.

Within this system, personality is essentially defined as the way one deals with stress. More specifically, personality is described as the product of genetic hardwiring interacting with early environmental influences and is viewed as an inevitable and self-limiting obstacle, separating the individual from his or her true nature or essential self. The purposes of studying the Enneagram are to fully claim strengths, modify weaknesses and reconnect with one's healthy, true nature.

Although the nine types are given slightly different names by different authors, the descriptions of each type's strengths and weaknesses do not vary among authors. The type names listed were assigned by well-known Enneagram experts Jerome Wagner and Don Riso and Russ Hudson. Both type names convey the spirit of each type. Also listed is a sample of the universally agreed-upon personality strengths and weaknesses of each type.

In order to improve psychological health, individuals must acknowledge unhealthy coping mechanisms and pursue a path of self-correction.

TYPE		STRENGTHS	WEAKNESSES
Wagner's Labels	Riso and Hudson's Labels	Universal Descriptions	
The Good Person	The Reformer	Conscientious Honest Persevering	Impatient Unrealistic Overly critical
The Loving Person	The Helper	Accepting Supporting Sympathetic	Martyr Demanding Infantilizing
The Effective Person	The Achiever	Energetic Self-assured Goal-oriented	Ignores feelings Image-conscious Self-promoting
The Original Person	The Individualist	Creative Expressive Good taste	Dramatic Eccentric Overly sensitive
The Wise Person	The Investigator	Logical Thoughtful Perceptive	Miserly Overly detached Postpones action
The Loyal Person	The Loyalist	Prepared Honorable Determined	Worrier Indecisive Security conscious
The Joyful Person	The Enthusiast	Optimistic Entertaining Enthusiastic	Sybaritic Superficial Unreliable
The Powerful Person	The Challenger	Autonomous Hard-working Direct	Intimidating Insensitive Non-listening
The Peaceful Person	The Peacemaker	Patient Receptive In harmony	Oblivious Low energy Obstinate

There are several means to do so. For example, Don Riso and Russ Hudson suggest that each type must continually walk a particular "spiritual path" practicing constructive behaviors, such as gratitude, courage, forgiveness or acceptance. In *Understanding the Enneagram: The*

Practical Guide to Personality Types, Riso and Hudson discuss a particular "capstone" for each type, an ultimate positive outcome for staying the course and, thereby, reconnecting with the healthy authentic self.

Several authors address the interaction between individuals of different types. In *Are You My Type? Am I Yours? Relationships Made Easy Through the Enneagram,* Renee Baron and Elizabeth Wagele discuss what each type likes and dislikes about every other type. Helen Palmer's *The Enneagram in Love and Work: Understanding Your Intimate and Business Relationships* describes how each type interacts with every other type in romantic relationships and in work settings. On the Enneagram Institute Web site, Don Riso and Russ Hudson offer information on relationships and type compatibility.

The consensus among these experts is that although some types may have a natural affinity for certain other types, no type is uniquely best-suited for any other type. The ultimate determiner of compatibility is level of mental health. In other words, any mentally healthy individual of any type can be compatible with any other mentally healthy individual.

Independent exploration of Enneagram guidelines for making the most of one's personality strengths is strongly encouraged. Many books and Web sites on the subject are available. (Refer to the chapter notes for some of my favorite resources on Enneagrams.[13])

Chapter 12

"Down in Front!"

Managing Psychological Weaknesses

The philosophy that reason (rational thought) is essential to happiness has been around a long time. Roman emperor Marcus Aurelius said it, as did Greek philosopher Epictetus. Today's cognitive behavioral psychologists say it, too. This philosophy underlies strategies for achieving the second goal aimed at improving marital satisfaction: managing psychological weaknesses by directing thoughts, emotions and behaviors. In order to manage psychological weaknesses, experience positive emotions and behave self-responsibly, we must "vigorously and calmly" choose our thoughts.

As explored in chapter 11, being a self-responsible partner means accepting responsibility for putting forth the best possible version of self, which requires making the most of talents and positive personality traits. Why is it that we often fail to do so? To the outsider, it seems like the simplest and most obvious way to improve one's life. But for the individual, putting the focus on strengths and talents requires much more than recognizing psychological weaknesses.

Andrew's Story

Andrew has been married for over twenty years and is in his forties.

> **Andrew:** It seems like my wife would rather exercise than spend time with me.

Dr. M.: Say more.

Andrew: Well, we're looking at fifty now and she's determined to stay in shape. Her workouts take up a lot of her free time.

Dr. M.: What about exercising together?

Andrew: We don't like the same workouts. She trains for triathlons. I lift weights and play golf.

Dr. M.: So, she won't play golf with you?

Andrew: She doesn't consider it nearly active enough.

Dr. M.: Bikes?

Andrew: We used to ride together, but she's a maniac now. She thinks twenty miles an hour is a good pace. I hold her back…like when she tried to teach me to play tennis.

Dr. M.: Tell me.

Andrew: She is really expert and belonged to a tennis club before we met. I was terrible at it. All net serves and wild swings. It was no fun for her.

Dr. M.: She complained?

Andrew: No, never. She used to say I was a natural, that I had great hand-eye coordination.

Dr. M.: So, even though she encouraged you and never complained, you were worried that it wasn't fun for her. Was it fun for you?

Andrew: It was frustrating! And I guess I felt a little foolish being shown up by a girl.

Dr. M.: (Smiles.) You were frustrated and you don't like being shown up by girls. Let's set aside, for the moment, your wife's lack of interest in the types of exercise that you enjoy. Do you see anything you could address?

Andrew acknowledged that though he initially hoped his wife's preference for vigorous exercise would rub off on him, this did not happen. He also identified four personal weaknesses that got in the way of the couple sharing a sport:

1. Negative self-talk about his tennis performance. Andrew told himself that his wife offered encouragement strictly out of her

wish to be a supportive partner and that she couldn't possibly be having fun playing with him.

2. Tendency to give up when frustrated. Andrew felt frustrated by the challenges of tennis as well as by his wife's bike riding pace and gave up on both.
3. Need for approval. Andrew thought that if he couldn't excel at tennis, he could excel at thoughtfulness by not asking his wife to waste time on a hapless student.
4. Aversion to being shown up by a girl.

Although this client had a natural ability that his wife saw as a talent for tennis, he let psychological weaknesses get in the way of this opportunity for them to share a sport. Additionally, Andrew wanted to blame his "maniac" girl for the fact that they didn't exercise together.

Beyond Assigning Blame

In order to manage weaknesses, we must, once again, move beyond conventional wisdom. Conventional wisdom encourages assignment of blame. So, we blame others (i.e., inept, neglectful or abusive parents, ruthless schoolmates, sadistic coaches or nuns) for our faults or we blame ourselves.

The problems with assigning blame are that it not only fosters resentment but also renders us unlikely to change. If we blame others, we tell ourselves it is too late to do anything but exact revenge. If we blame ourselves, we say it is too late to do anything but self-denigrate.

Ethan's Story

Ethan is an unmarried man in his early thirties.

Ethan: My problem is I'm unmotivated.

Dr. M.: Say more.

Ethan: I guess I'm just lazy.

Dr. M.: For example?

Ethan: Well, my therapy assignments.

Dr. M.: Hmm…hmmm.

Ethan: I'm supposed to be reading that book and exercising more, but I'm not.

Dr. M.: And you say it's because you're unmotivated.
Ethan: I've always been like that.
Dr. M.: Do you *think* about doing assignments?
Ethan: I think about it a lot.
Dr. M.: Then you are motivated.
Ethan: (Frowns.)
Dr. M.: If the thought occurs to you, you're motivated.
Ethan: Okay, then I'm just lazy.
Dr. M.: You can look at it two ways. Laziness is a deeply-ingrained personality trait or it is a habit.
Ethan: A bad habit…like smoking or swearing.
Dr. M.: Exactly. If you tell yourself laziness is a personality trait, you may think there's nothing to be done about it. If you tell yourself it is a habit, you can decide to learn new habits.
Ethan: So, I can learn to follow through?
Dr. M.: You already know how to follow through. It's your choice. You either persevere with a given behavior or you don't.
Ethan: (Chuckles.) I *have* been persevering…at calling myself lazy.

Conventional wisdom holds that undesired behavior is due to undesirable personality traits and that behavior change requires personality change. Modern psychology knows, though, that becoming mentally healthy does not begin with changing personality. Nor is it about changing first reactions. It is about choosing healthy second reactions, claiming our freedom to practice desired behaviors and, thereby, rewiring our brains.

Cognitive Restructuring

Cognitive restructuring is the practice of choosing thoughts rather than settling for whatever comes to mind. Based on the theory that thoughts perpetuate unwanted emotions, cognitive restructuring promotes the practice of reframing negative thoughts and establishing new sets of association. This emphatically does not mean lying to oneself or rationalizing. It means rationally evaluating negative emotional reactions (based on self-preservation instincts and past experiences) and reforming destructive mental habits. It means cultivating alternative viewpoints, positive emotions and, ultimately, healthy behaviors.

Consciously redirecting thoughts improves marital satisfaction because we refocus away from partners' faults and failures and onto personal distortions of reality. We adopt realistic expectations, manage counterproductive reactions, practice forgiveness and find the humor in almost any situation. We route around destructive impulses and habits and become as constructive as humanly possible.

Adopt Realistic Expectations

Albert Ellis, M.D., a trained psychoanalyst, was the intellectual founder of what is now known as cognitive behavioral therapy (CBT). He called his approach rational emotive behavior therapy (REBT). Two of his earliest books, *How to Live with a Neurotic* (1957) and *The Art and Science of Love* (1960), specifically applied his ideas to sex and marriage. Another Ellis title, *How to Stubbornly Refuse to Make Yourself Miserable about Anything* (1988), presents the essentials of REBT. According to Dr. Ellis, unhappiness is guaranteed if we fail to refute our own irrational beliefs and expectations. He held that three universal beliefs, known as "Ellis' musterbations," are at the root of all unhappiness:

1. I must do well.
2. You must treat me well.
3. The Universe must make life easy for me.

The third is the belief I encounter most often. On some days, when I awake feeling out of sync, one of my most entrenched automatic thoughts is, *I bust a gut every day being good and doing good, so the Universe ought to reward me with an easier life.* Ridiculous, right? Frustration begins to arise as I drag myself out of bed, complete my interminable grooming routine, swallow all those herbs and vitamins, pack a lunch and walk four city blocks to my office. It's nothing but bad hair, same old wardrobe, split fingernail, hot and humid weather, heavy tote, moving van blocking the shady side of the street, etc. When I go from mildly frustrated to fit-to-be-tied, my husband calls me Betsy and asks what's Betsy done with his Christine. The only way to shake it off is to breathe deeply and laugh about the absurdity of expecting the Universe to revolve around me.

Even when we see the absurdity of Ellis' third musterbation, we often stake our happiness on an insidious variation: Although the Universe has not yet made life easy for me, life will be made easy for me in the future. We maintain hope that our luck will change on the other side of certain milestones. Under the spell of "somewhere over the rainbow," we obsess about how much easier and happier life will be as soon as we achieve these goals:

- Get a driver's license
- Graduate high school
- Move away from home
- Get a degree
- Find the right person
- Make it to the weekend
- Get a better job
- Get pregnant
- Earn more money
- Remodel your house
- Move to a new city
- Relocate to the country
- Win the lottery
- Retire

Tune into Five Senses

As famed Beatle singer and songwriter John Lennon put it, "Life is what happens to us while we're busy making other plans."[14] So, why not pay attention to our lives? Rather than chasing after future satisfaction, try appreciating the here and now. Tune out fear-based worrying and catastrophizing and tune into what our five senses tell us about the present. It is what twelve-step programs mean by "one day at a time" and what hatha yoga and meditation students gain from practice.

Many people's qualities of life improve while watching fireworks on a summer night, savoring the hint of hot pepper in a cheese sauce or recognizing the opening bars of a favorite song; and any romantic relationship improves as partners fully engage their senses. No, this is not a pitch for better sex. This is a pitch for boosting emotional intimacy via individual attention to our senses.

Not just hugging but *relishing* the warmth of a spouse's hug. Not half-listening but *actively listening* to a partner. Not barely registering but *fully noticing* the vulnerability in familiar gestures. As one client who told me that he could always get over a grudge by watching his wife's endearingly invariable breakfast routine put it, "The little things are the big things."

High Performance Users of Our Brains

In the early 1960s, Aaron T. Beck, M.D., a trained psychoanalyst, further developed CBT. He devised a now famous diagnostic tool, *The Beck Depression Inventory*, and conducted much of the initial research into the theory that cognitive distortions underlie depression. Over the next four decades, Dr. Beck and his students applied cognitive techniques to the treatment of depression, anxiety disorders, suicidal ideation and relationship problems and Dr. Beck published *Love is Never Enough: How Couples Can Overcome Misunderstandings, Resolve Conflict, and Solve Relationship Problems through Cognitive Therapy.*

In 1978, a student of Dr. Beck's, David Burns, M.D., published *Feeling Good: The New Mood Therapy,* a detailed presentation for the public of the theories and strategies of CBT. Addressing treatment of depression as well as low self-esteem, procrastination, anger, sadness and perfectionism, *Feeling Good* often holds first-place among the self-help industry's therapist-recommended books. In subsequent books, Dr. Burns applies CBT to management of anxiety, shyness and relationship problems. His newest contribution is *Feeling Good Together: The Secret to Making Troubled Relationships Work.*[15]

Drs. Ellis, Beck and Burns and many others encourage us to become "high performance users of our own brains."[16] Though it is unrealistic to expect to live a stress-free life or to find a perfect spouse, we *can* realistically expect to direct our own thoughts, emotions and behaviors. Independent exploration of various applications of CBT is strongly recommended.

Taking Matters into Our Own Hands

In order to improve our marriages, we must go beyond recognizing our psychological weaknesses and directing our thoughts. We must direct our behaviors, too. There are six specific guidelines for taking matters into our own hands:

1. When in doubt, don't
2. Try the direct approach
3. The Four Principles
4. Anger management
5. Practice forgiveness
6. Find the humor

1. When in Doubt, Don't

How we react to our spouses means everything. Something this important is best handled, as Marcus Aurelius put it, "without allowing anything else to distract you." Everyone has suffered the unhappy consequences of half-listening to a spouse, blurting out a spontaneous comment or failing to take seriously those little signals that a partner's patience was wearing thin. Paying attention, listening carefully and "following right reason seriously" are essential to marital satisfaction.

You might think, *Hey, lighten up. If you can't be spontaneous with your spouse, who then?* There is always a place for spontaneity. Spontaneity is great for random acts of kindness, gestures of affection and all-purpose frolicking. It is not so great for making your way through the minefield of everyday stressors and touchy situations. And it is completely counterproductive when confronted with a spouse's unhealthy, offensive or abusive behavior. So when it comes to spontaneity, follow Benjamin Franklin's rule of thumb: When in doubt, don't.

2. Try the Direct Approach

When clients complain about spouses' behaviors, my first inquiry is about how their spouses react to direct requests for behavior change. Occasionally, clients realize that although they have repeatedly registered complaints, they have not tried the direct approach.

Carole's Story

In her mid-twenties, Carole has been married less than a year.

Carole: My husband and I had a huge fight this weekend.

Dr. M.: What happened?

Carole: I ran out of gas on the way to the grocery store and it made me really mad. We only have the one car. It's his old clunker and the fuel gauge is broken. I've told him a million times that it makes me nervous when I go places without him, but he just says *he's* never had a problem. Isn't that the rudest thing?

Dr. M.: Maybe he's trying to reassure you.

Carole: He's trying to get out of spending money to fix it.

Dr. M.: Oh, you're still mad about it.

Carole: Yes!

Dr. M.: Say more.

Carole: Well, I had to walk to a station, borrow a gas can, walk back, etc., all through a not so great part of town…but I told myself the whole time not to tear him up over it. Just to use it as an object lesson.

Dr. M.: Object lesson?

Carole: Yeah, he may not worry about it happening to him, but he flippin' needs to worry about it happening to *me*! What made me twice as mad was how he acted when I told him about it. He was all like, "Chill. Nothing bad happened, so it's no big deal." He did not even care that something bad *could* have happened and that, hello, I was majorly inconvenienced. I seriously wanted to smack him.

Dr. M.: Have you directly asked him to help you figure out how to prevent running out of gas?

Carole: I tell him all the time how much it worries me.

Dr. M.: That's an *indirect* request for help.

Carole: Oh, so I have to lay it out for him?

Dr. M.: Unmistakably.

Carole: Lame!

Dr. M.: You or him?

Carole: Him!

Dr. M.: You are shifting onto him responsibility for what you want. It's not his need. It's yours. So, take responsibility for it. State it directly, ask for cooperation.

Carole: But he should care more that I'm not inconvenienced, that I'm not in harm's way.

Dr. M.: Again, that's you shifting responsibility onto him.

Carole: But I'm his wife.

Dr. M.: That doesn't make him responsible for your needs and wants.

Carole: I thought it did.

Dr. M.: A lot of people think that way. Especially unhappily married and divorced people.

Carole: (Laughs) I guess it's worth a try.

Sometimes, it's that simple. Most clients, though, tell me that they have tried the direct approach and their spouses ignore, oppose, accuse or blame them. When the direct approach elicits such undesired responses, it is time to bring out the four principles.

3. The Four Principles

Rather than trying to change our partners, we need to change our reactions to our partners' undesired behaviors. Four basic behavioral principles can be applied in adult/adult as well as parent/child relationships. Recently after a discussion on the four principles, a middle-aged client sadly shook her head and said, "Gee, I wish somebody had told me about this when I was twenty."

A. Reinforce desired behavior. In parenting, this is called "catch them being good." A little praise goes a long way with children; adults also respond well to acknowledgement and appreciation. Make it your mission to seize every opportunity to compliment and thank your spouse. Thank him or her for cooking such a delicious dinner, washing your car, turning down the television—any behavior of which you'd like to see more.

Also apply this principle any time your spouse mysteriously chooses *not* to engage in one of his or her typical undesired behaviors. For example, if one of your pet peeves is that your spouse leaves out your tools, don't fail to acknowledge the one time he or she puts them away. "I appreciate your putting away that hammer" is all it takes.

If your reaction to this principle is, *He should always put away my tools because he knows how I feel about it* or *she needs to know I'm upset because she's an adult who should know better,* you haven't yet caught on to the basic premise of this book. It is not about what your spouse *should* do. It is about accepting the reality of whatever your spouse does and choosing your reactions.

If your reaction to this suggestion is *it's never that simple with my spouse*, you may be underestimating the power of staying positive and keeping it light. Even if you believe reinforcement won't work, do yourself and your partner the favor of trying this approach more than once and in more than one situation. Use your knowledge of what pleases your partner and show some enthusiasm.

B. Do NOT reinforce *un*desired behavior. In parenting, this is referred to as "ignore the tantrum." We've all seen a child throwing a tantrum in the grocery store and heard the parent trying to intervene:

> **Parent:** Please stop screaming.
> **Child:** No!
> **Parent:** I mean it! Calm down.
> **Child:** (Screams.)
> **Parent:** You're not going to get your cookie.
> **Child:** (Howls.)
> **Parent:** Look at that little boy. He's being *good*.
> **Child:** (Hits parent.)
> **Parent:** Stop that!
> **Child:** (Hits parent again.)
> **Parent:** (Holds child's hands.) You're going to be in so much trouble when we get out of here.
> **Child:** (Continues to scream.)

If you want someone (of any age) to stop doing something and the direct approach proves unsuccessful, ignore the behavior. For example, anyone getting unwanted phone calls, text messages, e-mails or visits from an ex-spouse is always encouraged to ignore 100 percent of future communications.

Responding in any way, whether being polite or telling off the ex-spouse, has the same effect. Any sort of attention to a behavior increases frequency of the behavior. If the relationship is one that you do not wish to maintain, the only way to clearly communicate this is to consistently ignore both the undesired behavior and the person.

If the relationship is one you wish to maintain, you won't improve the situation by ignoring the person. You do, however, want to ignore the undesired behavior and interrupt unhealthy patterns of interaction. This means changing your part of the interaction and offering your spouse a dignified exit from his or her part. So, how does one go about this?

Learn to use the non sequitur: say something that has absolutely nothing to do with whatever has just been said or done. The secret to using this technique is keeping it light.

Partner A: So, are you ever going to call your mother?
Partner B: I think it looks like rain.
Partner A: Did you hear me?
Partner B: I don't really have a comment.
Partner A: Oh, that's so like you.
Partner B: I'm going to bring in the kids' bikes.

OR

Partner X: I hate it when you leave the toilet seat up.
Partner Y: Would you like to go for a walk after dinner?
Partner X: Did you hear me?
Partner Y: It's a beautiful night for a walk.

One of my favorite examples of the power of the non sequitur comes from my work with Sally, an elderly farm wife, who complained that since retiring from her office job, frequent daily interactions with her cranky old husband, Tom, were depressing her. Sally explained that Tom ruined her mood every day by coming in from the field, the barn or town spewing negativity and thoughts of doing harm to barnyard animals and human beings. If his complaints and threats weren't depressing enough, his habit of turning his anger on her when she tried to point out the positive side of things was triggering fantasies of runaway tractors.

Sally was more than a little skeptical of my suggestion that she try a few non sequiturs. So, we brainstormed feasible non sequiturs: her husband's favorite foods, pastimes, people, memories, anything he was eagerly anticipating. Then we role-played, sounding exactly like actors in an absurdist play.

> **Sally:** (playing her husband) There is no more useless creature than that stupid goat.
> **Dr. M.:** (playing Sally) I baked a cherry pie.
> **Sally:** I've got half a mind to shoot it.
> **Dr. M.:** Would you like a slice?
> **Sally:** Then I'm going uptown to give that skunk of a bank president a piece of my mind.
> **Dr. M.:** I was just about to cut a slice for myself.
> **Sally:** (chuckling) Have you gone deaf?
> **Dr. M.:** I'm having mine a la mode.

After a few more role-plays, Sally agreed to try our approach every day until our next appointment.

At her next appointment, Sally reported that her husband never once commented about her non sequiturs and went along with all of them. Tom continued to enter the house fuming and fussing but he also came to the kitchen for pie, looked over her shoulder at snapshots that had arrived in the mail, glanced at the progress she'd made on a quilt or rolled his eyes at the latest church auxiliary gossip, never once commenting about her lack of engagement with his complaints. She observed that he actually seemed glad to be distracted from his ranting and raving and dropped the negativity more quickly each day. Sally also commented that she no longer found the interactions depressing, that she actually felt amused by them and that maybe her past habit of getting caught up in his complaints had actually made the situation worse!

By cheerfully saying something totally unrelated instead of simply remaining silent, the likelihood of provocation is lessened. For most couples, there are too many potentially provocative interpretations of silence: obliviousness, disrespect or the silent treatment. The non sequitur ignores the undesired behavior without communicating disapproval. If we express annoyance at a spouse's behavior, we risk starting an argument in which case both spouses end up angry and reinforcing each other's undesired behaviors.

Communicating disapproval through words, gestures or facial expressions is an ineffective strategy for discouraging unwanted behaviors. Though it may appear that disapproval discourages unwanted behavior, especially in children and animals, coercion inspires only temporary compliance and almost always does more harm than good. The long-term effects on loved ones—emotional distancing, loss of respect and feelings of distrust and resentment—are grossly counterproductive for any relationship.

C. Let natural consequences emerge. In parenting, this might be called "let them get burned." This is the answer to the question, "Well, if I can't show disapproval, what am I supposed to do? Let them get away with murder?" Get out of the way and let natural consequences emerge! In Al-Anon, this is called letting them "hit bottom" and not enabling.

When natural consequences emerge, people suffer. A natural consequence of not studying for the driver's test is not getting your driver's license. A natural consequence of not getting your driver's license is not being able to borrow the family car. The natural consequence of not being able to borrow the car is a preadolescent social life.

A natural consequence of drinking too much is having a hangover. A natural consequence of being hungover is feeling too sick to go to work. The natural consequence of habitually skipping work is losing your job.

The harshness of these unpleasant realities is what makes them effective learning experiences. It is what makes us look for ways to protect ourselves. Anyone who enables or protects others from natural consequences actually interferes with the learning process.

Some natural consequences are just too harsh to let happen. Fortunately, it is equally effective to *assign* consequences. You do not teach a child to stay out of the street by letting her get hit by a car.

A child can be taught that if she plays in the street, she goes inside for the rest of the day.

You do not let your spouse learn the dangers of reckless spending by waiting for the family to slide into bankruptcy. If ever there were an argument for the direct approach, this is it. A spouse who abuses credit cards, for example, can be shown figures that document how his behavior is threatening the family's financial security. If the direct approach fails, exercise your right to protect your credit rating, your children's futures and your retirement fund. Fulfill your fiscal and fiduciary responsibilities by informing your compulsively spending partner that you will cut up the credit cards and take over monthly bill paying chores.

If you're thinking, *Oh, yeah, that'll go over big*, please keep reading. Since psychotherapy clients in financial trouble are common, I have worked with both the big spenders and those who financially support them. It is common to hear the stories of wives and husbands who have accumulated thirty thousand dollars (the average) or far more in credit card debt, who generate no income yet spend thousands on luxuries, hobbies or travel or who expect spouses to provide financial support for adult siblings or parents. As most everyone knows, inability to resolve money conflicts is one of the top reasons for divorce. By the time a client is bringing up this subject in psychotherapy, it is usually past time for decisive action.

If the fiscally irresponsible spouse is my client, I point out that he is abusing his spouse with this behavior and that the natural consequence of abusive behavior is loss of the relationship. Although this assessment doesn't make the spender feel good, no one who exhibits this behavior has ever challenged the point. In fact, most clients who are fiscally irresponsible reluctantly (sometimes tearfully) agree with the assessment. In order to make right this injustice, some clients cut up credit cards, curtail self-indulgent spending and repay debt. Some of my clients have taken second jobs for the sole purpose of paying off credit cards, gotten part-time or fulltime employment to pay for luxuries, adopted the *less is more* philosophy or cut off handouts to freeloading relatives.

Frequently, clients who abuse credit cards are in relationships with individuals whom they describe as controlling. Though this pronouncement may be accurate, it is not realistic to plan to change the controlling spouse. The focus of effective psychotherapy is always self-correction: changing one's spending and earning habits, modifying reactions to a spouse's "controlling" behavior or accepting the reality that a great mistake (see chapter 3) has been made.

If my client is the spouse being financially abused, the goal is to change her reactions. She may learn to make direct requests for behavior change or to apply the four principles. She may decide to take over all joint-money management chores. She may decide the sacrifices required to continue marriage with an unreformed partner are too great. She may assign a consequence and let it emerge.

D. Do not punish! We all impose limits on our behaviors. No shoplifting, no littering, no cursing. Whatever your particular limits, *no punishing* belongs on the list.

Punishing is lazy, unimaginative and intended to inflict pain. It takes many forms:

- Physical abuse
- Verbal abuse (yelling, name-calling, sarcasm, mean-spirited "jokes")
- Withdrawal of affection (refusing to soften when the punished one makes a gesture of conciliation)
- The silent treatment
- Museum trips (pointing out all the offender's faults and past transgressions)

When we punish, we damage. We hurt the one we punish. We undermine the relationship. We weaken our personal integrity.

Most of us, unfortunately, do not know the difference between consequences and punishment, because we were raised by people who did not know the difference. For example, you may have been told that if you played in the street, you would be sent into the house, which would have been an assigned consequence and a helpful learning experience.

All too often, we experienced not only the assigned consequence but also a few forms of punishment given by parents who vented anger while disciplining. Your parent angrily yelled at you, grabbed you by the arm and/or spanked you all the way into the house. Then you were told that you brought all this rough treatment on yourself by scaring your poor parent who loves you so much.

As many of us may know from experience, punishment raises anxiety, gets in the way of the primary lesson and teaches fear and resentment. Many of us have been subjected to our parents' and other adults' misguided attempts to teach self-discipline. If you believe that the person with whom you chose to share your life deserves to be punished, you are failing to think self-responsibly. Also, you are mistaken. There is no place for punishment in loving relationships.

4. Anger Management

Many people's favorite negative emotion is anger. Not that we enjoy being subjected to other people's anger, but as many clients have told me, we get satisfaction and a feeling of power from directly and indirectly expressing our own anger. Conventional wisdom's myths that fighting is healthy and "holding in" anger is harmful are rubbish and nonsense (as discussed in chapter 2). So, what's an angry person to do?

Manage the Physiology of Anger

The body sensations of anger and anxiety (tense muscles, rapid and shallow breathing, increased heart rate, etc.) are the result of sympathetic nervous system (SNS) chemical secretions. When threat is perceived by the neocortex and limbic system, especially the amygdala, the hypothalamus sets in motion additional mechanisms for self-preservation. Adrenaline and other corticosteroids prepare the body to fight or flee.

What must be considered is the fact that the brain does not distinguish life-threatening from ego-threatening. The same SNS hormones are secreted, albeit in varying amounts, whether we are staring down the end of a handgun or overhearing an insult muttered by a co-worker. It is up to our minds to downgrade the level of threat when appropriate and calm bodily overreactions.

Whether we fight because we are angry or are angry because we fight, we can shut down the flow of SNS hormones by activating the relaxation response. Aerobic exercise does the trick. Mental distraction works, too. Most effective of all are relaxation techniques including diaphragmatic breathing, progressive muscle relaxation, yoga and meditation.

Diaphragmatic breathing is the natural way of breathing. Just watch how babies and animals do it: tummies rising and falling, sides expanding and contracting. Many adults inhale and exhale, utilizing only the upper lobes of the lungs. Diaphragmatic breathing techniques retrain lungs to fully inhale and exhale. Fully exhaling is the same as deeply sighing, which triggers the relaxation response.

Diaphragmatic Breathing

Inhale and exhale both through the nose. Expand the abdominal area as you inhale and "deflate" the abdominal area as you exhale. Fill your lungs with air as if filling a glass with water: from the bottom to the top. Empty your lungs as if you are emptying a glass of water.

Basic Technique	**Advanced Technique**
Inhale to a count of four	Inhale to a count of four
Hold four counts	Exhale to a count of eight
Exhale to a count of eight	and relax muscles
and relax muscles	Wait (with empty lungs) four counts
Repeat five to ten times	Repeat five to ten times

Progressive Muscle Relaxation

Using muscle relaxation to calm the SNS has roots in the practice of yoga. Edmund Jacobson, M.D., promoted progressive muscle relaxation (PMR) in the 1920s, a method for training muscles to relax on command. PMR involves tensing then relaxing muscle groups. It is essential when practicing PMR to exhale as you relax a muscle group. This trains your brain to associate exhaling and releasing muscle tension.

Tense and then relax each muscle group twice, with ten seconds of muscle tension followed by ten seconds of relaxation. Notice the difference in sensation between tension and relaxation. Once you have completely relaxed one muscle group, try to keep it relaxed as you tense and relax other muscle groups.

Muscle Areas	Tense and Relax
Hands	Make tight fists
Arms	Tighten biceps
Shoulders	Pull shoulders toward ears
Face	Raise eyebrows, tighten forehead and scalp Wrinkle nose and squeeze shut eyes Clench jaws and press together lips
Neck	Press chin against chest
Back	Arch back by pushing out chest
Abdomen	Tighten abdominals
Chest	Take a deep breath and hold it
Buttocks/lower back	Squeeze together buttocks
Legs/feet	Straighten legs and curl toes under

After tensing and relaxing each muscle group twice, deepen your relaxation by resting while breathing diaphragmatically.

Manage the Psychology of Anger

Anger is an emotion based on the assumption that we are being treated unfairly. We are essentially ready to fight against reality. Whether we believe an election was stolen or our spouse has unreasonable expectations, we come from a place of righteous indignation. The psychological underpinnings of our indignation can be complex and mysterious, sometimes based in reality and sometimes not. Reactions can stem from associations to childhood experiences, narcissism, desires to intimidate, manipulate or defend. Regardless of origins, angry reactions are indelible black marks against us on our spouses' slates of marital satisfaction.

Distinguish Anger from Frustration

Distinguishing anger from frustration is more than a semantic exercise. We often tell ourselves we are angry when, in fact, we are merely frustrated. Consider this: Although a two-year-old throwing a tantrum certainly looks and sounds angry, he is simply demonstrating the intensity with which humans can react when an obstacle gets between us and what we want.

Correctly labeling the emotion allows us to choose relevant and constructive behaviors. First, ask yourself, *Is there anything unfair to me in this situation*? Be honest. Just as there is nothing unfair about Mother putting breakable objects out of reach, there is nothing unfair about the old guy in the car ahead of you driving five miles an hour under the speed limit. If, honestly, there is no inequity, there is no one to blame. If there is no one to blame, we are experiencing frustration.

Now, for some good news: Resolving frustration is a one-person project. Simply determine what need is not being met, identify the obstacle and devise a way around it. Rather than pounding the steering wheel and cursing the drivers around him, the self-responsible driver recognizes that though he is going nowhere fast, he is not being treated unfairly. Instead of working himself into a state of road rage, he averts a tantrum by calming his physiology (regulating breathing and releasing muscle tension) and reframing his thoughts (accepting that public roadways must be shared, brainstorming alternative routes or resolving to leave home earlier, ride the bus or move close enough to work to walk).

Sometimes, we are, in fact, treated unfairly and, under such circumstances, feeling angry is understandable. In the face of unfairness, however, behaving angrily is counterproductive. This is where conflict resolution comes in.

Resolve Conflict

According to conventional wisdom, resolution of marital conflict requires either the spouse with the weaker case to gracefully give in or both spouses to compromise. Whether you keep the peace or attempt compromise, sacrifice will be required. In the end, one partner or both will give up their first choice preferences. Invariably, we focus on the thousands of times we have given in to our spouses and on our spouses' lack of reciprocation, which leads to dissatisfaction, which leads to whining, scorekeeping and end-around scenarios. The self-responsible partner knows that once conflict arises, there is no way to erase it.

Refusing to be the one who sacrifices invites a partner to increase the conflict. When we consistently choose to get needs met at a partner's expense, marital satisfaction plummets. If we choose to examine our narcissistic expectations and censor our combative reactions, marital satisfaction soars.

Distinguish Unfair from Abusive

If we wish to maintain marital stability, even when a spouse's behavior is unfair, we do well to manage angry reactions. If, on the other hand, a spouse's behavior is punishing, mentally cruel or physically abusive, we do well to use fight or flight reactions as our guide. We must act to make abuse stop or plan ways to escape it (refer to chapter 3).

Now, a word about the well-intentioned mainstay of conventional wisdom "Never go to bed angry." It sounds like such good advice. Unfortunately, most of us interpret the saying to mean that the day's marital conflicts must be resolved before we go to sleep. Talk about diving headfirst into the shallow end! It's late. You're tired. You have to get up early the next day to go to work or to get children to school. Conflict resolution is difficult when we are at our bests and even the sober are not at their bests at bedtime. Late night attempts at conflict resolution rarely succeed and most of us make a bad situation worse by attempting.

The only way to make this bit of conventional advice constructive is to give it a self-responsible meaning. In other words, if conflict is unresolved at bedtime, take responsibility for your own emotional state. Whether you are hurt, miffed or outraged, it is not your spouse's responsibility to soothe you. You may want an apology, but what you must do is calm down and get a good night's sleep. You may want immediate gratification, but what you must do is think long-term. You must soothe yourself and promise yourself and your spouse to work toward resolution in the near and well-rested future. You must persist in love. (Refer to the chapter notes for additional resources on anger management.[17])

5. Practice Forgiveness

By failing to forgive a spouse's innumerable transgressions, we stress ourselves. Minds that are fixed on score-keeping and acts of revenge keep brains and sympathetic nervous systems on red alert. As decades of studies document, holding grudges alters neurochemistry, ruins peace-of-mind and psychological well-being and endangers physical health (e.g., depression, compromised immune function, cardiovascular damage).

Unless we have acquired the emotional maturity to stop punishing, we believe offenders deserve punishment. We feel justified in seeking revenge or, at the very least, fervently hoping that the unforgiven get what they deserve. Ironically, the ones who dependably get what's coming to them are those who are unwilling to forgive.

Forgiveness requires cognitive restructuring. In order to forgive, we must cancel unmet expectations and wire around sets of association that trigger negative emotions. Forgiveness never just happens with time. Forgiveness results from conscious redirection of thoughts.

As farfetched and idealistic as it may seem, a few clients have chosen to mentally bless loved ones with whom they are angry. Every time an injustice comes to mind, they think or even whisper, "Bless you." From a CBT standpoint, blessing those with whom we are angry redirects negative self-talk. From a brain science standpoint, this exercise rewires neural connections. Those who have used this approach swear by it.

Psychologist Everett Worthington, Ph.D., offers a guide to achieving forgiveness called the *Pyramid Model of Forgiveness*.[18] The acronym REACH serves as a reminder of the five steps of the model:

Recall the hurt.
Empathize.
Altruistic gift of forgiveness.
Commit to forgive.
Holding onto forgiveness.

Dr. Worthington's model is based, in part, on his own process of forgiving the men who murdered his mother. Thankfully, most of us have nothing nearly so heinous to forgive.

This model is compatible with principles of self-responsibility because the emphasis is on the wronged individual rather than on the offender. It employs cognitive restructuring by centering expectations for change on the thoughts of the wronged. Suggestions for writing down or talking over thoughts with others reflect understanding of how our brains fire up new neural pathways and transfer new information to memory.

The Dalai Lama expresses a unique forgiveness he learned from his friend who spent nearly twenty years detained in Chinese prison and labor camps. The friend shared with the Dalai Lama that he encountered danger. The Dalai Lama asked what kind of danger, and his friend's response was, "Oh, danger of losing compassion for the Chinese." [19]

Few on the international front reflect the attitudes of the Dalai Lama and his friend. Warring nations and sects, militantly ignorant leaders and neighborhood bullies continue to show no mercy. The world *zeitgeist* of dominance and aggression thrives because individuals say, "Nobody else forgives. Why should I?" Despite an unforgiving macrocosm, individuals who value peace in their minds and their relationships allow themselves to feel compassion and practice forgiveness.

Forgiving is not the same as enabling and it is not the same as saying, "It doesn't matter. Walk all over me." Active rather than passive, forgiveness involves psychologically raising the bar, expecting more from oneself than resignation, suffering in silence or claiming victim status. Extending forgiveness may be the single exception to Clare Booth Luce's oft-quoted observation, "No good deed goes unpunished." No matter what sins your partner may have committed, consider reaching for the mental and physical health benefits associated with practicing forgiveness.

Those who are hard on others are often harder on themselves. If forgiving others proves difficult, take a look at your track record on self-forgiveness. Compassion for self, despite glaring imperfections, requires establishing new expectations and consciously and persistently redirecting unforgiving thoughts.

6. Find the Humor

Sense of humor—not to be confused with punishing behaviors such as sarcasm and mean jokes—effects partner selection and improves marital satisfaction. In a study published in 2006, Canadian researchers showed undergraduate students photos of attractive people of the opposite gender paired with funny and unfunny statements seemingly authored by the individuals pictured. Women were significantly more likely to rate photos of men as "desirable relationship partners" if the men's statements were funny. No equivalent effect was found among men. Researchers concluded that although men cite their desire for a sense of humor in a mate, they are actually seeking someone who appreciates their humor.[20]

In *The 100 Simple Secrets of Great Relationships,* David Niven, Ph.D., lists a sense of humor as the thirty-first secret.[21] He references a 2002 study by De Koning and Weiss in which they assessed the functions of humor in close relationships. Levels of conflict were compared in couples who both thought the other had a good sense of humor and in those who thought that neither had a good sense of humor. Not surprisingly, humorous couples reported 67 percent less conflict.[22]

A sense of humor's value to relationships is found in its positive effects on both frame of mind and neurochemistry. Introducing humor allows us to see familiar situations with new eyes,[23] to expose our rigidity and to see truths that everyone knows but nobody admits.[24] Laughter, which evolutionary psychologists believe existed long before humor, enhances communication and facilitates social bonding. Additionally, laughter feels good because it stimulates the brain's reward system.[25]

According to American essayist Agnes Repplier, "Humor brings insight and tolerance." Self-responsible partners are receptive to spouses' use of humor as a constructive attempt to reveal their take on reality, which increases the likelihood of insight. Self-responsible partners also use humor to lighten moods and communicate benign intentions, which increases the likelihood of tolerance.

Chapter 13

Growing Yourself Up

Emotional Independence

In order to increase emotional independence, the third goal aimed at improving marital satisfaction by becoming self-responsible, one has to know three things:

- What behaviors are emotionally independent
- What emotional independence is not
- What specific behavior changes increase emotional independence

During my junior year in high school, I took Introduction to Psychology. Although I remember eagerly anticipating the class and finding the subject interesting, my only specific memory is of the concept of psychological dependence and independence, introduced one day just before the dismissal bell. Everything I now know about psychological dependence and independence is wired together with images of classmates' clock-watching and fidgeting, sounds of desks scraping and everyone talking at once and an insight about how one's thinking can quickly reorganize around a new idea.

I got a ride home that day in my friend's car. Unlikely as it seems, we six sixteen-year-olds talked about psychological dependence and independence. In our rudimentary understanding, dependence meant adopting the viewpoints of others and independence meant thinking for oneself. Two of my friends said they were independent. The other three said they were dependent. While stopped on the driveway at my house, one of my friends asked, "So which are you, Chrissie?" That is when I spoke my epiphany. "Well," I said as I climbed out of the backseat, "I'm dependent and that's going to change."

Learned Dependence

Human infants must have caretakers in order to survive. Via instincts to gaze and smile, we endear ourselves to caretakers and experience the rewards—food, warmth, soothing—of human contact. If we are hungry, uncomfortable or in pain, we cry out. Mother appears and we soon feel relieved. This interactive cycle fosters psychological dependence. We learn the benefits of drawing others to us and we learn the consequences of failing to do so. Ultimately, we learn that we must please others or seek approval in order to get what we need and want.

My niece's two-year-old son offered a brilliant demonstration of toddler style approval-seeking. Within seconds of my arrival, he lured me to his play area by taking my hand and, in the most endearing way imaginable, talking to me as we walked. "I'm cute," he said. "I'm funny," he continued. "I'm craaazy." He had won me over the moment he reached for my hand.

Learned Independence

Over time, we teach ourselves psychological independence as we venture away from parents and caretakers. This happens when we are adolescents, but much earlier, too, as kindergartners, preschoolers, toddlers and as we learn to crawl and walk. Picture one of the babies in your life crawling or toddling away then stopping to look back. The quality of your response to that backward glance shapes a child's psyche. If you cheer him on, you encourage independence. Now, picture him rushing back to you. When you welcome him back with open arms, you doubly encourage independence. He learns that he can strike out on his own without losing your approval.

Approval-seeking as adults (from parents or other family members, peers, mentors and romantic partners) is not mentally unhealthy, if practiced in moderation. Human beings, after all, are hardwired to construct social networks. Experiencing others' approval bathes our synapses in feel-good neurochemicals and usually inspires reciprocation, which leads to round after round of pleasing and reciprocating. Caring about others' approval becomes unhealthy only when it dominates our psyche and leads to self-defeating behaviors.

Psychologically emancipating ourselves means:

- choosing our thoughts, emotions and behaviors,
- honoring our intuitions,
- setting goals and deciding to sacrifice what we must in order to achieve them,
- accepting consequences of our choices.

This means relying on internal resources rather than on external influences. Although the process begins the first time we crawl beyond our mothers' reaches, fully claiming our independence takes a lifetime.

I overheard a thirty-something female talking on her cell phone downtown one day. Her side of the conversation caught my attention:

> He asked me to point out to him when he does that thing I don't like. [Pause.] I thought that, too, at first. It made me remember why I liked him. But then it sort of struck me…[Pause.] Exactly! What am I? His mother?

This struck me as uncommon insight on both ends of the phone line. Though the term *psychological dependence* probably never crossed their minds, both parties recognized dependent behavior.

Asking someone to point out an annoying behavior seems, on the surface, like a good faith gesture. On closer examination, it is the same as saying, "Since I'm not a good judge of my own behavior, I'll depend on you to tell me if I'm annoying you." Or worse, "You're the hypersensitive one, so I'll depend on you to point out what you don't like then I'll either try to please you or rebel against you." A conversation between two people practicing this might go something like this:

> **She:** You're doing that thing again.
> **He:** What thing?
> **She:** That thing I don't like.
> **He:** (Stony silence.)
> **She:** You told me to tell you!

He: Well, do you have to be so cranky?
She: Cranky? I'm just doing what you asked.
He: You're nagging.
She: Nagging?
He: Yeah, just like my mother.
She: (Getting upset.) Why do you always say that?
He: Why do you always have to ruin everything?

Conversations like this are unproductive and only lead to both partners getting upset.

Emotional Evenness

Because partners can be strongly affected by each other's emotions, relationship satisfaction is affected by the degree to which partners indulge their impulses in order to vent negative emotions. For example:

She: That woman really made me angry. She was not listening. I pointed out three times that the warranty on the water heater is still good, but she kept making the same completely obtuse statement.
He: (Joking, provocatively.) Why can't you women just get along?
She: Listen, I'm pissed and not in the mood for comedy.
He: Fine. I was about to offer to take over getting this worked out, but since you're turning on *me* now…
She: Typical. I handle 90 percent of this kind of crap, anyway. Why not make it 100 percent?
He: Hey! I've had about enough of your attitude.

Cultivating emotional evenness means practicing emotional neutrality and behavioral control rather than joining a partner in behaving badly.

Partners sometimes assume that distressed spouses would appreciate being rescued. Too often, though, the outcome is one in which would be rescuers become the target of partners' frustration. We mistakenly assume that negative emotions are directed at us and then engage in attempts to placate or justify. Or we feel angered and react aggressively. If we, instead, assume that spouses can rescue themselves, we not only avoid making targets of ourselves but also offer spouses a vote of confidence. Here are examples of conversations where the husband first attempts to rescue his wife and then allows her to rescue herself:

She: That woman really made me angry. She was not listening. I pointed out three times that the warranty on the water heater is still good, but she kept making the same completely obtuse statement.

He: If you want, I can try talking to her.

She: Oh, *now* you offer to help.

He: Do you want me to talk to her or not?

She: Don't bother talking to *her*. Get her boss or the owner…somebody who knows what they're doing.

VS.

She: That woman really made me angry. She was not listening. I pointed out three times that the warranty on the water heater is still good, but she kept making the same completely obtuse statement.

He: You hardly ever get mad over stuff like this.

She: I know!

He: Do you think she was being obtuse *deliberately*?

She: Yes!

He: It had to be bad to get *you* upset.

She: Yeah, but I'll calm down and try again tomorrow.

If your spouse is, in fact, negatively reacting to something you have said or done, it is crucial that you remain neutral to displays of disapproval:

He: I'm meeting with the banker tomorrow about the new house loan.

She: Don't forget about that big balance on my credit card.

He: You haven't paid that off?

She: You told me not to!

He: I told you not to use the money you inherited from your grandfather.
She: So, I didn't.
He: You were supposed to pay it off with the money your mooching sister owes you.
She: She's not a moocher. I volunteered to help her.
He: Well, when does she plan to pay you?
She: I'm not really sure.
He: So, we'll have wishy-washy you and your mooching sister to thank when we don't get the loan.
She: Well, maybe it's time to do what I wanted to in the first place and use Grandpa's money.
He: Just forget the whole thing! I'm not stepping foot in that bank under these circumstances!
She: Don't be ridiculous!
He: Then get the money from your sister!
She: Jeez, she's right! You're insane!

VS.

He: I'm meeting with the banker tomorrow about the new house loan.
She: Don't forget about that big balance on my credit card.
He: You haven't paid that off?
She: No, my sister hasn't paid me what she owes me.
He: Well, when does she plan to pay you?
She: I think it's time to dip into my inheritance.
He: No, it's time to get your mooching sister to pay up!
She: You're right, but we have to act quickly if we want this house. I'll pay off the card today with Grandpa's money.

Staying optimistic, constructive and self-confident regardless of others' dark moods characterizes emotional independence.

Emotional Imperturbability

Ever heard anyone say, "Happy wife, happy life"? In my experience, this is not said by husbands who sincerely work to enhance their wives' lives.

Rather, it is said by men to express dissatisfaction with or resignation to their wives' annoying, emasculating demands. For example:

He: I'm thinking of buying an AR-15 to use for target practice.
She: Aren't those illegal?
He: Not anymore.
She: Are you serious?
He: Yes.
She: I hate guns!
He: (Singing John Lennon lyrics.) Happ-i-ness…bang-bang…shoot-shoot…is a warm gun...
She: I'm a pacifist!
He: I'm not planning to shoot living things.
She: I don't want a gun under my roof!
He: Are you putting your foot down?
She: It's the principle of the thing.
He: You're actually telling me I can't have a gun?
She: You should honor my feelings on this.

Emotional dependence alert! If the husband in this situation succumbs to his wife's demand that her feelings be honored, he acts on his emotional dependence and, at the same time, resents being treated like a child. If the wife clings to her assertion that a gun under her roof violates her principle of pacifism, her emotional dependence is showing, too. Emotionally independent people do not worry that a spouse's behavior reflects poorly on them. Besides, whether your spouse hunts animals or wears his pants too high, the only people in your life who think it is your responsibility to do something about it are the blissfully *non*-self-responsible ones.

Just as it is possible to disagree with friends and colleagues without expressing, or even experiencing, anger or hurt, it is possible to do the same with spouses.

He: I'm thinking of buying an AR-15 to use for target practice.
She: Aren't those illegal?
He: Not any more.
She: (Joking.) Planning on becoming a sniper?

He: (Joking.) I'll need a Swarovski scope for that.
She: You're really interested in shooting?
He: I was a junior member of NRA.
She: You were?
He: Yeah! A one-hole shooter at age twelve.
She: That means all the bullets in the same spot?
He: You got it.
She: Hmmm…
He: When your brother took me to the gun range last weekend, I remembered how much fun I used to have shooting.
She: This is going to take some getting used to.

What Emotional Independence Is and Is Not

IS	**IS NOT**
Internal locus of control	External locus of control
Proactive	Reactive
Self-soothing	Self-indulgent
Engaged	Disengaged

External locus of control means believing that external forces control everything from how happy we feel to whether our dreams come true. When we believe others are calling the shots, we adhere to the standards they impose. Obedient children give external locus of control a good name. On the other hand, adults engaging in groupthink have committed history's most heinous acts.

Adherence to romantic partners' standards eventually causes conflict. Most adults resent having their lives controlled by others and seek opportunities to even up perceived imbalances. Also, if we believe our spouses control everything, we feel justified in shirking responsibility and blaming them for problems.

Internal locus of control means living by internal standards—being authentic, expressing preferences, acting according to conscience, behaving with integrity. It means cultivating emotional neutrality to others' disapproval. If taken to extremes, internal locus of control can take unhealthy forms, too. World leaders, corporate executives and ordinary people do harm when they march to their own tragically misanthropic drummers and stubbornly refuse to be influenced.

If you are self-righteously trampling others, be prepared to watch your approval ratings plummet. If you are trampling your partner, be prepared to lose intimate connections. If your partner is trampling you, ask yourself whether you have made a great mistake.

Debbie's Story

Debbie is a forty-two-year-old, stay-at-home mother of four. Her husband, a construction contractor, has intermittently been living with another woman for nearly a year. Debbie has abused alcohol, experienced depression and felt suicidal during this time. She initiated psychotherapy when she first decided to divorce her husband then changed her mind about divorce and discontinued therapy. She has repeatedly vacillated about divorce and resumed and interrupted psychotherapy.

Debbie: A lot has happened since I saw you last. The good news is I've contacted my attorney and told him to go ahead with the divorce.

Dr. M.: What brought that on?

Debbie: Well, it has to do with the bad news. I overdosed on alcohol and pills and ended up in the hospital.

Dr. M.: When did this happen?

Debbie: About a week ago. I convinced them it was an accident, so they released me without making me go to the mental health unit.

Dr. M.: Was it an accident?

Debbie: I didn't want to die. I could never do that to my children. I wanted to stop hurting, though.

Dr. M.: Go on.

Debbie: I did this after I found out my husband has also been involved with a woman for whom he built a house. I really flipped out.

Dr. M.: You were angry.

Debbie: Well, yes! At him, of course, but at myself, too, for being so weak! I've been trying everything to get him back. I kept hoping he'd take pity on me or, at least, want what's best for the kids and stop the affair…affairs, I should say. I'm ridiculous. Pathetic.

Dr. M.: Well, I'd call you emotionally dependent.

Debbie: That's why I've come back. I have to change that about myself…for my own good and for my children's. (Starts to cry.) Dr. Meinecke, my seventeen-year-old daughter is the one who found me unconscious and called the ambulance.

Dr. M.: Tell me what you mean when you say you're angry with yourself for being weak.

Debbie: I guess I should say I'm angry with myself for losing my independence. Before I got married, I felt secure in myself. I had confidence to burn. But that all changed when I married a control freak. Did I ever tell you that he tells us how many squares of toilet paper to use?

Dr. M.: He's serious?

Debbie: Yes. The kids just laugh at him and use however much they want. But it really upsets me, not only because he acts this way but because I put up with it.

Dr. M.: You've always said that you stay married because of your financial and emotional dependence.

Debbie: And for my children. I thought they needed their father, but he shows no interest in them.

Dr. M.: Let's go back to your having confidence to burn.

Debbie: Yeah, what a waste. I've figured out this much. For the past eighteen years I've traded real independence for some kind of fake independence based on the "safety net" of marriage.

Dr. M.: Well said.

Debbie: I see now that the security of marriage was an illusion. I have to get back to providing my own emotional security.

Dr. M.: Exactly.

Debbie: I think I'm just out of practice.

For the can't-we-all-just-get-along majority of people, developing stronger internal locus of control takes determination and perseverance.

If expectations have been established and precedents set, asserting independence will invite criticism and resistance. This will also afford ample opportunities to practice showing up for one's self.

Get Out of the Middle

Many of us experience stress and conflict due to dueling emotional dependencies, simultaneously trying to please two external influences: our families of origin and our spouses, for example. We also try to avoid conflict with both and, in doing so, satisfy no one, least of all ourselves. Marital satisfaction depends on establishing and honoring clear priorities:

1. Behaving self-responsibly
2. Nurturing marriage
3. Everything else

As if newlyweds don't have enough to worry about, families often stress them with pressure to honor holiday traditions. Trouble is inevitable for individuals stuck in external locus of control, because they want to please both their partners and their families. Characterized by fear, external locus of control fosters anger, impulsivity and counter-dependence (adolescent-like rebellion):

Groom: Christmas is my family's most important holiday.

Bride: It's my family's most important, too.

Groom: It's really my mom's *only* important holiday.

Bride: (Fearing her family's disapproval.) Don't do this to me!

Groom: (Fearing his family's disapproval.) Come on! We can spend Thanksgiving *and* July Fourth with *your* family.

Bride: What about my nephews and nieces?

Groom: What about my mom?

Bride: (Fearing husband's disapproval.) Just great! I can have my family mad at me or you mad at me!

Groom: (Fearing setting precedent of always giving in to wife, said only half-jokingly.) Well, you don't want *me* mad at you!

Bride: (Fearing setting precedent of always giving in to husband, said in all seriousness.) Is that some kind of threat!?

Characterized by self-confidence, internal locus of control fosters self-examination and cooperation.

> **Groom:** Christmas is my family's most important holiday.
> **Bride:** It's my family's most important, too.
> **Groom:** It's really my mom's *only* important holiday.
> **Bride:** I suppose we could alternate years. Lots of couples do.
> **Groom:** Maybe we can do better than that.
> **Bride:** Which, for you, means every Christmas with your family.
> **Groom:** (Nods.) Think of it as every Christmas in sunny, southern California.
> **Bride:** (Not getting defensive.) You know, another way to think about it is that every year I'd get to spend Thanksgiving, *my* favorite holiday, with my family.

Not everyone will be happy with this couple's decision. No family member's absence goes unnoticed at holiday time. Loved ones will miss Groom and his Bride around the Thanksgiving dinner table. And for Bride's nephews and nieces, opening Christmas gifts at Thanksgiving or receiving them by mail may not be as good as receiving them on Christmas. What is most important, though, is the fact that Bride and Groom made their decision without doing harm to their relationship.

Proactive Not Reactive

The emotionally independent are *proactive*, which means getting out ahead of potential problems, setting goals and troubleshooting obstacles. Proactivity, as it relates to emotional independence, takes one of two forms. It is proactive to accept a spouse's point of view and change our behavior. It is also proactive to change a behavior once we realize that it goes against our own best interests.

For example, if emotionally independent Bride seriously regrets her decision to forego Christmas with her nephews and nieces, she will revisit the decision with Groom. Together, emotionally independent partners can negotiate changes because they are not thwarted by fear of a partner's disapproval. If one partner is emotionally independent and the other is not, the emotionally independent one accepts the consequences of his or her choice of partner and works to counter provocation.

Intense Does Not Mean Urgent

The emotionally independent are not reactive. Whether a partner disapproves of our behavior or we disapprove of a partner's behavior, emotionally independent individuals know that intense does not mean urgent. In other words, absent life-threatening circumstances, intense emotion does not require urgent action. In fact, urgent action typically weakens one's position.

For example, when we fail to moderate emotional reactions and respond to provocation with provocation, we are playing by the other person's rules. When we rush to our own defenses and respond to provocation with justification, we relinquish personal power and freedom. Rule of thumb: The more intense the emotion, the more measured the response.

Stop Justifying

Consider these two conversations between co-workers:

> **Co-worker 1:** (Frowning and glancing at wristwatch.) I stopped by your office around nine, but I guess you came in late today.
>
> **Co-worker 2:** Well, first my cat threw up on the carpet, which, of course, I had to clean up. Then there was the longest train I've ever seen. Twenty minutes at least. Then I had to go by the post office…
>
> **Co-worker 1:** Bummer. So, do you have that report ready?
>
> **Co-worker 2:** It's around here somewhere. I've got a million phone calls to return and that meeting at eleven, but I promise I'll look for it after that.
>
> **VS.**
>
> **Co-worker 1:** I stopped by your office around nine, but I guess you came in late today.
>
> **Co-worker 2:** What can I help you with?

Co-worker 1: Do you have that report ready?
Co-worker 2: I'll drop it by your office before noon.

In the second vignette, Co-worker 2 sounds more powerful because she is not offering excuses. Powerful people do not justify their opinions, preferences or decisions. They are not overly concerned with gaining others' understanding or approval. In this way, they set a good example for the emotionally dependent among us.

Stop justifying your legitimate opinions, preferences and decisions. Practice making simple responses and statements. This does not preclude providing relevant, funny or juicy details to friends and loved ones, but it does preclude defensively chattering away in an effort to dispel emotional discomfort.

While you are working to change unhealthy patterns, you will sometimes hear yourself saying things that you do not want to go on saying. As soon as you notice yourself repeating old habits, stop talking! Do not continue in a self-defeating attempt to save face. Literally stop mid-sentence. With romantic partners (assuming a spirit of teamwork and the absence of substance abuse), you can openly practice stopping mid-sentence and redirecting yourself:

He: I thought you were cooking dinner tonight.
She: Well, I was going to, but… I mean, really, how much is one person supposed to cram into one day? First, I was late to work—the cat threw up and there was this long train. Then Davis was on me about that report. If I could count on you to help out once in a while, I might feel like cooking more often, but since I have to do *everything*—shop, cook and clean up—we're having frozen pizza.

VS.

He: I thought you were cooking dinner tonight.
She: No, I'm beat. There's frozen pizza or leftover lasagna.
He: (Silence.)
She: (Fearing disapproval.) Well, I was going to, but, I mean how much is one person—stop, I'm doing it again. Pizza or lasagna?
He: Pizza sounds good.

Practice Healthy Self-Care

Pioneered by medical and mental health professionals, prescriptions for healthy self-care mean asking patients to make necessary lifestyle changes and to practice stress-management behaviors. Unfortunately, prescriptions for healthy self-care often go unheeded. This is because exercising, eating right, getting enough sleep, practicing yoga, meditation or relaxation techniques, abstaining from substance abuse, pursuing creative outlets, etc., require hard work and perseverance.

During the 1980s, the concept of self-care became popularized. It is now common to hear talk (especially among women) about needing to take better care of oneself. It is also irresistibly profitable for advertisers to perpetuate the fantasy that self-care can be easy. As a result of the self-care marketing blitz, many of us think that getting pedicures, choosing hand-dipped dark chocolates and buying 10,000-thread count bed linens equal healthy self-care.

Because this idea suffers from overexposure, it is necessary to distinguish among four related terms: self-care, self-soothing, self-indulgence and self-pampering. The emotionally independent are good at *self-care.* They take responsibility for their health, undertaking health-promoting routines and regimens and learning to *self-soothe:* Calming their own psychological discomfort and pain.

Popularly, the terms *self-care* and *self-indulgence* are used interchangeably, as in "Oh, go ahead, indulge. You deserve it." In a psychological context, emotionally *in*dependent women and men engage in healthy *self-care* and those who are emotionally dependent engage in *self-indulgence*. Emotionally dependent individuals indulge tendencies to avoid the effortful (self-care). They substitute quick and easy antidotes, which rarely improve and often worsen their situation, all the while telling themselves they are engaging in *self-care*. From a relationship standpoint, the emotionally dependent indulge their impulses to vent negative emotions. They also indulge their fantasies that others are to blame for their suffering or, at least, responsible to kiss it and make it better.

At times, we all engage in *self-indulgence* and we practice some degree of self-deception about these behaviors. Rather than shouldering the hard work and self-denial required for healthy *self-care*, we reach for temporary and largely symbolic fixes then tell ourselves that these measures count as self-care. At best, such indulgences do no harm and qualify as *self-pampering* behaviors. At worst, such indulgences are destructive to self and others and qualify as compulsions and addictions.

Remember your mother teaching you to blow on the scrape on your knee? Ever hear the advice to let babies older than six months put themselves to sleep even if it means letting them cry? Many experts feel such early experiences provide lessons in *self-soothing*.

The majority of adults, unfortunately, haven't the foggiest notion how to constructively calm and manage their own emotional pain. Rather than working to develop a repertoire of healthy, *self-soothing* behaviors, we seek temporary and ultimately destructive remedies. Anxious? Pop a pill. Angry? Go blow some money. Sad? Drown your sorrows. Lonely? Turn on the television set. Bored? Log online for sex.

We also depend on other people to distract us from emotional pain. Most of us get married, in part, because we want someone other than Mother to calm our fears and offer us bandages. It is never a mistake to seek comfort in the sweet embrace or wise words of a spouse. The mistake is to believe that a spouse is obligated to be a perpetual source of emotional support. It is also not a spouse's role to teach us *self-soothing*. We must learn this skill on our own.

Learn to Self-Soothe Feelings of Loneliness

Many of us are fearful of being alone because we then have no one to distract us from our darkest, most anxiety-producing thoughts. We scare ourselves silly obsessing about past mistakes and humiliations and asking "what if?" about illness, catastrophe, loss and death. A lot of us have done a great deal of harm to ourselves, because we do not know how to soothe feelings of loneliness.

Fear of feeling lonely is one of the reasons people stay in abusive relationships. Fear of feeling lonely can drive a person to spend evenings phoning friend after friend, insensitively keeping each one tied up far too long and, eventually, wondering whether her friends are screening her calls. Fear of feeling lonely compels people to go shopping and charging, drinking and driving, gambling and losing. Fear of feeling lonely keeps people numbing out in front of the television set, eating for comfort and logging on to destructive Web sites.

Bear Down and Ride

Practice being alone. Stop running from reality. Being alone is an inescapable fact of the human condition. Many of my clients who fear loneliness have taken on the assignment of spending entire weekends in mindful solitude. This means being alone without resorting to sleeping around the clock, telephoning, e-mailing, web-surfing or watching television or movies.

Before you assign yourself this task, prepare by doing two things. To calm physical sensations of anxiety, learn relaxation techniques (diaphragmatic or yoga breathing, progressive muscle relaxation, imagery). To calm psychological symptoms, generate rational responses to panic-inducing thoughts and make a list of healthy distractions. *Important note*: This assignment is not for anyone who is actively suicidal.

Healthy self-soothing can be learned through relax and distract strategies, flood and relax strategies or some combination of both. Relax and distract strategies are internally generated substitutes for mother's soothing—the kinder, gentler approach. These involve practicing relaxation and pursuing constructive individual activities, especially those during which you lose track of time: exercise, music (making or listening), reading, any creative pursuit, physical labor, household projects and improvements or acquiring new skills (e.g., cooking/baking, studying a foreign language, knitting).

Flood and relax strategies are crash courses in self-soothing that temporarily increase anxiety—the sink or swim approach, the psychological equivalent of jumping in the deep end and thrashing around. These involve seeking opportunities to experience whatever you fear and to calm your fight or flight response with deep breathing, muscle relaxation and positive self-talk. If you fear public speaking, for example, speech classes and auditions for community theatre provide many flood and relax opportunities.

To overcome the fear of loneliness, you must deliberately immerse yourself in solitude. Learning to meditate, attending silent retreats, writing about feelings of loneliness, walking in nature or quietly sitting with yourself provide opportunities to practice developing your capacity for self-soothing. Typically, my clients who choose this assignment have made significant strides toward tolerating being alone.

Dana's and Nancy's Stories

One high-functioning, thirty-something female with a history of unstable and psychologically abusive romances is Dana. She decided it was time to interrupt her years-long pattern of spending evenings and weekends partying with one of several opportunistic men. Dana reported that undertaking the mindful solitude assignment not only changed her attitude toward being alone, but also resulted in newly painted walls in three rooms of her house. Soon after, as these things often go, Dana found a healthy relationship, got married and gave birth to her first child.

Another single woman, Nancy, recognized that her non-stop socializing was a strategy for coping with anxiety about being alone. Get-togethers at her home or out with friends kept her occupied until bedtime almost every night of the week. After practicing relaxation techniques and soothing self-talk, Nancy went the mindful solitude assignment one better, devising a strategy in which she selected one day a week, one week a month and one month a year during which she spent evenings and weekends home alone.

Effortful Not Stressful

When we exert maximum effort, whether physical or mental, we sometimes make the mistake of telling ourselves that the activity is stressful. An undertaking becomes stressful only when we tell ourselves, *This is awful, horrible. I can't stand it.* Whether we feel angry, jealous, envious, neglected or sad, the first step toward resolution is to stop denying or avoiding the emotion. The next step is to remind ourselves that grappling with negative emotion, though effortful, does not have to be stressful.

William's Story

William, a thirty-something, gay male client, had been avoiding experiencing his grief over a failed relationship because he feared being "overwhelmed." For weeks, William had been sleeping away his leisure time, abusing alcohol and snapping at everyone who asked him how he was handling the loss. When I asked William what exactly he meant by being overwhelmed, he dramatically predicted "suicidal depression or descent into madness." Ultimately, he accepted the flood and relax challenge. He went home from one of our sessions, curled up in a ball and sobbed. The result was not the feared experience of decompensation but, rather, an experience of profound relief.

Healthy Self-Focus

Occasionally, clients who are trying cognitive and self-responsible approaches to improve relationships question whether all of this self-focus could lead to emotional disengagement from their partners. Although this is a legitimate question, there are different forms of self-focus and emotional disengagement.

*Un*healthy self-focus is the narcissistic, other-people-exist-to-make-my-life-easier type. Healthy self-focus is the development of two avenues of self-correction. First, we develop an observing ego: the ability to see ourselves with objectivity (as much as humanly possible). Second, we learn to recognize and care about how our behavior affects others.

Healthy Emotional Disengagement

Emotional disengagement comes in unhealthy and healthy forms, too. Chronic emotional disengagement can lead to marital dissatisfaction. Conversely, selective and temporary emotional disengagement can effectively defuse negatively charged situations and improve marital satisfaction. Emotions are wired into our networks of association. Think about almost anything—holidays, sunsets, school buses, classic cars, baseball gloves, war memorials—and experience the emotions wired into your neural networks. Recall times you witnessed middle-aged adults ranting about childhood run-ins with parents, siblings and schoolyard bullies. Think of your all-time favorite loved ones and feel your mood improve.

To illustrate, I sometimes tell clients a story about my paternal grandmother who developed symptoms of Alzheimer's disease and lived with my parents through the last years of her life. Once when I was visiting, she said to me, "I don't know who you are, but I sure do like you." Though the connection to how exactly she knew me was lost, the connection to how she felt about me endured.

Those of us whose cognitive powers are fully intact can connect to whichever emotions we chose. We can fire up a whole new world of positive emotional engagement. And, if we want less melodrama, we can learn to dis-identify with negative emotions.

Dis-identifying with negative emotions does not mean disengaging from the person whose behavior triggered negative emotions. It means redirecting our own thought streams. When we dis-identify with negative emotions, we no longer think, *Oh, yes, irritability, impatience and intolerance. That's me.* We think instead, *Serenity, patience and tolerance. I choose these emotions.*

When I was in high school, my grandmother gave me her old sewing machine on the condition that I sew a "dressy" dress for her. She brought over a relatively simple pattern for a fully lined chemise. The devil, as they say, is always in the details and the fabrics she chose were the devil to work with. The slippery, sliding pink satin lining and fray-if-you-breathe-on-it floral nylon overlay frustrated me to tears. My mother, an expert seamstress, showed me how to make French seams, but did not rescue me from my bargain with my grandmother.

Although at the time I did not think in terms of dis-identifying with negative emotions, it is what I did. I had not yet learned adult lessons that would render me capable of cognitive reframes such as:

- Nothing in life is free.
- Grandma is not a seamstress, so she had no idea how difficult it would be to work with the fabrics.
- Having only one bad memory associated with a grandmother is a tribute.

Instead, I focused on the fact that Grandma actually wore the dress! Every time I saw her in that pink dress and the carefully selected accessories (beige hat, low heels, handbag with jeweled clasp and pink rhinestone brooch and earrings), I felt touched and proud. Although images of the challenge of working with those fabrics exist within that associative network, the emotions associated with this experience are positive.

When it comes to spouses, shifting cognitive focus allows us to avoid unhealthy emotional disengagement. We must push ourselves to understand our negative reactions rather than pushing our partners to understand our unfulfilled needs. In this way, we practice self-responsibility and break old chains of association. We also prevent destructive mutual disengagement that occurs when partners blame each other for negative emotions.

Gina's Story

A thirty-eight-year-old writer, Gina has been married eight years.

Gina: He thinks he's too good to get an ordinary job.

Dr. M.: He said that?

Gina: Well, he's always talking about not compromising his artistic integrity.

Dr. M.: Which means?

Gina: He won't work in commercial art.

Dr. M.: That would be like you writing greeting cards.

Gina: Sure, but I would do it if I were the one generating no income.

Dr. M.: So, this is about money.

Gina: Well, it's been tight since I've been freelancing. Now, my COBRA's about to expire and we'll have to buy our own health insurance.

Dr. M.: He doesn't share your concern?

Gina: No! He keeps saying, "Don't worry, it will work out." He doesn't seem to care that I'm losing sleep over it.

Dr. M.: You're having insomnia?

Gina: (Nods, near tears.) I just can't believe he isn't stepping up…getting a real job with benefits.

Dr. M.: You're making this about his under-functioning.

Gina: Yes!

Dr. M.: To avoid dealing with your anxiety.

Gina: (Questioning expression.)

Dr. M.: What are you doing to reduce your anxiety?

Gina: There's more to it than that.

Dr. M.: Let's talk about what you're doing to reduce your anxiety.

Gina: (Half-smiling.) You mean besides blaming my husband?

Healthy Interdependence

If we consistently rely on others to meet our emotional needs and only feel good about ourselves as long as everyone else feels good about us, we are emotionally dependent. If, on the other hand, we see, as Tom Hanks' character did in *Joe Versus the Volcano*, that each person has to be his or her own hero, we open ourselves to the benefits of taking the self-responsible approach to life. As we take responsibility to meet our own physical, psychological and emotional needs, we increase our emotional independence; practicing emotional independence prepares us to engage in healthy interdependence.

Healthy interdependence is essential to mature love, the alternative to conventional models of emotional dependence, unrealistic expectations and blame. It is characterized by emotional engagement, teamwork and commitment to putting more into a relationship than we get out of it. Healthy interdependence involves accepting responsibility for our own emotional states and, at the same time, contributing to our spouses' qualities of life.

Chapter 14

Extreme Makeovers

Redefine the Marital Relationship

When it comes to marital satisfaction, change is inevitable. We may wish it were not so, but it's one of the few things in life of which we can be sure. It's easy to flip-flop, as Roxie Hart, in the Broadway show *Chicago*, sings, between "that funny, sunny, honey hubby" and "that scummy, crummy, dummy hubby." Whether relationships are founded on traditional or postmodern ideals, partners find the master key to long-term satisfaction in their willingness to redefine the marital relationship as often as necessary. By locking into obsolete definitions, we bar ourselves from marital satisfaction.

Definitions vary of romantic relationships. In the Lake Lugu region of Himalayan China, for example, the language of a contemporary matriarchal society has no words for husband, wife, marriage or virginity. Couples practice *zouhun*, loosely translated as "walking marriage." In walking marriage, a woman has a man (known as *azhu* or close male friend) with whom she spends her nights, but the man walks back to his own home every morning. Women raise children within their families of origin and couples share neither daily routines nor possessions.[1] In contrast, Western couples typically choose definitions that involve less personal freedom and more perceived security.

No matter how couples initially define their relationships, original definitions soon prove unrealistic. When this happens, couples' degree of adaptability determines their potential for success. Redefining along the lines of *zouhun* stretches the limits for most and copying models found among parents, siblings, friends or pop icons is futile. How others define (or appear to define) their marriages has nothing whatsoever to do with you and your spouse.

So, what are couples in search of marital success to do? Successful redefinition can be accomplished if both partners are willing to accept and accommodate change. Rather than clinging to the way it "should" be or "used to" be, get creative! Change your expectations. Restructure your cognitions. Fire and wire new neural pathways.

Honor the Freshness Date

Every relationship's freshness date eventually expires. As soon as the thought, *It's not what it used to be*, crosses your mind, a new marital definition is needed. This is when things get uncertain, but as Dr. John Gottman says: "Despite what many therapists will tell you, you don't have to resolve your major marital conflicts for your marriage to thrive."[2]

Marriages thrive when partners are self-responsible and adapt to new realities. Those who refuse to redefine escalate dissatisfaction and may find their marriages redefined by default when partners seek dissolution. Spouses who accept new realities guarantee opportunities to undertake the difficult yet ultimately relationship-enhancing task of modifying their expectations and changing troublesome aspects of their approaches to marriage.

Robert's Story

Robert is in his twenties, bisexual and married to a woman.

> **Dr. M.:** So, what was the understanding before you got married?
>
> **Robert:** Well, that Jill is straight, I'm bisexual and our marriage would be monogamous.
>
> **Dr. M.:** And now?

Robert: We're talking about our naïveté. Whether what we agreed to then is realistic for a lifetime.

Dr. M.: Do you want to stay together?

Robert: We still love each other.

Dr. M.: But it could get more complicated.

Robert: Well, we're honoring our vows. Neither of us is interested in anyone else…yet. What we're most concerned about is whether to start a family. We both want children and there's pressure from our parents. So, this is what I'd like some help thinking through.

This relatively postmodern couple seems to understand the basics of self-responsible relating. They also appeared to accept the reality of change. I counseled that though facing potentially painful decisions, all avenues were open for constructively redefining their relationship.

Expired Pair-Bonds

Most couples initially adopt some variation of the make-newlywed-happiness-last-forever definition. As long as neither partner has a demoralizing dip in happiness, initial definitions work. Realistically, though, feelings change. As stressors intrude and pair-bonds expire, existing definitions become obsolete.

Couples who cling to previously agreed upon but untested ideals doom themselves to marital dissatisfaction. Ongoing marital harmony depends upon partners' commitment to face reality and hammer out new, shared definitions.

Francine's Story

Francine is a thirty-two-year-old lesbian.

Francine: (Frustrated.) Redefine? What does that *mean*?

Dr. M.: Before your affair, how did you and your partner define your relationship?

Francine: Happy, I guess.

Dr. M.: What else?

Francine: Like newlyweds. Hopeful. Trusting.
Dr. M.: And now?
Francine: Unhappy. Messed up. She doesn't trust me.
Dr. M.: So, the definition went from happy newlyweds or, let's say, untested newlyweds to betrayed and betrayer.
Francine: (Shrugs.)
Dr. M.: That's reality.
Francine: (Nods.)
Dr. M.: Untested newlyweds is the old definition. Now, it's post-affair betrayed and betrayer.
Francine: That's dismal.
Dr. M.: That's reality.
Francine: (Chuckling.) Would you please stop saying that?
Dr. M.: Dismal is couples making their post-affair relationship a cesspool of punishing and groveling—
Francine: You got that right.
Dr. M.: Well, it doesn't have to turn out that way.
Francine: Promise?

Gay or straight, redefinition becomes inevitable when affairs occur. Even if affairs are never discovered or acknowledged, lies, split affections and guilt erode intimacy. If affairs are acknowledged, righteous anger, jealousy, distrust and grief render the prior definition obsolete.

Expired Pair-Bonds who Remain Faithful

Not all expired pair-bonds grapple with sexual infidelity. Many couples remain faithful after infatuation fades. Regardless, when sex is no longer novel, satisfaction wanes and definitions of what constitutes "good sex" diverge. Satisfied couples are those who successfully redefine the basis on which they relate sexually.

Many of my female clients of all ages tell me some variation of this tale:

Once upon a time, when her relationship was new, the Princess looked forward to sex. A mattress-romp with Prince Charming was one of her favorite things. Then an evil spell was cast upon her. Now, though she loves Prince and feels sexually attracted to him, sex is a boring and messy duty to be avoided or finished posthaste. The prospect of Prince endlessly exercising his God-given conjugal rights brings Princess to tears. So, she asks the court physician for a referral and makes an appointment with a psychologist. During her first appointment, the Princess says:

- I'm almost never in the mood.
- He wants it *all* the time.
- I wish I could say I enjoy it once we get into it, but I'm not even sure that's true.
- I'm making lists in my head of what not to forget to do when we're done.
- I'd rather clean toilets.
- Does this mean I'm frigid? Depressed?
- Can you break the spell?

And the psychologist says:

- There is nothing wrong with the Princess.
- Like everyone else, she is hardwired for disenchantment.
- She is definitely not frigid. Although no one in her right mind has an affair to prove the point, a new attraction would put the matter to rest.
- Unless Princess has certain other symptoms, she is not depressed.
- The magic that breaks this spell is redefinition.

Only One *First* Time

No matter what Madison Avenue, pop culture and the sex industry pretend, there is only one *first* time and some first times are better than others. As evil as it seems, the inevitable closing of any couple's one-to-four-year window is not an evil spell. The evil spell is cast by unrealistic expectations.

As infatuation fades, feelings about sex with spouses change (refer to chapters 2 through 5). The only requirement for constructive redefinition in this realm is openness to rethinking satisfaction-sabotaging, conventional notions about sex. Good sex for the long-term is about nurturing the relationship and giving the gift your partner wants rather than the gift you want him or her to have.

When to Redefine

Redefinition may be called for if you are thinking any of these "what if" statements:

- What if my feelings change?
- What if my partner stops contributing equally?
- What if I'm not being treated special?
- What if I'm feeling diminished?

If you aren't happy with your spouse's current definition of any aspect of your marriage, your preference is that he or she change. And now you know that this is unlikely. If you are prepared to redefine by matching your partner's definition, you can simply start reality-testing your expectations and changing your reactions to your spouse.

Feelings Change Like the Seasons

When relationships are new, it feels like glorious spring. Then comes summer, the season in which couples take their comfort for granted. Next, autumn arrives, bringing splendid days along with warnings of winter's harshness. Inevitably, a seemingly endless, frozen and slippery winter tests couples' endurance. After winter's ordeal comes the renewal of another spring. Recognizing the seasons of a marriage offers alternatives: constructively hunkering down until the spring thaw or claiming the promise of Albert Camus's words, "In the depths of winter, I finally learned that within me there lay an invincible summer."

When your spouse behaves in ways that annoy and disappoint you, he or she may be improving your chances of staying married. Results of one 2005 study indicate that having a clear picture of spouses' faults may promote marital longevity. Dr. Lisa Ann Neff found that newlywed couples who glossed over their partners' negative aspects tended to divorce during the subsequent four years. "Loving your partner is not enough," Neff concluded. "You have to love the partner and have an accurate perception of him or her."[3]

Holly's Story

Holly is thirty-five and has been married for six years. Her story can easily be translated to apply to many women.

Holly: I don't think I love my husband anymore.

Dr. M.: What's changed?

Holly: My feelings.

Dr. M.: You used to feel love for him and now you don't.

Holly: (Nods.)

Dr. M.: Describe your feelings when you loved him.

Holly: (Thinks a while.) I felt happy. When I heard the garage door go up, I felt excited that he was home.

Dr. M.: And now?

Holly: I feel annoyed. Disappointed. He doesn't try that hard anymore.

Dr. M.: Well, he might not be trying, but his behavior is outside your control. Before we talk about whether or not you love him anymore, let's talk about being happy and excited to see him and how you might reconnect to those feelings.

Information-Gathering and Wise Decision Making

Becoming a self-responsible partner as we've discussed involves managing negative feelings. This is not to say that negative feelings have no value. In fact, while assessing any situation, noticing feelings (negative and positive) triggered in the limbic system and right and left hemispheres is the first of three ways to gather information.

The other sources of information are intellect and intuition. Intellect refers to the rational mind, the left hemisphere, where we evaluate pros and cons. Intuition refers to what is sometimes described as "gut instinct." Tellingly, books written on the subject of intuition often fail to satisfactorily define it. Recently, though, brain science has shed new light on the subject. Intuition is now believed to be associated with information stored in and communicated from the right hemisphere to the left hemisphere. According to clinical psychologist Louis Cozolino, Ph.D.:

> The blending of the strengths of each hemisphere allows for the maximum integration of our cognitive and emotional experience with our inner and outer worlds. When we are awake, the right hemisphere constantly provides information to the left, although that hemisphere may not necessarily register, understand, or allow the information into consciousness.[4]

Intuition, then, would be experienced in those moments when the left hemisphere registers previously inhibited bits of the information streaming from the right hemisphere.

When information has been gathered and it's time to decide what changes to begin practicing, wise decision makers exclude feelings (especially negative) from the process. Conventional wisdom's "follow your heart" lingo directs people into the land of non-discernment. Stress generated by intense feelings hinders one's ability to ask, "Which of these bits of information are the *important* ones?" If you want to make *un*wise decisions, let your feelings be your guide. If you want to make wise decisions, go with intellect and intuition.

And how, exactly, does one go about overriding intense feelings in order to make wise decisions? Dr. Cozolino suggests teaching clients to go "*up left*" instead of "*down right.*"[5] I explain it to clients this way: The brain's chief priority is self-preservation. Sensory input is first routed *down* to the fear center (amygdala), where degree of threat to survival is determined, then on to the *right* hemisphere, where our earliest, nonverbal memories are scanned for images of danger. If input is even loosely associated with past negative experiences, we become alarmed. Then we can either repeatedly loop around *down right* in fear and past associations or we can continue routing.

If we continue routing, activation moves *up* to the frontal lobes and our brain's centers for inhibition of emotion and on to the *left* hemisphere and our rational mind. So, *up left* means utilizing our brain's power to inhibit negative emotion and generate rational thoughts. This, in a nutshell, is what is meant by becoming expert users of our brains.

Self-responsible partners learn to experience negative feelings without acting on them, without passing judgment or blaming a spouse and without denigrating themselves. They also learn to shift focus from feelings and memories about what's wrong with a spouse to rational thoughts of what's right. In *Too Good to Leave, Too Bad to Stay*, Mira Kirshenbaum suggests:

> If there's even one thing you and your partner experience together and look forward to (besides children) that reliably feels good and makes you feel close, there's the possibility you'll be able to clean

out the crap between you and have a viable relationship. If you had just met, there'd be the possibility of your falling in love. Quick take: Real love needs real loving experiences.[6]

Partner Stops Contributing Equally

First, ask yourself why you hold onto this impossible ideal. Was there ever in the history of the world an actual fifty-fifty partnership? Not likely. If you made the great mistake of marrying a chronically under-responsible, emotional adolescent, trying to get 50 percent out of him or her is futile. If, on the other hand, you found a self-responsible adult who, overall, has the best interest of the relationship at heart, respecting his or her limits is essential.

Paul's Story

Paul has been married for twenty years and is forty-four years old.

Paul: We had another big blowup.

Dr. M.: Tell me.

Paul: She was having a bunch of teacher friends over and wanted me to rush out and buy fresh mums for the front porch.

Dr. M.: And?

Paul: I told her that was ridiculous.

Dr. M.: Good call.

Paul: Yeah, she got really mad. Called me a slacker.

Dr. M.: Frankly, I think she made a mistake asking you to rush out and buy mums.

Paul: Thank you!

Dr. M.: However…

Paul: Oh, here we go.

Dr. M.: There are so many other ways to handle that situation.

Paul: Go buy mums?

Dr. M.: You could have…as a gift.

Paul: But I thought it was ridiculous.

Dr. M.: Hm-hmm…

Paul: The whole thing was ridiculous! I didn't want people coming over in the first place. It ruined our whole Saturday.

Dr. M.: Now, we're getting somewhere.

It is almost always helpful to ask yourself, *Would I want to live with me?* If either my client or his wife had asked this question, their situation, I believe, would have turned out differently. When his wife, Kim, noticed the faded mums, she could have done a dozen things other than demand that her husband go to a garden center for fresh ones. It can be distressing to live with someone who expects others to be at her beck and call.

Although in a perfect world Paul's wife would never have asked him to run the errand, Paul made a provocative choice by passing judgment on Kim's request. It can be distressing, as well, to live with someone who attempts to justify refusal to do a favor by calling it ridiculous. Paul was unprepared to react constructively because he had not first managed his negative reaction to his wife's desire to host the meeting. So, he experienced her urgent request as insult added to injury.

This is not to suggest that self-responsible spouses never ask favors of their partners. Consider your partner's level of tolerance for doing favors and ask accordingly. If you are discontent with your partner's level of willingness to do favors and instead try to manipulate, you will succeed only in annoying him or her. Self-responsible spouses take no for an answer without hard feelings.

Now, ask yourself why you're keeping track of whether your partner is contributing equally.

- Do you pride yourself on accepting nothing less than the best and define the best marriage as one in which partners contribute equally?
- Do you worry that others take advantage of you?
- Are you under the mistaken impression that your daily routine would feel easier if your partner did an equal share of tasks such as housecleaning, bill paying and grocery shopping?
- Do you maintain performance standards that few people, including your spouse, live up to?

Regardless of the particulars, if you cast yourself as the over-functioner, that leaves only the role of under-functioner for your spouse. When you find yourself keeping track, it's time to reality-test your expectations.

Not Being Treated Special

Everyone loves special treatment. According to conventional wisdom, marriage licenses guarantee special treatment. Married taxpayers get deductions. Married prisoners get conjugal visits. Married people, generally, feel entitled to receive from each other budget-busting trinkets and gifts of service (e.g., car windshields scraped, shoulders massaged or dinners prepared). We expect to have our preferences honored, such as choosing not to be employed or to stay at home with children. At the very least, we expect partners to give the gift of non-interference with favorite activities.

Regardless of specifics, expecting to be carried around on a pillow reflects adolescent fantasies about finding someone who will treat us like royalty. Self-responsible husbands give up the dream of being king of the castle. Self-responsible wives forego the fantasy of a knight in shining armor and give up the dream that gender equality involves reparations.

If you define marriage as a lifetime of giving and receiving special treatment, it is only a matter of time until your "world full of yes" turns (as Roxie Hart's did) to "one big world full of no." Those who extend special treatment to spouses struggle with chronic disappointment because reciprocation proves inadequate or nonexistent. Those who *expect* special treatment can never get enough. Healthy partnerships are those in which mutual respect is an everyday occurrence and special treatment is strictly voluntary.

Note to victims of abuse: Sometimes victims stay in abusive relationships because of the special treatment that follows episodes of psychological or physical battery. Victims are repeatedly seduced by the remorseful batterer's extravagant gifts and acts of penance. The insanity of this is often apparent to everyone but the victim, who clings to the desperate hope that special treatment will become the norm. It is also important to understand that nonviolent relationships are characterized by moderation and may actually have fewer incidents of special treatment than violent relationships. Healthy partners are neither abusive nor obsequious.

Feeling Diminished

Feeling diminished is different than not being treated special. Feeling diminished results from being devalued. We are devalued when others cruelly criticize, abuse or neglect us. The wives-submit-yourselves-to-your-husbands paradigm has wife-devaluation as the central premise. The hen-pecked husband paradigm offers equal opportunity misery. If your partner chronically devalues you, you have made a great mistake. Short of religious conversion, 12-step programs and intensive psychotherapy, mentally cruel partners do not change.

Becky's Story

Becky is a forty-something client who has been married eighteen years.

Becky felt devalued and sought redefinition of her marriage in an extreme manner. At her initial evaluation, she told me that her family physician asked her to make the appointment because, during her yearly physical exam, Becky mentioned her plan to abandon her husband and three teenage sons. Her stated goal for psychotherapy was to decide whether to follow through with the plan that she had been working out for several months. Becky's fantasy was to disappear one day, leaving all of them wondering what the heck happened to her.

Becky said that she had been miserable in her marriage for many years, but felt that she would not be acting in her sons' best interests were she to divorce their father. Now, to her utter dismay, her sons (aged fourteen, fifteen and seventeen) showed little respect for her. In fact, their behavior strongly resembled their father's. Becky especially resented their tag-team mockery of her efforts to provide a mother's guidance. She felt completely alone—one female against a pack of self-involved males. She also admitted that she wanted her husband to be forced into single-parenting the teenage monsters she felt he had created.

Becky had a high school girlfriend who lived in a large city in another state and she had decided to move there. She had visited the girlfriend, found a place to live and applied for jobs. The only reservations she had centered on concerns that leaving might negatively affect her future relationship with her sons.

In addressing this client's goal, we discussed potential consequences of abandoning her sons, likely effects on her relationship with each one and alternative actions she could take. We discussed Becky's responsibility to examine her expectations of her sons and her reactions to their disrespectful behavior. Regarding her marriage, Becky had only one desire: to escape it. At our third session, she told me that she was taking a flight the next day for a job interview and felt certain that she would be hired. Becky said she would likely not be returning home and thanked me for my input. That was the last time I saw her.

Sometimes, couples equally devalue one another. A typical, mutual-devaluation shouting match might go something like this:

> **He:** You need to shut your trap when I'm watching football with the guys!
>
> **She:** You need to stop yelling at the TV like a moron!
>
> **He:** Hey! That's what guys do!
>
> **She:** Hey! They can't hear you!
>
> **He:** (mimics wife) Is it *intermission* yet? Could you be any stupider?
>
> **She:** No one is *more stupid* than you.

Redefining a marriage as "over" may be the best course of action in some cases. If, however, you have compelling reasons for sticking with your expired pair-bond, there are self-responsible ways to potentially improve your day-to-day existence.

- Learn to withstand criticism and react constructively.
- Learn to agree with criticism.
- Learn to use the non sequitur or to say nothing at all when criticized.

Although these techniques may prove challenging to carry out, they are surefire when consistently practiced. Here are example conversations between partners using the these three techniques:

Withstand Disapproval and React Constructively:

> **He:** You need to shut your trap when I'm watching football with the guys!
>
> **She:** I'm going to start taking the kids to my sister's when you have the guys over.
>
> **He:** Who will fix the snacks?
>
> **She:** Order pizza. Have people bring junk food.

He: Hell, you don't have to go all radical on me.
She: When are they coming over next?
He: Two weeks.
She: It'll be good. You'll have the place to yourselves.

Agree with Criticism:

He: You need to shut your trap when I'm watching football with the guys!
She: What did I say?
He: (mimics wife) Is it *intermission* yet? Could you be any stupider?
She: (laughs) You're right. Sounds like I'm at the symphony.
Flabbergasted, he shuts his mouth.

Use the Non Sequitur:

He: You need to shut your trap when I'm watching football with the guys!
She: Your friend Murray has sure lost a lot of weight.
He: (No comment.)
She: He told me he did it by drinking ten glasses of water a day.
He: He did it by giving up beer.
She: Now, that's radical.

Sometimes, we feel diminished, because we misinterpret a partner's behavior. Since there are multiple possible interpretations of most behaviors, it pays to remember that feeling diminished can have more to do with an individual's immediate state of mind than a partner's intent. Self-responsible partners take stock of their own quirks, expectations and reactions. They ask themselves relevant questions:

- Am I overly sensitive?
- Do I have unrealistic expectations?
- Am I behaving provocatively?

If assessment leaves you feeling less than confident about your behavior, give your spouse the benefit of the doubt.

Feeling diminished is not always the result of a spouse's mistreatment. Sometimes we diminish ourselves with negative self-talk. And, occasionally, clients have questioned whether increasing their self-responsibility quotient diminishes some other valued aspect of themselves.

Clint's Story

Clint has been married for six years and is twenty-nine.

Clint: What about authenticity?

Dr. M.: Say more.

Clint: Showing my true feelings.

Dr. M.: Fine, if your goal is to maintain status quo.

Clint: But doesn't it diminish a person's authenticity to be so…restrained?

Dr. M.: How so?

Clint: Well, it's inauthentic to hide your true feelings.

Dr. M.: This is a situation where you have conflicting values.

Clint: (Questioning expression.)

Dr. M.: You value showing your true feelings and you value getting along with your spouse. Only you know whether you can have both.

Clint: Not usually.

Dr. M.: You can be authentic regarding one value but not the other.

Clint: So, I have to take responsibility and choose.

Clients have also questioned whether increasing self-responsibility emotionally distances spouses.

Enez's Story

Enez is forty-nine and has been married for over twenty years.

Enez: I'm starting to feel the shift in my head. I'm getting it about managing my own expectations and reactions. But I have a question. Doesn't this put emotional distance between my husband and me?

Dr. M.: How do you mean?

> **Enez:** I'm holding back. Not being honest about my feelings.
>
> **Dr. M.:** So, you're worried that not being honest about your anger, for example, reduces your emotional intimacy.
>
> **Enez:** Exactly.
>
> **Dr. M.:** Do you think, then, that complete freedom of expression is essential to intimacy?
>
> **Enez:** Well, I don't think you can just say *anything*.
>
> **Dr. M.:** So, being completely open about feelings is less important than…
>
> **Enez:** I'm thinking it's more important to be compassionate than honest.
>
> **Dr. M.:** Tell me.
>
> **Enez:** It's like what you always say about not having a right to impose our negativity on others. I agree with that now. I'm thinking that expressing negative emotions probably distances us more.

Sometimes, clients wonder whether being self-responsible is being "phony."

Alicia's Story

Alicia is in her late thirties and has been married for ten years.

> **Alicia:** I feel like a phony when I don't show my true feelings.
>
> **Dr. M.:** Well, at least you're a phony with good judgment.
>
> **Alicia:** (Laughs.)
>
> **Dr. M.:** You know, if your goal is to be a self-responsible spouse, you're the furthest thing from phony if you're being true to that goal.
>
> **Alicia:** (Laughs again.) I just thought of the weirdest thing. It's like when I had a cat as a kid. She didn't like me because I used to dress her up in doll clothes. Then even though I really, really wanted to keep treating her like a doll, I stopped—because I wanted her to stop running from me.

Restraint and Integrity

Some clients so thoroughly get the hang of behaving self-responsibly that they go above and beyond initial psychotherapy goals. One such client, Iris, initially identified the goal of deciding whether to go through with her wedding. She felt uncertain for several reasons.

Iris's Story

Iris is thirty-something and engaged to be married. Though Iris felt love for her twice-divorced fiancé, she had questions about whether he would be a true partner. Over the preceding three years, she had allowed him to live rent-free in her home. Iris had bankrolled a business for him, paying for a workspace as well as marketing and selling his artistic creations. She had paid for joint vacations and agreed to foot the bill for a pricey, destination wedding. When Iris tried to set limits on her spending, he pressured her to "stop being so selfish" and do even more for him.

After the first session, this accomplished and beautiful woman acknowledged that she was being shamelessly financially exploited. Iris expressed doubt, however, about whether she could go through with ending the relationship. Just thinking about it skyrocketed her anxiety! She not only dreaded causing her fiancé suffering, but also noted that her confidence in her own judgment had been undermined. How could she be sure what was the right thing to do?

After a few more visits, Iris concluded that regaining control of her life and rebuilding her diminished self-confidence were the right things to do. She believed that this meant taking responsibility for and accepting the consequences of her great mistake. Although she vacillated for a few weeks, in part due to the tens of thousands of dollars she had invested in this man, Iris finally decided to end the engagement.

Once Iris made the decision, she felt less anxiety and more anger. She felt that her soon-to-be-ex-fiancé had essentially stolen her money and time. She blamed him for not genuinely reciprocating her love. Iris wanted to punish him, set him straight, tell the world what a leech he had been. But, again, she chose to practice self-responsible behavior.

Iris adopted a "mantra" that I often suggest to clients who are experiencing strong negative emotions. By repeatedly reminding herself to practice *restraint and integrity,* she subdued her anger and focused her intentions. Iris identified a new goal of extricating herself without deliberately punishing (diminishing) her former fiancé. First, she broke the news that she no longer intended to marry him and cancelled their destination wedding.

Dr. M.: So, how did it go?

Iris: Oh, Dr. Meinecke, I am now 100 percent sure I made the right decision.

Dr. M.: What happened?

Iris: Well, I told him I won't marry him because I want him to be someone he's not…that I should never have tried to change him…and that I made mistakes that I plan to correct.

Dr. M.: And?

Iris: He accused me of ruining his life and stormed out. He hasn't spoken to me since, even though I find him asleep on my couch every morning. And get this! Our friends tell me that he is saying I refuse to explain why I called it off and is claiming that I must be having an affair.

Next, Iris "evicted" her fiancé. His reaction was to take up residence in the workspace she still provided. For a few weeks, she considered allowing him to rent the workspace and continue their business relationship. Eventually, reason trumped emotion and she and he completely parted ways.

This client's final goal for our work together was to gain confidence that her days of getting involved with under-functioners were over. Once again, Iris demonstrated thorough understanding of self-responsibility.

Iris: You know, I don't think it even matters why I did this in the past.

Dr. M.: Say more.

Iris: Well, there could be a lot of reasons that I was attracted to psychological adolescents and went along with their manipulations, but going into that seems like…oh, I don't know…maybe like looking for justification.

Dr. M.: What do you want to discuss then?

Iris: I want to recognize telltale signs.

Dr. M.: Of under-functioning men?

Iris: Dr. Meinecke! I could write a book about that. I mean in myself! Signs that I'm not behaving self-responsibly.

Dr. M.: Wow! Our work is finished!

Iris: (Laughs.) Really? Well, just let me run a few thoughts by you.

Moira's Story

Here's another example of a client who completely "got it." Moira is a late-thirties stay-at-home mother of two (also accomplished and beautiful). Moira initiated psychotherapy after her husband of ten years told her he planned to divorce her because he no longer cared to deal with her "anger problem." Moira's goals for psychotherapy were to decide whether her marriage could be salvaged and to discover whether she, in fact, had an anger problem. When it became clear that her husband would not be dissuaded from divorce, Moira added the goal of keeping her children's welfare front and center.

The self-responsible approach to getting through her divorce had three aspects: 1) acknowledging that she had, throughout her marriage, vented frustration over her husband's emotional detachment and lack of follow-through on commitments made to her and to their children; 2) managing her impulses to continue venting during the divorce and 3) fulfilling her responsibility as a parent to put first her children's welfare. Moira chose to practice reacting constructively (and rewire her brain) whenever provoked by her husband's behavior. Like Iris, she adopted the *restraint and integrity* mantra, successfully subduing her anger and focusing her intentions.

Moira maintained her self-responsible ways even after she learned about the other woman in her husband's life.

Moira: Can you believe it?

Dr. M.: Can you?

Moira: Part of me says, "No way, he was not having an affair. He wouldn't do that." The other part says, "Sure he was. It explains so much." The thing is, I want to know details... confront him about it.

Dr. M.: Hmmm...

Moira: Don't worry. I'm taking the high road. Restraint and integrity. Restraint and integrity. I always think of that. If you ever write a book, make that a heading. Seriously. I've got all my girlfriends saying it. The other night they were dreaming up ways to get even with Rat Bastard and Skanky Whore. (Laughs.) Their words, not mine...and one of them goes, "She'll never do any of it. She's changed. Remember...restraint and integrity."

Dr. M.: You have changed.

Moira: In this situation, I'm delaying gratification and I feel good about it.

Dr. M.: Say more.

Moira: I'm bound to run into them together somewhere. I'm willing to wait for my moment.

Dr. M.: And when you do?

Moira: He'll be a nervous wreck, expecting the worst. I can't wait to be the model of restraint and integrity.

Dr. M.: I want to hear about this, when it happens.

These clients learned the essentials of self-responsible behavior, which all but guarantees better future relationships.

Chapter 15

...But I'm Not Stupid

The whole world loves love and the United States of America loves marriage. There is no place in the Western world where couples get married more than in America.[1] We love marriage so much that married couples marry each other again, staging ceremonies to renew their vows.

Americans love marriage so much that in some states, among them Louisiana, Arkansas and Arizona, we pass covenant marriage laws, allowing well-intentioned (we presume) brides and grooms to opt for making it more complicated to divorce. We tolerate the use of state and federal tax dollars to support marriage-promotion Web sites[2] and billboards. We tune into reality television shows like *My Big Fat Fabulous Wedding* and *Wife Swap* and we go to movies with titles like *The Proposal* and *27 Dresses*.

The some-people-are-more-equal-than-others debate continues in many states. But I strongly believe all men and women, gay and straight, should be able to marry and no one should be denied this civil right.

Laura's Story

Laura has been in a committed lesbian relationship for two years. She has been a client of mine, off and on, for several years. She invited her partner, Liz, who has two teenage children, to join her at a session soon after the Iowa Supreme Court legalized gay marriage.

Laura: We want to talk about marriage.

Dr. M.: A little surprising, isn't it?

Laura: You know the saying, "The afternoon knows what the morning never expected."

Liz: We're really surprised. And now that we have the right, we're thinking about exercising it.

Laura: It's exciting but our concern is the kids.

Dr. M.: Tell me.

Laura: Of course, they already know we're a couple...

Liz: Even though we never spend the night together unless they're at their dad's.

Laura: Dr. Meinecke knows that.

Liz: (Nods.) So, they're totally cool with the *idea* of us getting married, but we're concerned about how they would handle the reality of it.

Laura: They have a lot to deal with just being teenagers, although their issues are completely different. Cassie is graduating and will be starting college...

Liz: And Lauren, as I'm sure you know, has been smoking pot.

Dr. M.: (Nods.) Yes, I heard that you put her in treatment.

Liz: Well, she's still using...when she goes to her dad's. And with her friends, too.

Dr. M.: She actually smokes pot with her dad?

Liz: He's an idiot.

Dr. M.: Okay, so you think the kids have enough going on and shouldn't be asked to also adjust to the two of you getting married.

Laura: Exactly. But we're also worried that there might be a limited window of opportunity here.

Dr. M.: You mean the talk about a ballot initiative. It sounds like that won't happen until 2012 at the earliest.

Liz: Or maybe never.

Dr. M.: So, it all boils down to whose needs come first.

Laura: I knew that's what you'd say! (To partner.) Didn't I tell you that's what she'd say?

Liz: (Joking.) Not that again. Kids' welfare ahead of our own?

Dr. M.: Kids' welfare ahead of political statement, for sure.
Liz: Okay, seriously, I'm getting tired of always putting kids first.
Dr. M.: Somebody has to!
Laura: (To Liz) You know their dad's not.
Liz: (To Laura) I think we know what we're going to do.
Laura: Yup, our work is here is done.

Despite America's profound love of marriage, we divorce more and end cohabitation relationships more, too.[3] In *The Marriage-Go-Round*, sociologist Andrew J. Cherlin addresses the state of marriage in America today:

> Americans are conflicted about lifelong marriage: they value the stability and security of marriage, but they tend to believe that individuals who are unhappy with their marriages should be allowed to end them. What Americans want, in other words, is for everyone else to have a covenant marriage.[4]

Dr. Cherlin offers the insight that Americans are stuck on the marriage-go-round because they hold two conflicting values: marriage and individual freedom. Essentially, Americans are still sorting out the dilemma faced by the founding fathers. As Benjamin Franklin famously concluded, "Any society that would give up a little liberty to gain a little security will deserve neither and lose both." When it comes to marriage, Americans want both.

Hopefully you now have come to the conclusion: *I don't have to make this an either/or situation. I can honor my marriage and my individual freedom by adopting the self-responsible spouse model.*

When high school seniors, surveyed between 2001 and 2006 by the Survey Research Center at The University of Michigan, were asked how likely they were to stay married to the same person for life, 62.7 percent of females and 57.1 percent of males responded "very likely." As we all know, despite relatively high expectations, only about half of marriages last a lifetime. The likelihood of lifetime marriage is, in fact, steadily decreasing.

The United States Census Bureau calculates statistics about percentages of first marriages that reach milestone wedding anniversaries. Among men and women who married in 1955, 96.1 percent and 94 percent, respectively, reached their fifth anniversaries. Those who married in 1980 and 1990, however, achieved this milestone less often than their 1955 counterparts did so. Specifically, 89.8 percent of men and 87.3 percent of women who married in 1980 and 90.1 percent of men and 86.9 percent of women who married in 1990 reached their fifth anniversaries. The downward trend seems likely to continue. Related data, collected in 2001, report the median duration to divorce is about eight years and seven years to separation.

And how many lasting marriages qualify as happy ones? A survey taken between 2004 and 2006 by the National Opinion Research Center of the University of Chicago asked married people age eighteen and older to rate the happiness of their marriages. Almost 63 percent of men rated their marriages as "very happy" while 59.5 percent of women gave the "very happy" rating.

Many of my clients have experienced the benefits of practicing mature love. Some started young, before marriage. Others started sometime after disenchantment set in and before dissolution. Regardless of marital status and life stage, those who abandon old patterns of thought and behavior and adopt a self-responsible approach succeed in relationships.

Sarah's Story

A thirty-year-old newlywed, Sarah was referred to me by her family physician after she became depressed as a college student. Notably, in the beginning, this client regularly expressed how much she hated psychotherapy. Regardless, Sarah continued sessions, off and on, for the next ten years.

> **Sarah:** You won't even believe what my brother is lying about now. So, you know that his ex-wife is pregnant and he's been telling his fiancée that he isn't the father. Now, he's admitting that he's the father but, get this, he's accusing his ex-wife of getting pregnant by putting a date-rape drug in his drink when he came over to pick up their son.
>
> **Dr. M.:** Tell me more.
>
> **Sarah:** My ex-sister-in-law told our parents and they told my brother to stop lying. So, now he's furious with them and me for not buying his story.

Dr. M.: What did you say to him?
Sarah: All I said was, "Really?" He knew, though, that I didn't believe him, and he went off about how much he hates that I've changed. (Chuckles.) He blames you.
Dr. M.: Me?
Sarah: Yeah, he's always known I go to therapy. Anyway, he said I used to look up to him and do things his way, but now I'm too rational and think I know everything.
Dr. M.: He was trying to goad you into behaving badly.
Sarah: Exactly. And before, I would have. Well, I did say one thing. I said that after all our parents have done for us, he should try apologizing like I've learned to do.
Dr. M.: And?
Sarah: He went off again, reminding me of all the things I used to do to upset them. I just ignored that.
Dr. M.: Good.
Sarah: Yeah, he left after that. Later, though, he sent me and my parents the most vicious e-mails, saying that he is "officially estranged" from us. I showed it to my husband and he just rolled his eyes and said, "Your brother needs help bad." Luckily, my husband didn't know me when I acted like that, too.
Dr. M.: Well, you never lied like your brother does.
Sarah: I know, but I'll never forget the time you told me I was high-maintenance.

Sarah first practiced behaving self-responsibly in her relationships with sorority sisters, post-college friends, co-workers, her parents and her narcissistic older brother. By the time she married at age thirty, she had established new habits that will serve her well in married life.

Brent's Story

Brent is a successful advertising executive in his early fifties. Brent initiated treatment due to chronic insomnia and migraine headaches. Discussion of possible emotional triggers identified work pressures and marital distress as frequent precursors to both sleepless nights and throbbing migraines. At the beginning of treatment, Brent was considering early retirement and, despite being a devout Catholic, was contemplating divorce.

At our third appointment, Brent asked whether I would object to his wife, Joelle, attending one of his sessions. Brent told me that Joelle accused him of presenting a one-sided picture of their marriage and making her look bad. She also feared that I might not be "pro-marriage" and might be advocating for divorce.

I assured Brent that I rarely object to a spouse's request to join a session, that other clients' spouses have reacted in similar ways and that I welcome being "checked out" by insecure spouses. Although I appreciated Brent's concern about whether I might object, I particularly wanted to know whether he objected. He said he did not object and expressed a belief that Joelle's fears would be put to rest if she met me and got an opportunity to give input. So, the joint appointment was scheduled.

Joelle, an attorney who left a corporate position to stay home with the couple's children, described her husband, Brent, as completely self-absorbed and miserably negligent in showing sympathy for the stressors of her life and appreciation for her sacrifices. Joelle acknowledged that she readily vents anger at him, triggering arguments a few evenings each week. The only positive comments she offered were about her husband's success as a provider and his strong interest in parenting their children.

With Brent's permission, I outlined for Joelle the basics of treatment for insomnia and migraine headaches as well as the central philosophy of self-responsibility. I also offered assurance that the focus of Brent's sessions would always be on his behavior not hers. Ultimately, Joelle also entered individual psychotherapy with a Christian counselor.

Over time, Brent's persistence in practicing mature love boosted his confidence in the couple's ability to redefine their marriage. With marital tensions significantly lessened, he focused exclusively on redefining his work life. As might be expected, the more capably he managed his expectations and reactions on these two fronts, the more his insomnia and migraines lessened.

Dr. M.: Are things still going well at home?

Brent: Never better. We've been attending a marriage enrichment series at our parish and I think it's really good.

Dr. M.: Is your wife still going to counseling?

Brent: No, she's finished. A faster learner than I am, I guess. I just keep focusing on taking the beam out of my own eye before I worry about the speck in hers.

Dr. M.: Excellent.

Brent: I'd say I generate a thousand impressions a year on that.

Dr. M.: Like ads popping up on a Web site.

Brent: Yeah, at least three times a day I send a banner across my brain that reminds me to focus on the beam in my own eye.

Karen's Story

Karen is a thirty-nine-year-old divorced mother of an eleven-year-old girl.

Karen: I've had a couple of sessions with my daughter's counselor. She says we need to work on healthy boundaries.

Dr. M.: How's it going?

Karen: Slowly. My ex and I got into a lot of bad habits with her. Just like we did with each other.

Dr. M.: Is he still using her as his confidante?

Karen: Not as much. My mother is still his best friend, though, which bothers me. It's just so bizarre. They were not that close when we were married.

Dr. M.: And?

Karen: And, nothing. I "get" that their relationship is none of my business. I'm all about not taking personally what any of them say or do. It helps a lot. I just remind myself not to be provoked into repeating old patterns.

Dr. M.: Tell me.

Karen: Well, they all tend to get angry and blame me. Before, I felt angry and acted angry and tried to convince them they were wrong. What's so obvious to me now is how I was doing just as much provoking as they were. And, as impossible as this used to be, I take responsibility for being the one to interrupt the pattern. I do just like you told me: I offer them a way out of it. I say, "Hmmm...I'll have to think about that" or I change the topic.

Dr. M.: Is anyone taking you up on it?

Karen: Not my ex, for sure. He's doing his usual punishing. I never go there with him, though. Not anymore. And, of course, I *learned* all this drama from my mother.

Dr. M.: And your daughter learned it from you.

Karen: (Nods.) We're all controlling—controlling daughters of controlling mothers. I think my mother is starting to accept that when I say I'm not going to argue, I actually mean it. So she lets things drop. She always has to have the last word, though. She says stuff like, "Well, okay, I guess we're just going to have a superficial relationship from now on."

Dr. M.: And when she says that?

Karen: I let her have the last word. It all seems so silly to me, now. Seriously, I can't believe my own behavior sometimes. I'm so different.

Dr. M.: That happens when you practice.

Karen: Yeah and it gives me hope, high hope, really, for future relationships. I don't know whether my mother will change her ways, but I think she will adjust to my new approach. The one I'm really hopeful for is my daughter. If I keep walking the walk, our relationship will improve, for sure. And I'm also thinking that she'll have a healthier attitude and save herself a lot of future heartache.

Mona and Ed's Story

A couple in their fifties, Ed and Mona's marriage is the second marriage for both of them. Ed and Mona are emotional, witty, affectionate, easily offended, controlling and prone to alcohol abuse. Their story played out like a three-act dramedy.

Act I – At first joint session

Ed: If we can't stop fighting, we are getting a divorce.

Dr. M.: Fighting or arguing?

Mona: Arguing. We love each other too much to be violent.

Ed: We need to learn how to stop arguing.

Act II – After several sessions

Ed: We are still arguing too much. We are getting a divorce.

Dr. M.: Are you both working to change yourselves?

Mona: Yes, but it's not helping.

Dr. M.: You both need a lot of practice at behaving self-responsibly. Give it more time.

Ed: I'm tired of her nagging.

Mona: I'm sick of you bossing me around.

Dr. M.: Do you still love each other?

Both: Yes.

Dr. M.: Then give it more time.

Both: It's hopeless.

Dr. M.: Would you consider separating rather than divorcing?

Both: No! We're getting a divorce.

And they did.

Act III – About a year later, the couple showed up at my office during the lunch hour asking to see me "for just a minute." Both radiated happiness.

Dr. M.: My goodness, what a surprise!

Mona: Well, we have an even bigger surprise for you.

Both: We got remarried!

Dr. M.: Oh, wow! When did you do that?

Both: Yesterday.

Mona: We should have listened to you.

Ed: Yeah, would have saved us a lot of money. Our divorce was our separation.

They are still together ten years later.

Rebecca's Story

A sixty-four-year-old retired English teacher, Rebecca has one adult son. She first entered treatment shortly after her divorce, with the stated goal of getting over her anger toward her ex-husband. She resumed treatment many years later, with the stated goal of learning to control her "sharp tongue."

Dr. M.: You know, I believe that everybody marries the wrong person.

Rebecca: Oh, that is so true. It's all about expectations and reactions and not blaming the other person.

Dr. M.: It is.

Rebecca: Well, I was certainly a wrong person. What I put my poor ex through was unforgivable. Yet he has forgiven me. You know, we're best friends now, even though he's remarried. We never had a *bad* marriage. He just had a bad wife. Of course, he had his faults, still does, but he's definitely the better person.

Dr. M.: You clearly met your goal to get over your anger at him.

Rebecca: Oh, yes, if I had learned before we got married what I've learned since we divorced, things would have been different. I doubt we would have divorced. I would have been a better parent, too. I really had no idea how to be a wife or mother.

Dr. M.: Are you turning your sharp tongue on yourself here?

Rebecca: Hmmm...I think I'm just being honest. I was too young, too emotionally immature, too caught up in fantasy, too worried about what I was getting out of it. And, of course, too judgmental.

Dr. M.: Are you giving yourself credit for making amends and being a loving friend to both, now?

Rebecca: I need to work on that, don't I?

Marriages that Stand the Test of Time

Discouraging divorce statistics aside, about half of marriages last a lifetime. It is safe to say, too, that about half of lasting marriages are happy ones. One out of every four married couples, then, succeeds by both measures of longevity and satisfaction.

Research tells us that, absent dementia, happiness improves with age. Accordingly, couples celebrating silver, golden and diamond anniversaries are often asked about their secrets to happiness or to making love last. Many offer conventional comments: Never go to bed angry. Happy wife, happy life. Pray without ceasing. Don't have children. Some are not happy and have made a marriage last without the mutual benefit of love. Many, though, are truly happy and have succeeded at love.

One such couple is the subject of a documentary film called *A Man Named Pearl*. Filmmakers Scott Galloway and Brent Pierson present the story of Pearl Fryar, a factory worker in Bishopville, South Carolina, who put his small town on the map after he turned his three and a half-acre yard into a topiary masterpiece. Released in 2008, the film's main subject is Pearl's extraordinary passion for beautifying his yard, but there is subtext, too, about beating the odds against successful, lifelong marriage.

The Fryars reveal their secrets to making their love and their marriage last for thirty-eight years. Their radiant smiles as they talk about each other tell part of the story. Their words about managing expectations and emotional reactions tell the rest.

Now, in their late sixties, Pearl wonders why Metra married him, a man who "really had nothing to offer," and Metra says, "I thought you had potentials. I guess they panned out over the years." Then Pearl tells the interviewer, "We've always been so close, since we were thirteen years old to now. She's my life. In thirty-eight years of marriage, I've never seen her get riled."

When the interviewer asks Metra about the effects of Pearl spending evenings and weekends in his yard, she offers these thoughts: "You have to learn to let the other person live, too. Not one person overshadow the other. I let him go and be Pearl. You can look at the yard and see that. That's his."[5]

Regardless of age and stage, anyone can choose to practice self-responsibility, gain emotional growth and reap the benefits of mature and everlasting love.

Chapter 16

The Love We Make

A few years ago on the day after Thanksgiving, my husband and I were sitting in my brother and sister-in-law's kitchen, talking about our plans for the next day. My brother was joking about how he couldn't do anything fun until after he finished the Saturday morning chores that my sister-in-law would "make" him get up bright and early to do. "Oh, " I said, telling him of my theory, "everybody marries the wrong person." The three of them burst out laughing. "That," my sister-in-law said, "would be a great book title."

I smiled. "Yes, it is going to be."

However, predictably, the idea puzzled other family members. When we got together with my newly married niece and her husband, my sister-in-law mentioned what I had said. The twenty-somethings did not burst out laughing. Instead, they exchanged blank looks and my niece said, "What does that mean?" When I mentioned to my mother and mother-in-law that I was writing a book called *Everybody Marries the Wrong Person*, they both said the same thing, "Well, *you* didn't, did you?"

Conventional wisdom insists that if you don't marry the right person, you must (by expressing your opinions and influencing them to change for the better) make your wrong person into the right person. As you now know, this is disaster waiting to happen. In order to succeed at marriage, we must reject conventional wisdom and cultivate self-responsible behaviors. This requires:

- Forsaking fantasy and embracing reality.
- Remembering that since there are no *right* people, no one is likely to be significantly better than your current spouse.
- Accepting that some degree of marital dissatisfaction is guaranteed.
- Letting go of the desire to blame your partner for marital dissatisfaction.
- Resolving to manage your own quirks, expectations and reactions.
- Accepting responsibility for the consequences of your behavior and rescuing yourself, if your choice of partner qualifies as a "great mistake."

From first attraction until death parts us, the odds are against marital success. Both external and internal forces relentlessly threaten relationship satisfaction. Life events expose expectations and elicit reactions, most of which are not worthy of the self-responsibility seal of authenticity.

For example, if couples make it to engagement, we encounter dire threats to happiness while planning the conventional wedding. The billion-dollar-per-year wedding industry exploits childhood fantasies, normalizes pop culture excesses and fosters self-indulgent spending frenzies. Entrepreneurs chanting "you only get married once" lure lemming-like brides and grooms and their loved ones into party busses and stretch limousines and toward the brink. Soon after the customary dream-trip honeymoon, which is almost always tainted by impossibly high expectations, reality (e.g., in-laws, career demands, financial pressures, health crises, parenting duties, outside interests of every description) begins casting its shadow over the fantasy.

Internal forces (e.g., sex and gender differences, psychological incompatibility and self-serving expectations) also present major threats to happily-ever-after. Although couples soon realize that marriage is much more difficult than expected, we are often immobilized by our fantasies, hoping against hope that:

- our partners will change for the better and/or
- our partners will honor the "in good times and bad times" vow and indefinitely tolerate *our failures* to change for the better.

What are we to do? Adopt the self-responsible approach to relationships! Sir Paul McCartney's karmic equation in his song lyrics to "The End": "And in the end the love you take/Is equal to the love you make" is a poet's way of saying that it is all up to you.[6]

Just as surely as infatuation is followed by disenchantment, disenchantment can be followed by mature love. What is conceived by mutual attraction and mutual admiration can be made viable in our rational minds. Disenchantment can be overcome as we banish conventional misconceptions and fantasies. Mature love can develop as we manage personal expectations and reactions, focus on our partner's strengths and choose to be both loving and lovable. Marital success can be enjoyed as self-responsible partners take and make love in their own mutually agreed upon, dynamic and rational, uniquely satisfying ways.

Acknowledgments

Thanks to my husband Deems, my brother Mike and sister-in-law Juli, and my friend-since-kindergarten, Cathy, for bursting out laughing the first time I said, "Everybody marries the wrong person." Their enthusiasm inspired me to write about the concept.

Thanks also to family and friends who looked puzzled and to my mother and mother-in-law, both of whom said, "Well, you didn't, did you?" Their confusion prompted me to fully clarify the concept.

Thanks to my clients for sharing their romantic relationship stories, particularly to those who generously allowed me to use their words as examples.

Thanks to fellow authors, Andy Schell and Dr. Diane McDermott, who read early drafts and encouraged me as I sought publication.

Finally, thanks to Dr. Joan Dunphy of New Horizon Press for saying, "We would like to make you an offer."

Notes

This section is intended to provide a starting point for independent investigation.

PART ONE: WHAT IT MEANS

Chapter 1: Out with the Old

[1] Carolyn Hax, "Stop holding emotions inside," *The Des Moines Register*, September 15, 2008.

[2] Steven D. Levitt and Stephen J. Dubner, *Freakonomics: A Rogue Economist Explores the Hidden Side of Everything* (New York: HarperCollins, 2005), vi, 90.

[3] Daniel Gilbert, *Stumbling on Happiness* (New York: Vintage Books, 2005), 86.

[4] Stephanie Coontz, *Marriage, a History: How Love Conquered Marriage* (New York: Penguin, 2005), 309.

[5] The briefest history/timeline of feminism:

- Pre-First Wave feminism—Mary Wollstonecraft (1754-1797), known as the mother of feminism and British author of *Vindication of the Rights of Women* (1792), died of septicemia after giving birth to her second daughter, Mary Wollstonecraft Shelley, author of *Frankenstein*.
- First Wave feminism 1848-1920—Lucretia Mott (1793-1880); Susan B. Anthony (1820-1906); Elizabeth Cady Stanton (1815-1902); Carrie Chapman Catt (1859-1947). Fought the women's suffrage fight, which celebrated ratification of the Nineteenth Amendment in 1920. Elizabeth Blackwell (1821-1910) was the first woman to graduate medical school.
- Second Wave feminism 1960s and 1970s—Betty Friedan (1921-2006), known as the mother of modern feminism, first President of National Organization of Women (NOW) founded in 1966; Simone De Beauvoir (1908-1986), existentialist author of *The Second Sex (1949)*; Gloria Steinem (1934-), founder of Ms. Magazine; 1980s and 1990s—guerilla theater group, *Ladies Against*

Women; Susan Faludi (1959-), author of *Backlash: The Undeclared War Against American Women* (1991) and *Stiffed: The Betrayal of American Men* (1999).

- Third Wave feminism 21st century—"New feminism"; women who grew up feeling less of what second-wavers called oppression; critical of the white, middle-class heterosexual emphasis of second-wavers; interest in ending all types of discrimination. Support and active involvement by men has occurred in all the movements.

[6] This information was gathered from material provided at the exhibition in 2000 at Faulconer Gallery, Grinnell College, Grinnell, Iowa, including the pamphlet *Corot to Picasso: European Masterworks from the Smith College Museum of Art* by Clare Renken.

[7] Barack Obama, "Remarks by the President at Fatherhood Town Hall," (Town Hall Meeting, The White House East Room, June 19, 2009) http://www.whitehouse.gov/the_press_office/Remarks-by-the-President-at-Fatherhood-Town-Hall/.

[8] *2007 Stress in American* survey reported the following percentages by age group claiming relationships as a top stressor: 80% of 18-34 year-olds; 83% of 34-54 year-olds; 73% of 55+ year-olds.
APA.org—American Psychological Association media Room—2007 Stress in America press Kit, p.16.

[9] Louis Cozolino, *The Neuroscience of Psychotherapy: Building and Rebuilding the Human Brain* (New York: Norton and Co., 2002), xv, 16.

[10] Pam Willenz, "Marital Satisfaction Affected By Both Spouse's Mental Health, Says New Study," APA Online,
http://www.apa.org/press/releases/2004/10/marital-depress.aspx

Chapter 2: I May Be Dumb…

[1] Natalie Angier, "Men. Are Women Better Off With Them, or Without Them?" *The New York Times,* June 21, 1998; Linda C. Gallo, et. al., "Marital Status and Quality in Middle-Aged Women: Associations with Levels and Trajectories of Cardiovascular Risk Factors," *Health Psychology* 22, no. 5 (2003): 453-463.

[2] Richard E. Lucas, et. al., "Reexamining Adaptation and the Set Point Model of Happiness: Reactions to Changes in Marital Status," *Journal of Personality and Social Psychology* 84, no 3 (2003): 527-539.

[3] Thornton Wilder, *The Bridge of San Luis Rey* (New York: Harper & Row, 1927), 59-60.

[4] Julia Seton, *The Science of Success* (Whitefish, MT: Kessinger Publishing, 1997).

[5] David D. Burns, *Feeling Good Together: The Secret to Making Troubled Relationships Work* (New York: Broadway Books, 2008), 59.

[6] Joan Borysenko and Larry Rothstein, *Minding the Body, Mending the Mind* (New York: Addison-Wesley, 1987).

[7] Katherine Ellison, *The Mommy Brain: How Motherhood Makes Us Smarter* (New York: Basic Books, 2005).

[8] J.P. Lorberbaum, et. al., "Functional MRI of mothers responding to infant cries," *Biological Psychiatry* 43, no. 8, suppl. 1 (April 1998): S25.

[9] Martin E.P. Seligman, *Authentic Happiness: Using the New Positive Psychology to Realize Your Potential for Lasting Fulfillment* (New York: The Free Press, 2004), 206.

[10] Allan Pease and Barbara Pease, *Why Men Don't Listen and Women Can't Read Maps* (New York: Broadway Books, 1999), 227.

[11] Robert T. Michael, et. al., *Sex in America, a Definitive Survey* (New York: Warner Books, 1994).

[12] Ibid.

[13] Ed Bradley, "Finding the 'Lord God Bird,'" CBS News, http://www.cbsnews.com/stories/2005/10/13/60minutes/ main940587.shtml.

[14] Neal A. Grauer, "Neuroscience's Act II," *Hopkins Medicine,* Spring-Summer 2006, 12.

[15] John Medina, *Brain Rules: 12 Principles for Surviving and Thriving at Work, Home, and School* (Seattle, WA: Pear Press, 2008), 271.

[16] Joseph LeDoux, *Synaptic Self: How Our Brains Become Who We Are* (New York: Viking, 2002), 301-324; Jeffrey Schwartz and Sharon Begley, *The Mind and the Brain: Neuroplasticity and the Power of Mental Force* (New York: Regan Books, 2003).

[17] These authors address neurogenesis:

- Pierce J. Howard, *The Owner's Manual for the Brain: Everyday Applications from Mind-Brain Research,* 3rd ed. (Austin, TX: The Bard Press, 2006), 112, 522.
- Sharon Begley, *Train Your Mind, Change Your Brain* (New York: Ballantine Books, 2008).
- Peter S. Eriksson, et. al., "Neurogenesis in the Adult Human Hippocampus," *Nature Medicine* 4, no. 11 (November 1998): 1313-1317.
- Elizabeth Gould, et. al., "Neurogenesis in the Neocortex of Adult Primates," *Science* 286, no. 5439 (October 15, 1999): 548-552.
- Elizabeth Gould and C.G. Gross, "Neurogenesis in Adult Mammals: Some Progress and Problems," *The Journal of Neuroscience* 22, no. 3 (February 2002): 619-623.
- Fred H. Gage, "Neurogenesis in the Adult Brain," *The Journal of Neuroscience* 22, no. 3 (February 1, 2002): 612-613.
- Gerd Kempermann and Fred H. Gage, "New Nerve Cells for the Adult Human Brain," *Scientific American* 280, no. 5 (May 1999): 48-53.
- Ayumu Tashiro, et. al., "NMDA-receptor-mediated, cell-specific integration of new neurons in adult dentate gyrus," *Nature* 442 (August 24, 2006): 929-933.

[18] Alvaro Pascual-Leone, et. al., "The Plastic Human Brain Cortex," *Annual Review of Neuroscience* 28 (July 2005): 377-401.

Chapter 3: Red Flags

[1] American Psychiatric Association, *Diagnostic and Statistical Manual of Mental Disorders DSM-IV-TR*, 4th ed., text rev. (Washington, D.C.: American Psychiatric Association, 2000).

[2] Michael S. Kimmel, "Male Victims of Domestic Violence: A Substantive and Methodological Research Review" (a report to The Equality Commission of the Department of Education and Science, 2001); Linda Berg-Cross, "Intimate Relationships, Psychological Abuse and Mental Health Problems," *The Register Report* (Spring 2005): 20-27.

[3] Books

- Ginny NiCarthy, *Getting Free: You Can End Abuse and Take Back Your Life* (Seattle, WA: The Seal Press, 2004).
- Michele Harway and James O'Neil, eds., *What Causes Men's Violence Against Women*? (Thousand Oaks, CA: Sage Publications, 1999).

Hotline

- National Domestic Violence Hotline (NDVH): 1-800-799-SAFE (7233) or 1-800-787-3224 (TTY)

Web sites

- www.ndvh.org
- www.batteredmen.com
- www.apa.org/about/gr/issues/women/trauma.aspx

[4] Carolyn Hax, "Forgive husband for not wanting kids," *The Des Moines Register,* June 20, 2009.

[5] Sandra Blakeslee, "A Small Part of the Brain, and Its Profound Effects," *The New York Times*, February 6, 2007.

[6] Nasir H. Naqvi, et. al., "Damage to the Insula Disrupts Addiction to Cigarette Smoking," *Science* 351, no. 5811 (January 26, 2007): 531-534.

PART TWO: INFATUATION

Chapter 4: Nature's Cruel Joke

[1] Daniel G. Amen, *Change Your Brain, Change Your Life* (New York: Times Books, 1998), 86-87.

[2] Jim Harrison, "Easter Morning," *Saving Daylight* (Port Townsend, WA: Copper Canyon Press, 2006), 60.

[3] Christopher Lasch, *The Culture of Narcissism: American Life in an Age of Diminishing Expectations* (New York: Norton & Company, 1979), 8.

[4] Ibid., 199.

[5] Allan Pease and Barbara Pease, *Why Men Don't Listen*, 227; Robert T. Michael, et. al., *Sex in America, a Definitive Survey* (New York: Warner Books, 1994).

[6] Lasch, *The Culture of Narcissism,* 199.

[7] Seligman, *Authentic Happiness,* 188.

[8] These authors address female sexuality including recreational sex:

- Natalie Angier, *Woman: An Intimate Geography* (New York: Houghton Mifflin, 1999).
- Michael, et. al., *Sex in America, a Definitive Survey.*
- Camille Paglia, *Sex, Art, and American Culture: Essays* (New York: Vintage Books, 1992).
- Naomi Wolf, *Promiscuities: The Secret Struggle for Womanhood* (New York: Random House, 1997).

[9] Deborah Blum, *Sex on the Brain: The Biological Differences Between Men and Women* (New York: Viking, 1997), 94.

[10] Daniel Amen, *Making a Good Brain Great* (New York: Three Rivers Press, 2005), 37-38.

[11] Kurt Vonnegut, *Galapagos* (New York: Random House, 1985), 25.

[12] Shanhong Luo and Eva C. Klohnen, "Associative Mating and Marital Quality in Newlyweds: A Couple-centered Approach," *Journal of Personality and Social Psychology* 88, no. 2 (2005): 304-326.

Chapter 5: Hot Sex Here

[1] Pierce J. Howard, *The Owner's Manual for the Brain: Everyday Applications from Mind-Brain Research,* 3rd ed. (Austin, TX: The Bard Press, 2006), 301-316; Helen Fisher, *Why Him? Why Her? Finding Real Love By Understanding Your Personality Type* (New York: Henry Hold & Co., 2009).

[2] R. Douglas Fields, "Sex and the Secret Nerve," *Scientific American Mind* (February 2007): 21-27.

[3] Etienne Benson, "Pheromones, in context," *Monitor on Psychology* 33, no. 9 (October 2002): 46.

[4] Donatella Marazziti and Domenico Canale, "Hormonal changes when falling in love," *Psychoneuroendocrinology* 29, no. 7 (August 2004): 931-936.

[5] Etienne Benson, "Study finds sex differences in relationship between arousal and orientation," *Monitor on Psychology* 34, no. 4 (April 2003), 51. Benson reports on a study by Northwestern University psychologist J. Michael Bailey, Ph.D., and student Meredith Chivers that offers a case in point regarding controversy in the realm of sex research.

[6] Mary Catherine Bateson (lecture, Des Moines, Iowa, 1990s).

[7] Elizabeth Wurtzel, *Bitch: In Praise of Difficult Women* (New York: Anchor Books, 1999), 344.

[8] James McBride Dabbs and Mary Godwin Dabbs, *Heroes, Rogues, and Lovers: Testosterone and Behavior* (New York: McGraw-Hill, 2000), 62-63, 164.

[9] Robert Sapolsky, *The Trouble with Testosterone* (New York: Scribner, 1997), 155.

[10] Michael, et. al., *Sex in America*, 10-12, 15-25.

[11] Rebecca Clay, "Sex research faces new obstacles," *Monitor on Psychology* 34, no. 4 (April 2003): 57.

[12] Alexandra M. Minnis and Nancy S. Padian, "Reliability of adolescents' self-reported sexual behavior: A comparison of two diary methodologies," *Journal of Adolescent Health* 28, no. 5 (2001): 394-403.

[13] Alfred C. Kinsey, Wardell B. Pomeroy, and Clyde E. Martin, *Sexual Behavior in the Human Male* (Philadelphia: W.B. Saunders, 1948); Alfred C. Kinsey, Wardell B. Pomeroy, Clyde E. Martin, and Paul H. Gebhard, *Sexual Behavior in the Human Female* (Philadelphia: W.B. Saunders, 1953).

[14] William Masters and Virginia Johnson, *Human Sexual Response,* (Boston: Little Brown, 1966).

[15] Ruth K. Westheiemer, *Encyclopedia of Sex* (New York: Continuum, 2000); Eve Ensler, *The Vagina Monologues* (New York: Villard Books, 1998); Gail Sheehy, *Sex and the Seasoned Woman: Pursuing the Passionate Life* (New York: Ballantine Books, 2007).

[16] Sheldon Rampton and John Stauber, *Banana Republicans: How the Right Wing is Turning America into a One-Party State* (New York: Tarcher/Penguin, 2004).

[17] Michael, et. al., *Sex in America*, 1, 112, 114, 113.

[18] Marabel Morgan, *The Total Woman* (New York: F.H. Revell, 1973).

[19] Deborah Smith, "Women and sex: What is 'dysfunctional'?" *Monitor on Psychology* 34, no. 4 (April 2003): 54.

[20] Camille Paglia, *Sex, Art, and American Culture* (New York: Vintage, 1992), 269.

[21] The Boston Women's Health Collective, *The New Our Bodies, Ourselves* (New York: Simon and Schuster, 1992), 131-150, 153-236.

[22] Natalie Angier, *Woman: An Intimate Geography* (New York: Houghton Mifflin, 1999), 72.

[23] Howard, *The Owner's Manual for the Brain*, 310.

[24] Wilder, *The Bridge of San Luis Rey*, 146.

Chapter 6: Mutual Admiration Society

[1] Simone De Beauvoir, *The Second Sex* (New York: Knopf, 1952).

[2] Steven Johnson, *Mind Wide Open: Your Brain and the Neuroscience of Everyday Life* (New York: Scribner, 2004); Daniel Goleman, *Social Intelligence: The New Science of Human Relationships* (New York: Bantam Books, 2006); The complete "Reading the Mind in the Eyes Test" and scoring key can be found in *The Essential Difference* by Simon Baron-Cohen (New York: Basic Books, 2004), 187-199.

[3] Goleman, *Social Intelligence*.

[4] E. Boatella-Costa, et. al., "Behavioral gender differences in the neonatal period according to the Brazelton scale," *Early Human Development* 83, no. 2 (February 2007): 91-97.

[5] Simon Baron-Cohen, *The Essential Difference: Male and Female Brains and the Truth about Autism* (New York: Basic Books, 2003), 178.

[6] These authors address attachment styles:

- Kendra Van Wagner, "Attachment Styles," About.com, http://psychology.about.com/od/loveandattraction/ss/attachmentstyle.htm. Links to quiz "What's Your Romantic Attachment Style?"
- Louis Cozolino, *The Neuroscience of Psychotherapy: Building and Rebuilding the Human Brain* (New York: W.W. Norton & Co, 2002), 201-211.
- Carol Garhart Mooney, *Theories of Attachment: An Introduction to Bowlby, Ainsworth, Gerger, Brazelton, Kennel, and Klause* (St. Paul, MN: Redleaf Press, 2009).
- Martin Seligman, *Authentic Happiness: Using the New Positive Psychology to Realize Your Potential for Lasting Fulfillment* (New York: The Free Press, 2002), 190-196.

[7] Willow Lawson, "New Friends: Negatives Attract," *Psychology Today* (November /December, 2005).

[8] To learn all about crying, read: Jack Katz, *How Emotions Work* (Chicago: University of Chicago Press, 1999), 175-203.

[9] Amy Worthen, "Emotions: Frida Kahlo & Diego Rivera," Des Moines Art Center, January 28, 2005.

[10] Collection owned by Jim and Patty Cownie of Des Moines, Iowa.

[11] Johnson, *Mind Wide Open,* 143.

[12] A. Pease and B. Pease, *Why Men Don't Listen*, 226.

[13] These authors address male/female neurochemical differences:

- Daniel Amen, *Sex on the Brain: 12 Lessons to Enhance Your Love Life* (New York: Harmony Books, 2007).
- Baron-Cohen, *The Essential Difference.*
- Antonio R. Damasio, *The Feeling of What Happens: Body and Emotion in the Making of Consciousness* (New York: Harcourt, 1999).
- Helen E. Fisher, *Why We Love: The Nature and Chemistry of Romantic Love* (New York: Henry Holt, 2004).
- Goleman, *Social Intelligence.*
- Howard, *The Owner's Manual for the Brain.*
- Pease, *Why Men Don't Listen and Women Can't Read Maps.*

[14] Howard, *The Owner's Manual for the Brain,* 795.

[15] Metta Spencer, *Two Aspirins and a Comedy: How Television Can Enhance Health and Society* (Boulder: Paradigm, 2006).

[16] R. Douglas Fields, "Beyond the Neuron Doctrine," *Scientific American Mind* 17, no. 3 (June/July 2006): 21-27.

[17] Annie Proulx, *The Shipping News* (New York: Scribner, 1993).

Chapter 7: So Much in Common

[1] George Orwell, *Animal Farm* (New York: Harcourt Brace Jovanovich, 1946).

[2] Eric R. Kandel, "The New Science of Mind," *Scientific American Mind* 17, no. 2 (April/May 2006): 64.

[3] Ibid., 64-65.

[4] Diane Ackerman, *An Alchemy of Mind: The Marvel and Mystery of the Brain* (New York: Scribner, 2004), 13.

[5] Elkhonon Goldberg, *The Executive Brain: Frontal Lobes and the Civilized Mind* (New York: Oxford University Press, 2001), 88.

[6] Robert Ornstein, *The Right Mind: Making Sense of the Hemispheres* (New York: Harcourt Brace, 1997), 83.

[7] A. Pease and B. Pease, *Why Men Don't Listen*, 57. For a fun "Brain-Wiring Test" see p. 57-65.

[8] Ackerman, *An Alchemy of Mind*, 193.

[9] N.A. Fox, "If it's not left, it's right: Electroencephalograph asymmetry and the development of emotion," *American Psychologist* 46, no. 8 (August 1991): 863-872.

[10] Howard, *The Owner's Manual of the Brain*, 805.

[11] Goldberg, *The Executive Brain*, 89.

[12] Ibid., 91.

[13] Larry Cahill, "Larry Cahill," University of California, Irvine, Faculty Profile System, http://www.faculty.uci.edu/profile.cfm?faculty_id=3276.

[14] Joe Kelly, "Dads and Daughters," Joe Kelly, www.DadsandDaughters.org.

[15] Amit Etkin, et al., "Resolving Emotional Conflict: A Role for the Rostral Anterior Cingulate Cortex in Modulating Activity in the Amygdala," *Neuron* 51, no. 6 (September 21, 2006): 871-882.

PART THREE: DISENCHANTMENT

Chapter 8: Bait and Switch

[1] "Human Genome Project Information," U.S. Department of Energy Office of Science, Office of Biological and Environmental Research, http://www.ornl.gov/sci/techresources/Human_Genome/homes.html.

[2] Howard, *The Owner's Manual for the Brain*, 264-265.

[3] Ibid.

[4] Baron-Cohen, *The Essential Difference*, 21-60, 61-84.

[5] "Lawrence Summers Video & Audio," boston.com, http://multimedia.boston.com/politics/obama-administration/lawrence-summers.htm.

[6] Susan Pinker, *The Sexual Paradox: Men, Women and the Real Gender Gap* (New York: Scribner, 2008), 7.

[7] Sandra L. Bem, *The Lenses of Gender: Transforming the Debate on Sexual Inequality* (New Haven: Yale University Press, 1993).

[8] A. Pease and B. Pease, *Why Men Don't Listen*, 56-57.

[9] Howard, *The Owner's Manual for the Brain*, 267, 906-907.

[10] Ruben C. Gur, et al., "Sex Differences in Brain Gray and White Matter in Healthy Young Adults: Correlations with Cognitive Performance," *The Journal of Neuroscience* 19, no.10 (May 15, 1999): 4065-4072.

[11] Howard, *The Owner's Manual for the Brain*, 268.

[12] Richard Haier, et al., "The neuroanatomy of general intelligence: sex matters," *NeuroImage* 25, no. 1 (March 2005): 320-327.

[13] Howard, *The Owner's Manual for the Brain*, 268.

[14] Cristina Lundqvist and Karl-Goran Sabel, "The Brazelton Neonatal Behavioral Assessment Scale Detects Differences Among Newborn Infants of Optimal Health," *Journal of Pediatric Psychology* 25, no.8 (2000): 577-582.

[15] These authors address differences between male and female brains:

- Ackerman, *An Alchemy of Mind*.
- Amen, *Sex on the Brain*.
- Baron-Cohen, *The Essential Difference*.
- Blum, *Sex on the Brain*.
- Goldberg, *The Executive Brain*.
- Johnson, *Mind Wide Open*.
- Joseph LeDoux, *Synaptic Self: How Our Brains Become Who We Are* (New York: Viking, 2002).
- Eleanor Maccoby and Carol Nagy Jacklin, *The Psychology of Sex Differences* (Stanford, CA: Stanford University Press, 1974).

[16] More on male/female differences:

- Fisher, *Why We Love*.
- Helen E. Fisher, *Anatomy of Love: The Natural History of Monogamy, Adultery, and Divorce* (New York: W.W. Norton, 1992).
- Eric R. Kandel, *In Search of Memory: The Emergence of a New Science of Mind* (New York: W.W. Norton, 2006), 315-316.

[17] A. Pease and B. Pease, *Why Men Don't Listen*, 20-23.

[18] Ibid.

[19] John Medina, *Brain Rules: 12 Principles for Surviving and Thriving at Work, Home, and School* (Seattle, WA: Pear Press, 2008), 85.

[20] "Zookeepers battle addict ape: Charlie chimp likes Joe Camel," *USA Today,* April 25, 2005, http://www.usatoday.com/news/offbeat/2005-04-25-chimp_x.htm.

[21] Daniel Goleman, *Emotional Intelligence: Why It Can Matter More Than IQ,* 10th ed. (New York: Bantam, 2006).

PART FOUR: MATURE LOVE

Chapter 10: In with the New

[1] Sue Monk Kidd, *The Secret Life of Bees* (New York: Penguin, 2002).

[2] Christine E. Meinecke, "Jerome Frank: Persuader and Exemplar," *Journal of Counseling and Development* 65, no. 5 (January 1987): 232.

[3] John Gottman, et al., *The Mathematics of Marriage: Dynamic Nonlinear Models* (Massachusetts: The MIT Press, 2002).

[4] Phillip Moffitt, "In Trust We Trust," *Yoga Journal* (May/June 2002), http://www.yogajournal.com/wisdom/654.

[5] Lewis Thomas, *The Lives of A Cell: Notes of a Biology Watcher* (New York: Viking Press, 1974).

Chapter 11: Strengths and Virtues

[1] Eva C. Klohnen and Shanhong Luo, "Interpersonal attraction and personality: What is attractive—self-similarity, ideal similarity, complementarity or attachment security?" *Journal of Personality and Social Psychology* 85, no. 4 (2003): 709-722.

[2] Sandra Murray, et al., "What the Motivated Mind Sees: Comparing Friends' Perspectives to Married Partners' Views of Each Other," *Journal of Experimental Social Psychology* 36, no. 6 (2000): 600-620.

[3] Sanjay Srivastava, et al, "Optimism in Close Relationships: How Seeing Things in a Positive Light Makes Them So," *Journal of Personality and Social Psychology* 91, no.1 (2006): 143-153.

[4] Shelly Gable, Gian Gonzaga and Amy Strachman, "Will You Be There for Me When Things Go Right?: Supportive Responses to Positive Event Disclosures," *Journal of Personality and Social Psychology* 91, no. 5 (2006): 904-917.

[5] Ibid.

[6] Fisher, *Why Him? Why Her?*, 3.

[7] Ibid., 7-17.

[8] Martin E. P. Seligman, et al., "Positive Psychology Progress: Empirical Validation of Interventions," *American Psychologist* 60, no. 5 (2005): 412, table 1.

[9] Ibid, 416.

[10] Ibid.

[11] Gilbert, *Stumbling on Happiness*, 263.

[12] Diane McDermott and C. R. Snyder, *Making Hope Happen: A Workbook for Turning Possibilities into Reality* (Oakland, CA: New Harbinger Publications, 1999), 209.

[13] Jerome Wagner, *The Enneagram Spectrum of Personality Styles* (Portland, OR: Metamorphous Press, 1996).

[14] "The Enneagram Institute World Headquarters," The Enneagram Institute, http:// www.enneagraminstitute.com/; Don Riso and Russ Hudson, *Understanding the Enneagram: The Practical Guide to Personality Types* rev. ed. (New York: Mariner Books, 2000), 321.

[15] Resources on Enneagrams:

- Helen Palmer, *The Enneagram in Love and Work: Understanding Your Intimate and Business Relationships* (New York: HarperOne, 1995).
- Renee Baron and Elizabeth Wagele, *Are You My Type, Am I Yours?: Relationships Made Easy Through the Enneagram* (New York: HarperOne, 1995).
- Don Riso and Russ Hudson, *The Wisdom of the Enneagram: The Complete Guide to Psychological and Spiritual Growth for the Nine Personality Types* (New York: Bantam, 1999).
- David Daniels and Virginia Price, *The Essential Enneagram: The Definitive Personality Test and Self-Discovery Guide* (New York: HarperOne, 2000).

Chapter 12: "Down in Front!"

[1] John Lennon, "Beautiful Boy," *Double Fantasy*, Geffen Records, 1980.

[2] David D. Burns, *Feeling Good Handbook: Using the New Mood Therapy* (New York: Penguin, 1990); David D. Burns, *Intimate Connections*

(New York: Penguin, 1985); David D. Burns, *Ten Days to Self-Esteem* (New York: HarperCollins, 1993); David D. Burns, *When Panic Attacks: The New, Drug-Free Anxiety Therapy That Can Change Your Life* (New York: Broadway, 2007); David D. Burns, *Feeling Good Together: The Secret to Making Troubled Relationships Work* (New York: Broadway, 2008).

[3] Katherine Ellison, "Mastering Your Own Mind," *Psychology Today* (Sept/Oct 2006): 72.

[4] David D. Burns, *Feeling Good: The New Mood Therapy* (New York: Signet, 1980), 135-177; Harriet Lerner, *The Dance of Anger: A Woman's Guide to Changing the Patterns of Intimate Relationships* (New York: Harper Paperbacks, 2005).

[5] Everett L. Worthington, Jr., "The Forgiveness Teacher's Toughest Test," *Spirituality & Health* (Winter 1999): 30-32; Everett L. Worthington, Jr., *Forgiving and Reconciling: Bridges to Wholeness and Hope* (Downers Grove, IL: InterVarsity *Press,* 2003), 73-166.

[6] Dalai Lama, "My Friend the Enemy," *Spirituality & Health* (Winter 1999): 33.

[7] Sigal Balshine and Eric Bressler, "The Influence of Humor on Desirability," *Evolution and Human Behavior* 27, no. 1 (2006): 29-39.

[8] David Niven, *The 100 Simple Secrets of Great Relationships: What Scientists Have Learned and How You Can Use It* (New York: Harper, 2003), 65-66.

[9] E. DeKoning and R. Weiss, "The Relational Humor Inventory: Functions of Humor in Close Relationships," *American Journal of Family Therapy* 30, no. 1 (2002): 1-18.

[10] Rod A. Martin, *The Psychology of Humor: An Integrative Approach* (Burlington, MA: Elsevier Academic Press, 2007).

[11] David Ritchie, "Frame-Shifting in Humor and Irony," *Metaphor and Symbol* 20, no. 1 (2005): 275-294.

[12] Vinod Goel and Raymond J. Dolan, "The functional anatomy of humor: Segregating cognitive and affective components," *Nature Neuroscience* 4, no. 3 (2001): 237-238.

Chapter 14: Extreme Makeovers

[1] Michael Palin, "Himalaya, Day 80: Lugu Lake," Prominent Palin Productions, Ltd., http://palinstravels.co.uk/book-3543.

[2] John M. Gottman and Nan Silver, *The Seven Principles for Making Marriage Work: A Practical Guide from the Country's Foremost Relationship Expert* (New York: Random House, 1999), 131.

[3] Lisa Ann Neff and Benjamin R. Karney, "To Know You Is to Love You: The Implications of Global Adoration and Specific Accuracy for Marital Relationships," *Journal of Personality and Social Psychology* 88, no. 3 (March 2005): 480-497.

[4] Louis Cozolino, *The Neuroscience of Psychotherapy: Building and Rebuilding the Human Brain* (New York: W.W. Norton & Co., 2002), 115.

[5] Ibid., 28-31.

[6] Mira Kirshenbaum, *Too Good to Leave, Too Bad to Stay: A Step-By-Step Guide to Helping You Decide Whether to Stay In or Get Out of Your Relationship* (New York: Penguin, 1996), 59.

Chapter 15: ...But I'm Not Stupid

[1] Andrew J. Cherlin, *The Marriage-Go-Round: The State of Marriage and the Family in America Today* (New York: Knopf, 2009), 16-17, 205.

[2] "TwoOfUs.org," National Healthy Marriage Resource Center, http://twoofus.org.

[3] Cherlin, *The Marriage-Go-Round*, 206.

[4] Ibid., 4.

[5] *A Man Named Pearl*, prod. and dir. Scott Galloway and Brent Pierson, 78 min., Tentmakers Entertainment, 2008, DVD.

Chapter 16: The Love We Make

[1] Sir Paul McCartney and John Lennon, "The End," *Abbey Road,* EMI Records Ltd., 1969.